A Media Ecology of Theology

A Media Ecology of Theology

Communicating Faith throughout the Christian Tradition

Paul A. Soukup, S.J.

BAYLOR UNIVERSITY PRESS

© 2022 by Baylor University Press
Waco, Texas 76798

All Rights Reserved. No part of this publication may be reproduced, stored in a retrieval system, or transmitted, in any form or by any means, electronic, mechanical, photocopying, recording, or otherwise, without the prior permission in writing of Baylor University Press.

Cover and book design by Kasey McBeath
Cover art: Shutterstock/Passatic

Paperback ISBN 978-1-4813-1775-7
Library of Congress Control Number: 2022940707

To Robert A. White, S.J., who started me on this road

To Franz-Josef Eilers, S.V.D., who put me back on it

To Walter J. Ong, S.J., whose writings provided important tools

To the students enrolled in many of the courses in which we explored these media ecologies.

CONTENTS

	Introduction	1
	The Culture of Faith-Seeking-Understanding	
1	Orality and Christian Theology	17
	A Media Ecology Perspective	
2	The Stories of Faith	33
	Narrative and Theological Meaning	
3	Educational Systems	49
	Managing the Content of Faith	
4	Writing and Printing	65
	Shifting Theological Authority	
5	Translation	77
	Experiencing Scripture as Applied Communication	
6	Art	95
	Shaping the Sacramental Imagination	
7	Music	119
	Hearing the Divine	
8	Architecture	139
	Building Up the Faith	
9	Ritual	153
	Expressing Belief in Action	
10	Film	171
	Expanding the Sacramental Horizon	

11 Social Media   187
    Opening Up the Theological Ecosystem

Conclusion   203
    Faith-Seeking-Understanding in Popular Culture

Bibliography   211
Index   227

INTRODUCTION

The Culture of Faith-Seeking-Understanding

Theology, however we define it—the systematic reflection on religious experience, the articulation of belief, the intellectual consciousness of faith—is how the Christian Church does its thinking. For some two millennia, Christians have thought about the experience of God in Christ Jesus. What they have thought has covered a vast amount of intellectual territory: the relations between Christianity and Judaism; the gratuitous saving work of Jesus; the person, identity, and natures of Jesus; the possibility of revelation and prophecy, as well as their interpretation; the nature of salvation; the day-to-day experience of God's covenant promise; Christian practices, sacraments, and Church membership; the role of forgiveness and reconciliation; sin; the ability of human thinking to know God; the fall and original sin; Christian behavior, morality, and spirituality—the list continues for centuries (Pelikan, 1971). And Christians have not finished thinking.

Why Christians have thought about these things and not others remains a question for historical investigation. How Christians have thought about these things also deserves exploration, which provides the focus for this book. Christian thinking does not happen in a vacuum. Christian thinkers draw on materials ready to hand, beginning with the Bible, both the Hebrew Scriptures and the Christian New Testament. Other sources include the prayers and practices of worship (Hilgartner, 2009) and even the decoration of Christian places (Pelikan, 1971, p. 4). In his history of Christian doctrine, Pelikan provides a sense of the sources that prompt theological reflection. He defines doctrine as "what is believed, taught, and confessed" (p. 3), describing it in more detail:

> Without setting rigid boundaries, we shall identify what is "believed" as the form of Christian doctrine present in the modalities of devotion, spirituality, and worship; what is "taught" as the content of the word of God extracted by exegesis from the witness of the Bible and communicated to the people of the church through proclamation, instruction, and churchly theology; and what is "confessed" as the testimony of the church, both

against false teaching from within and against attacks from without, articulated in polemics and in apologetics, in creed and in dogma. (p. 4)

Despite Pelikan's placing "churchly theology" in the second category ("what is taught"), each of the three areas provides material for theology. Theology, as a reflection on belief, takes root in every person wrestling with Christianity. The ongoing reflecting on the three areas "implies that both the subject matter and the source material for the history of the development of doctrine will shift, gradually but steadily, as we trace it through the history of the church" (p. 5). The forms of Christian theology also shift with culture and time.

Not surprisingly, this theological reflection occurs in whatever media those individuals wrestling with faith find best suited to their thought. Pelikan calls this overall effort "tradition," which "refers simultaneously to the process of communication and to its content" (p. 7). Again, not surprisingly, some people think more clearly than others; some think more effectively in different communication forms than others; some theology is clearer or better than others. Some media work better for theology than others. But the form matters. In a contemporary exploration of the impact of social media on theology, Horsfield and Teusner (2007) remind their readers, "it is important to specify *which particular mediated form* of Christianity we are talking about and to recognize that when that particular form was being shaped, it was contending with other mediated versions or potential mediated versions around at the same time" (p. 280, italics in original).

Firmly rooted in cultural experiences, much Christian thinking responded to important issues of the day. The acceptance of Jesus as savior by non-Jews and the later expulsion of Christians from the synagogues led to the Church's thinking about the relationship between Christianity and Judaism. Augustine, for another example, thought about the relationship between civil and religious society in *The City of God* because the barbarians were literally at the gates of Rome, and Augustine's world seemed at an end. Centuries later, enslaved Africans in America thought about God's promise of freedom. Each of these groups used the communication media at hand: preaching, writing, singing, and so on. The same import of history, culture, and media holds true for theology today. Christian theology thinks about the experience of God in multiple cultures because our world knows its cultural plurality more clearly. The Christian Church thinks again about liberation because the experience of millions in South America and other regions of the world points to a rereading of the biblical texts of liberation, developing a "liberation theology." The Church thinks about God's revelation from the perspective of women because women now do more of the Church's public thinking. The Church thinks about God and nature and people's responsibility to the environment because we as people have become conscious of our destruction of that environment. At each of these moments, the Church thinks with the tools it has, with whatever communication media allow its members to express and share their thoughts.

In these perspectives, "theology" refers to a reflection on belief. Each of the common definitions of theology includes some aspect of this: For Anselm in the eleventh century, theology is "faith seeking understanding." "[T]heology is an exercise of faith, a way of being faithful, and a way of living one's faith" (Switzer, 2010, ¶2). Aidan Nichols expands this a bit to argue that "The task of theology is the disciplined exploration of what is contained in revelation" (2009, orig. 1988, ¶10). Thus, theology moves forward, explores beyond the assertion of what the Church believes, but in a structured way, whether that structure comes from philosophy or some other way of knowing. Richard McBrien acknowledges this exploration in the lives of all Christians: "Theology comes into play at that very moment when the person of faith becomes intellectually conscious of his or her faith" (McBrien, 1981, p. 26). Such reflection on belief occurs in many places and occupies many people. Some of them work professionally as theologians—most often in church or university settings. Pelikan notes that this "professional" engagement has changed over time: "During the years 100 to 600, most theologians were bishops; from 600 to 1500 in the West they were monks; since 1500, they have been university professors. . . . Each of these life styles has left its mark on the job description of the theologian" (1971, p. 5). Today, some work as ministers and preachers or composers, people whose theological reflection takes place in the context of worship. And many come to theology only through the day-to-day challenges of living Christian faith. Theology, as it appears in this book, encompasses both the professional (academic or cleric) theologian and the individual believer or "popular" theologian—the theologian living and working in popular culture.

Though the Church thinks about whatever it wills, that thinking, whether done by professional or ordinary believer, does not occur without outside influence. As noted before, the experience of the poor in the contemporary world, the experience of women, the experience of the environment—almost all public experiences—come to the Church's attention both directly and, more often, in a mediated way. The means of communication very often tell all of us—religious people and the not so religious, the professional theologians and the most ordinary person—what the world is like. Despite its simplification, this statement holds as much truth today as in the 1960s: communication media do not tell us what to think but what to think about (Cohen, 1963).

Should any have doubts, decades of communication research support that finding (Bryant and Zillmann, 2002). The various communication media (the printed word, radio, television, film, online sources, and so on) make it possible for us to know what each other thinks about. And the same holds for what the Church thinks about.

Most, if not all, of the key themes of the Church's thinking gained importance because people recognized them as important and as present to them. Again, to use Augustine as an example, his response to Pelagius articulated and made sense of a problem, but only because he had heard of that problem through an exchange of letters. The fact that his sermons in response to that problem were written down and copied and sent to others meant that his thinking influenced more than those who heard them. They influenced Christians across the Mediterranean world and for generations to come, even to our own day. Church councils wrote down their decisions and communication technologies—the media of writing, copying, and preservation—kept them in the consciousness of the Church. Centuries later, Martin Luther's thinking about justification, and the interpretation of the Scriptures that supported it, took on a wider life when the printed versions of his writings spread throughout Germany and Europe as best sellers for the new business of book printing. Again communication technology, the media, and the business world facilitated and influenced the Church's thinking.

Whatever the initial religious experience and whoever did the initial thinking, that thought would not have entered into the consciousness of the Church had it not found its way into the means of communication available to the human community at the time. Preaching and speaking create a community, but one limited in size and constrained in time (Innis, 1951, pp. 33–60). A written text leads to a community of the book and the ideas of such communities enter into a wider circulation (Stock, 1983; Anderson, 1991). This reality marks any thinking, but especially Christian thinking, which grows from a community.

All of this raises at least three sets of questions about communication for the Church, which this book sets out to explore. First, questions about the context of communication: What do we know about that context today? How has that context taken shape in the past? What did that context look like for the reflection on belief? Second, questions about the structures of communication: How have the structures of communication affected the way that the Church thinks? How does each contextual structure work? Third, questions about the relationship of communication and theology: How does the Church's thinking, the systematic reflection on belief, take place in the communication context?

In this book, the overall approach to these questions follows a path set out by media ecology.

Contexts of Communication

First, the context itself: what does the context of communication do to the theology of the Church, both in the past and today? If the Church thinks about religious experience and if human experience includes a great deal more of mediated than of immediate experiences, then people think about what comes to them through the technologies of communication as well as their direct experience. People live in a world of ideas, in a culture that we now describe as a media culture. But, in an equally accurate way, we can say that every human culture consists of its media. How might we describe that culture and its interactions? How does that culture affect the Church's thinking?

Communication studies, especially in its American branches, has explored media effects, that is, how the world of communication media shape or influence individuals. Interest in that question goes back to the beginnings of radio research at least, as people investigated more administrative questions like the efficacy of advertising, the believability of news broadcasts, and the different effects of entertainment on different audiences. Over 40 years of experimental and observational studies identified a number of theoretical models. Two theories of political influence describe how people learn from media. The two-step flow of information (Lazarsfeld, Berelson, and Gaudet, 1944) suggests that people are more likely to learn from others who have learned from media sources. Agenda setting theory (McCombs and Shaw, 1972; McCombs, 2014) holds that communication media (originally the press, but now any "influencer") sets the agenda for segments of the culture by identifying important issues. Other theories, designed to explain more general effects, examined learning. Cultivation theory (Gerbner et al., 1980) suggests that a steady diet of media content cultivates attitudes and opinions about the world, particularly (in the focus of its studies) in terms of estimates of violent behavior. The social learning theory (Bandura, 1977, 1986) explains that people, but especially children, learn behaviors and social interaction by viewing others who enact those behaviors, if that behavior is somehow rewarded. Still other studies sketch out in more detail things that communication studies have discovered about how media messages affect people, in advertising, persuasion, politics, education, and so on (for summaries, see Bryant and Zillmann, 2002).

But the question about the context of communication runs more deeply than specific effects. As noted above, communication studies has long wrestled with the general form of this question. Scholars have debated and attempted to measure the mechanisms by which communication influences us, but we all sense this influence intuitively. Some, beginning with Aristotle, have suggested that the influence stems not only from a particular content but also from our own characteristics and the ways in which that content reaches us—a trusted source, for example, will have more influence than someone whom we know wants to sway us, a finding supported by a great deal of research on persuasion (for summaries, see Miller and Burgoon, 1978; Wilson and Sherrell, 1993). Most agree that the quality of kinds of information available to people influences the topics people think about, if not the content of their thought. Other influences work on people's thinking, too. It is not just the information but its availability, its form, and its suppleness.

More recent attempts to synthesize the larger role of communication in human society fall under the general heading of "media ecology." Media ecology describes a broad range of academic approaches to communication in society. Borrowing a biological metaphor, it takes as its premise that all human communication interacts, with its own forms and contents, with larger cultural and historical factors, with its technologies, and with a complex web of implicature. Like the biological ecology, the addition of any new factor or the change in an existing one will affect all the other interactions. We see evidence of these changes all around us. For example, the introduction of the "smart phone"—the Internet- and computer-enabled phone—turned the telephone into a general-purpose portable communication device that allows not just telephonic communication but texting, email, video, and so on. And that device has changed how people talk or do not talk (preferring text messages or other apps), how people get news (switching from newspapers to news feeds), how people watch video content (not in movie theaters or on television, but in short-form apps), and so on. One change in the physical dimension of communication affected other communication practices and probably a general attitude to communication.

Media ecology regards communication not so much as a tool or as a cultural force, but as an environment. Strate (2004) credits Postman with the naming of this approach:

> Postman did, however, provide a definition of media ecology as "the study of media as environments" (Postman, 1970, p. 161), explaining that the main concern is "how media of communication affect human perception, understanding, feeling, and value; and how our interaction with media facilitates or impedes our chances of survival. The word ecology implies the study of environments: their structure, content, and impact

> on people" (p. 161). These environments consist of techniques as well as technologies, symbols as well as tools, information systems as well as machines. They are made up of modes of communication as well as what is commonly thought of as media (although the term "media" is used to encompass all of these things). Thus, Postman also describes media ecology as "the study of transactions among people, their messages, and their message systems" in *The Soft Revolution* (1971: 139), which he co-authored with Charles Weingartner. (p. 4)

Media ecology encompasses human communication and, with its emphasis on modes of thought as well as symbols, suits theological investigation quite well. For theology, too, forms an environment for people, although only a part of the larger environment called religion or religious practices. As a kind of advanced analysis of religious symbols and meaning (as well as the construction of religious meaning), theology creates an environment for belief.

This book will examine these environments for theology, with a stress on the different media environments.

Structures of Communication

The second question asks, how have the structures of communication affected the way that the Church thinks? How does media ecology work? As we have seen, a media ecology describes a complex environment or set of environments in which communication media interact with a variety of social forces—educational, economic, political, religious, technical, and so on—while at the same time creating their own environment of thought, ideas, patterns of exchange, and other media. For example, evangelists set the oral Gospels in written form; later, copyists bound these into lectionaries or testaments; still others decorated the texts. At each stage, the Church continued to make use of the Gospels, but in ways influenced by the forms that the Gospels took—an illuminated manuscript affects people differently from a proclaimed gospel.

This ecology manifests the fact that people think in patterns that reflect the way that they share information among themselves, whether that occurs orally, in writing, in some combination, or in some other communication form. Media ecology attempts to describe the *forms* of communication, the kinds of information management, the things that characterize both the form and the communication exchanges, and what those forms allow (that is, their affordances); media ecology then draws attention to what people often take for granted in their communication. Clearly, such patterns of communicating and thinking appear in the Church's thinking, as they do in all human activity.

Over fifty years ago, Walter Ong, S.J. (1969) suggested one way to approach the ecology of communication, at least in terms of theology:

> The relationship of communications media and theology can be thought of in terms of the influence of communications media on theology or of theology on communications media, or in terms of the responsibility of the communications media vis-à-vis theology or of theology vis-à-vis the communications media. Here, however, I propose to consider none of these matters directly, but something more profound: the interlocking of communications media and theology. We know now that in a given culture many seemingly unrelated phenomena are somehow correlatives of one another. The intellectual activity of a culture and its technological activity are correlatives; styles in art and styles in politics are correlatives, and so on, although we must not imagine correlation here as one-to-one correspondence. We can suspect that the state of theological thinking and the modes of communication in a given culture at a given time are perhaps somehow correlatives, too. (p. 462)

His idea of correlatives offers a helpful construct that illustrates the ecology model: Some things fit together well and grow up together in and through interaction. Subsequent chapters will illustrate this point further.

Another way to think about the ecological system that communication creates comes from technology studies. Though attractive some years ago, few today would hold a position of technological determinism—the theory that the presence of a technology (as, for example, a communication technology like the printing press) determines or prevents some historical outcome, social structure, or cultural value (Hutchby, 2001, p. 442; Chandler, 2013). Instead scholars debate how human tools influence human action or history. Rather than a directly causal connection, human tools play a weaker role in leading to one of a number of possible outcomes. Hutchby explains this, using the metaphors of "text" and "affordance" to describe two approaches. First, technology as "texts":

> Grint and Woolgar (1997) suggest the intriguing notion that technologies should be treated as "texts" which are "written" (i.e. configured) in certain ways by their developers, producers, and marketers, and have to be "read" (i.e. interpreted) by their users or consumers. The writers of these technology-texts may seek to impose particular meanings on the artefact, and to constrain the range of possible interpretations open to users. Users, by contrast, may seek to produce readings of the technology-text which best suit the purposes they have in mind for the artefact....
>
> Neither the writing nor the reading of technology-texts is determinate: both are open, negotiated processes. (2001, p. 445).

Such an approach indicates one way that a technology has an influence while accounting for the fact that different cultures or groups use technologies in different ways. But Hutchby points out that no technology is completely open to any use whatsoever. So he proposes a second approach to understanding how technologies can influence human action, what he calls "affordances." Basing his thinking on Gibson's (1979) studies of perception, he argues that the affordance of an artifact, natural or artificial, offers a possibility for action (Hutchby, 2001, p. 447). The technologies do not determine their use, but constrain the overall possibilities, directing the use to particular possibilities. Because Gibson developed his original studies in terms of natural ecologies, they offer helpful possibilities for media ecology. This is not Hutchby's purpose, but his comments (worth quoting at length) do apply to communication media:

> There are of course many types of affordances: affordances of the natural environment; affordances of artefacts; affordances of other species within the environment; or of other members of our own species; and so on. These different sources may be interrelated or compounded on any given occasion of action.
>
> Secondly, it is important to see that affordances are not just functional but also relational aspects of an object's material presence in the world. Affordances are *functional* in the sense that they are enabling, as well as constraining, factors in a given organism's attempt to engage in some activity: for instance, walking, or hiding, photocopying a document, and so on. Certain objects, environments, or artefacts have affordances which enable the particular activity while others do not. But at the same time the affordances can shape the conditions of possibility associated with an action: it may be possible to do it one way, but not another. The *relational* aspect, by contrast, draws our attention to the way that the affordances of an object may be different for one species than for another. . . .
>
> Thirdly, especially when it comes to the world as experienced by humans, objects and their values can also be tied in with complex sets of concepts and conventional rules governing their use, so there is an important sense in which we can, and indeed must, *learn* about some of the affordances that certain things offer. (pp. 448–49)

Such an ecology of technology well describes what happens when an ongoing human activity like theology meets various communication contexts and tools.

The affordance model does not completely describe what happens when people encounter new technologies. Contemporary studies of the oh-so-many new communication technologies have sought to explain what happens through many models. Another of these models helpful to media ecology comes from the idea of "domestication"—how people actually make use of a given (communication) technology. Following Haddon, Ling (2004) suggests four steps: consumption or acquiring the technology, a process of adoption, negotiation regarding the role of the technology, and social interaction among users to further incorporate the technology (pp. 26–27). Here again the sociology of technology describes a complex ecology, where many factors work simultaneously.

In this spirit, the chapters that follow will describe a media ecology of theology. Ideas interact with various media, which in turn generate patterns and ideas in the theology itself. The communication media themselves offer affordances for thinking and managing information and subtly influence thinking in one direction or another. People reflect on their belief not only in the time and culture in which they live but also with the communication media available to them. Not everyone will use those media in the same way and not every theological expression will have the same value.

Communication for Theology

Third, how does the Church think in the communication context? Both well-established fields of inquiry, theology and communication each have long histories and a number of interactions, periods of mutual influence, and overlaps—as one would expect from an ecological perspective. One, a mostly non-ecologically oriented approach, attracted early interest from churches in the recent past.

Insofar as people view it as a set of technical or instrumental skills, communication often finds itself recruited to work in the interests of theology and its larger ecclesial parents, evangelization and instruction. Responding to requests from ecclesial offices—the Roman Catholic Church's Second Vatican Council, various Vatican offices, conferences of bishops, the World Council of Churches, the U.S. National Council of Churches of Christ, and similar groups—people have set out to explore a "theology of communication." The last fifty years have seen any number of thinkers attempting to bring theology and communication together (see Soukup, 1983, 2006, 2011 for overviews). The various inviting church groups often intended some reflection on instrumental communication or communication strategies, as well as moral guidance drawn from denominational documents. In the face of new media "revolutions" that moved quickly from satellite and cable television to the Internet to social media in a relatively short time, and confronted by religious entrepreneurs with television ministries or self-appointed online pastors, church officials sought guidance from theology. What should churches or church bodies do? What kinds of communication made not only good tactical sense but also fit the theological self-understandings of the churches? For example, should a church that theologically defines itself as nonhierarchical employ centralized mass media formats? Who has authority (and of what kinds) over these new kinds of theological expression? These kinds of concerns gave rise to the search for a theology of communication. Ironically, though with some exceptions, communication practitioners and scholars seemed readier to take up this challenge than did theologians or church leaders themselves.

But some approaches did take shape. A few examples of work from theological and communication scholars provides a sense. Dulles (1971, 1989) explored a theology of communication rooted in ecclesiology and highlighted the different communication approaches typical of different understandings of the church. His work indirectly addresses the overall theological environments for communication. Returning to the ancient tradition of theology informed by exegesis, Martini (1994) offered a theology of communication rooted in the reading of key texts, particularly Mark 7:31-37. Less an ecological approach than that of Dulles, Martini's reading of the Scriptures fits into the kinds of theology long known in the Church as practiced by bishops and preachers. From the perspective of communication, White (1986) develops a theological understanding of communication rooted in its sociological functions, noting four aspects: (1) the Church's role vis-á-vis society, (2) the necessary adaptation of theological ideas to the cultural logic and religious vocabulary of the times, (3) the development of popular styles of communication and religious expression, and (4) finding new models of the Christian community. Bonnot (2001) highlights what he regards as the most communicative concepts of theology as ideals for religious communication: the Trinity, creation and revelation, and the Incarnation. Plude (1995) calls attention to the media context of the communication world in which the Christian Church finds itself, outlining some of the consequences for religious communication, not least an emphasis on storytelling and the patterns of interaction fostered by newer communication technologies, ranging from organizational structure to the importance of individual expression. Examining how religious groups understand communication, Hosseini (2008) identifies functionalist, essentialist, and interactive approaches and argues that a "religious pluralism" best serves the theological constraints of communication technologies (p. 67). In this, Hosseini identifies the work of Hoover (1995) and Clark (Clark and Hoover, 1997) as particularly helpful.

The Church does its thinking in a number of other ways as well. When most people think of theology, they probably think either of the official thinking of the church—as for example in the Catholic tradition, papal statements, bishops' letters, Vatican materials, statements of national bodies, and so on—or of the work of professional theologians: university teachers, writers, and church employees. But these make up only one category of theological work. A second kind of theology, or at least of the Church in the process of thinking, meets people through preaching and pastoral counseling. In fact, this quite ordinary way for the church to do its thinking probably affects more people more directly than the first category. Admittedly, the first kind of thinking has a strong impact on the second, but the first group does not have the same day-to-day contact with Christians as does the second. Third comes a category of much more ordinary thinking about religious experience. Everyone at some time reflects on the experience of God. Some people give expression to their thinking in art, drama, storytelling, song—however they express themselves. Where these expressions enter into mass culture, we find still another theology, one often assembled from existing cultural tools or expressions.

As people more and more recognize the role of communication in their lives, they turn to media products, either directly or indirectly, to find meaning and to reflect, even on their religious experience. The chief environment for such reflection consists of popular culture. Clark (2005) has tracked such uses in the lives of teens and young adults. She explains the background in an earlier paper and her observation bears repeating:

> The media provide a primary language of shared, cultural experience through stories, images, and ideas. Whether we like it or not, the electronic and print media provide the common language, usually mediated through capitalism and consumerism, that is shared the world over. . . . Popular culture is not the location of the latest version of Christianity, but it is a context of culture. It is a primary language of the majority of people. So it seems to me that theology must take it seriously if theologians are to be taken seriously, as being truly interested in people. One of the obvious bridges between theology and media studies, therefore, is through this concern for the meaningful experiences of the people. Thus one thing that media studies can offer to theologians, I believe, is a better understanding of how these shared, largely hegemonic, worldwide, and highly problematic stories communicated in the various media become meaningful, even in terms of "religious" understandings, in peoples' everyday lives. (Clark, 1998)

Clark's assertion that popular culture provides an environment for theological reflection today should also serve as a reminder that popular culture has done so in the past. As subsequent chapters point out, a good deal of reflection on belief takes place in popular expression.

This should not seem unexpected. Gordon Lynch (2015) identifies four ways in which theology and religion interact with popular culture, and all of them can apply to the past as much as to the present day. He notes that people can approach religion or theology "in relation to the environment, resources, and practices everyday life (in particular asking about how popular culture shapes religious beliefs and activities or is appropriated by religious groups, how religion is represented in popular culture, and how religious groups interact with popular culture)"—an ecological approach, to use the terminology presented earlier. Further, Lynch writes that popular culture itself "may serve religious functions" (p. 21), again something that subsequent chapters will highlight. Third, churches and religious individuals may use the tools or sites of popular culture to further Christian goals, in a kind of missionary outreach. Finally, the materials of popular culture present opportunities for theological reflection (p. 36). Lynch sees this as "a critical dialogue between a particular religious text or theological concept and a specific aspect of popular culture. Through this process of critical conversation between popular culture and theological texts and concepts, writers have thus sought to use popular culture as a means of exploring issues including the nature of God, the possibility of meaning in life, the nature of sin and evil, and the nature of redemption" (p. 37). One need only recall Dante's *Divine Comedy* or Milton's *Paradise Lost* to realize that such dialogues have a long history in Western culture.

Where These Things Lead

The questions about theology and communication—about the context, about the structures of communication, about the relationship of communication and theology, about the affordances that communication provides theology—run through this book as they do throughout the ecosystem in which both areas of study exist. Although it examines theology and theological forms as its data, this book explores media ecology, viewing theological expression through that lens of studying and understanding communication. The history and variety of the theological practices of Christianity show the stamp of communication media, because Christianity in particular has over time seized on every communication tool both to propagate its beliefs and to understand them. The ecology of how this happens shows a good deal about communication in everyday practice. Because the changing ecosystem of communication often appears more clearly in the past, the history of the practices of theology offer interesting case studies across a two-thousand-year history of Christianity's reflection on its belief in both personal and institutional settings. The book, then, explores a media ecology focused on theology in a variety of places, times, and examples. Each study could stand alone; together they offer a picture of a complex ecology at work. They also provide some views of how the Christian Church does its thinking. None of the case studies intends or attempts to provide an exhaustive account of theology in a given medium; none attempts to provide a complete account of the media ecology of each medium. The case studies instead offer a glimpse, on the one hand, of what the media ecology approach can reveal about thought over time and, on the other hand, of how theological history illustrates the interaction of different media ecologies.

This book does not attempt to "do" theology, nor does it attempt to explain the meaning of various communicative expressions of theology. Reflections in various media must stand on their own, as Carpenter (1972) points out:

> It [artistic expression] bypasses language & seems to play directly on the nerve ends. The same applies to much contemporary dance, film & music, especially electronic music. When we ask the contemporary artist to explain himself in words, he refers us back to the work. Isadora Duncan said, "If I could tell you what it meant, there would be no point in dancing it." (p. 34)

A composer of religious music, a church architect, or a religious artist might say the same. This book, instead, aims to show how the form affects the expression, how people reflect on their belief.

The rest of this book examines eleven media forms and their connection to theology. Each chapter briefly summarizes the relevant media ecology approach and then considers the affordances of the medium for theology, for "faith-seeking-understanding," in Anselm's phrase. The book uses Anselm's formulation to distinguish the faith-seeking-understanding in various media from "theology," which today typically refers to written academic expressions. The "understanding" in faith-seeking-understanding encompasses more than formal logic and engages in different systems of information management than printed texts.

Chapter 1 explores the oral background of Christian theology. Christianity itself emerged from a mixed oral and scribal culture, one which knew and utilized writing but one in which only a small minority of people actually could read and write. Chapter 2 continues that theme by considering the ongoing influence of narrative as a way of thinking, one that takes root in the oral nature of early Christianity and continues to this day, although more in the wider culture than in theology and more in popular media forms than in writing.

The next chapters address some specific communication media used within the Christian tradition. Chapter 3 lays the groundwork with an overview of the educational systems that shaped the shifting ways in which theology manages information. Each medium can manage information and the educational system prepares students to work in the ecology created by the dominant media of the time. Chapter 4 brings writing and printing to the fore, calling attention to the communication tools that definitively shaped theology as it exists today. Chapter 5 offers a case study of the translation of the King James or Authorized Version of the Bible, an enterprise that illustrates the complexity of the media ecology and the combination of non-media forces that shaped it.

The next several chapters examine communication systems that differ from writing. Chapter 6 examines art and the shifting relationship of artistic expression to Christianity's reflection on belief. Chapter 7 turns to music, sensitive to its forms more than to specific musical lyrics. Chapter 8 calls attention to church architecture, a communication medium that people often take for granted, but one that gives a concrete meaning to an environment and an ecosystem. Chapter 9 considers ritual or the communicative behaviors that take place in religious environments.

Chapter 10 moves closer to the present time with discussions of film and other screen images, which connect both to art and to industrial production and mass mediated experience. Chapter 11 turns to one aspect of social media culture, examining its impact on nonacademic reflection on belief. Finally, a concluding chapter summarizes the book by looking at how the contemporary encounter between academic theology and popular culture shows how media ecologies can change over time.

1
ORALITY AND CHRISTIAN THEOLOGY

A Media Ecology Perspective

Most people typically regard theology as a written project, because its texts, gathered over the centuries, offer a testament to what Anselm termed an ongoing "faith-seeking-understanding," the reflection on belief typical of Christianity (Switzer, 2010). Taking theology simply, as faith-seeking-understanding or, more elaborately, as a systematic reflection on belief shows how theology bears the mark of the communication tools available to it at different points in its history. Christian theology evolved in a milieu that encompassed both an oral culture and a written culture, with the oral aspects predominant in its first millennium. If media ecology approaches are correct, then the media environment should leave some kind of an imprint on the theology.

Through a complex relationship of orality and early scribal culture (Kelber, 1994), the Christian Gospels provide a memorial of orality, of the utterances of Jesus, as for example, "When Jesus saw the crowds, he went up the mountain . . . and taught them, . . . Blessed are the poor in spirit . . ." (Matt 5:1–3 NRSV). They tell us that "with many . . . parables he spoke the word to [the crowds] . . ." (Mark 4:33 NRSV). And, especially in the Gospels of Matthew and Luke, they record enough sayings of Jesus that do not appear in the Gospel of Mark that Scripture scholars posited a lost gospel document "Q" (for the German *Quelle* or "source") as a collection of the sayings drawn upon by those who composed the Gospels (Funk and Hoover, 1994).

The Gospels record any number of instances of Jesus teaching, speaking to the people and to his disciples. Only once do they refer to him writing (John 8:6), though the Synoptic Gospels do refer to him reading. Christianity has no writings left by Jesus, and the written New Testament letters and Gospels date from the middle to the end of the first century of the Christian era—some thirty years and more after the death of Jesus.

Galilee and Judea at the time of Jesus formed a mixed communication culture—some people could read and write (notably the scribes, some religious leaders, and probably those working in state administration), others had some reading, and many lived in a purely oral culture: "Studies of literacy in the ancient Mediterranean world place the number of people who could read and/or write at somewhere around 5%, with a somewhat higher percentage projected for urban males (Rohrbaugh 1993: 115, Bar-Ilan 1992: 56; Harris 1986: 267 suggests 15% for urban males)" (Hearon, 2004, p. 102; and see also Wright 2017). Most likely, even the literate, like those in Roman and Greek cities, used scribes to write for them, as evidence in various texts indicates (for examples, see Kenyon, 1971, pp. 21, 82; Hadas, 1954, pp. 15–17). St. Paul certainly did so, as he explicitly remarks on the scribes recording his dictation (see Rom 16:22, 1 Cor 16:21, Col 4:18, 2 Thess 3:17). Public reading, by professional or enslaved readers, was also common (Kenyon, 1971, p. 85; Hadas, 1954, pp. 60–64; Hearon, 2004, p. 97; Ward and Trobisch, 2013, pp. 8, 12–13). This mixed culture of a small proportion of literates and many nonliterates creates an interesting media ecology.

Part of that ecology resulted in a written culture of administrative documents, poetry, drama, history, and even oratory circulating in writing, though often performed orally, as well as the collection of myths, stories, wisdom sayings, and events handed on by word of mouth and later written out for reading or performance. In such a situation, the oral shaped the written. Quoting Foley (1990), Kelber refers to these as "oral-derived texts" (Kelber, 1994, p. 199). He notes the difficulty in separating one modality of communication from another, but nonetheless urges an attention "to phenomena such as residual oral traces or orality filtered through textuality, transformation of voice and the rhetorical outreach of texts" (p. 194).

This situation calls into question any firm line between an "oral culture" and a "written culture," at least in the world of the Greco-Roman Empire during the early Christian era. Many of the written texts, including the Gospel texts, show signs of oral composition. The evidence of how Christian groups reflected on their belief in preaching, for example, or in hearing the Gospels, shows signs of a written substrate. Classical education fostered this mix (Soukup, 2012; see ch. 3).

The theological situation similarly moves between these worlds. The earliest theology consists of a biblical theology, of a Jewish community of believers in Jesus trying to understand the impact of Jesus by drawing on the Hebrew Bible. Later Gentile converts seemed to have first learned the stories of Jesus and the Hebrew Bible in order to add their own interpretations. Still later generations drew on the Greek philosophical tradition to pose questions about those stories.

The New Testament scholar James Dunn describes the provenance of the Gospels as "Jesus in oral memory" (2001). The early preaching of the disciples most likely consisted of their telling the story of Jesus and retelling his parables and other sayings. When Jesus sent the seventy-two out to preach the Kingdom of God (or even when the disciples talked among themselves), what would they say but to repeat what they had heard from Jesus (pp. 119–120)? An oral culture, even one with some writing, is a culture of stories and storytelling, of repeating and retelling the familiar. This seems consistent with the actions of Jesus and the disciples. The Gospels themselves bear the hallmark of oral composition, something that scripture scholars have described in their close analysis of the texts (Dunn, 2001, pp. 84–93).

Dunn reports on theories of how an oral tradition develops, of how Mark or the other Gospels received the materials assembled into the structure they now have. Following Bailey (1991), Dunn suggests five categories of oral material preserved in the day-to-day life of a Middle East village: proverbs; "story riddles" in which "in the story the hero is presented with an unsolvable problem and comes up with a *wise* answer;" poetry; parables or stories; and accounts of important figures (Dunn, 2001, p. 91). Villagers maintain accuracy in the parts of the oral tradition to varying degrees:

> Particularly valuable are Bailey's notes on how the community controlled its tradition. He distinguishes different levels of control. (1) No flexibility: poems and proverbs. (2) Some flexibility: parables and recollections of people and events important to the identity of the community. "Here there is flexibility *and* control. The central threads of the story cannot be changed, but flexibility in detail is allowed." (3) Total flexibility: jokes and casual news: "The material is irrelevant to the identity of the community and is not judged wise or valuable." (Dunn, 2001, p. 92)

The accuracy of this kind of oral transmission varies, then: it follows a general practice of preserving the core message with changes in the minor details. Dunn illustrates this point with examples, first from the Acts of the Apostles and then from the synoptic Gospels. Acts provides an interesting internal example, with three accounts of the conversion of Saul/Paul in Acts 9, 22, and 26. Here, the core message remains identical, but with each telling some details change (time of day, the role of the traveling companions, the choice of verbs, etc.). In the account of Jesus' calming the storm at sea, the main story again remains the same in Matthew, Luke, and Mark but with changed details. For Dunn, this provides evidence of the oral transmission rather than of the evangelists working with a written text:

> Once again it is quite possible to argue for a purely literary connection—Matthew and Luke drawing upon and editing Mark's (for them) original. The problem with the purely literary hypothesis is that most of the differences are so inconsequential. Why, for example, as literary editors would it be necessary for them to vary the description of the storm and the danger of the boat being swamped (each uses different verbs)? It is surely more plausible to deduce that Matthew and Luke knew their own (oral) versions of the story and drew on them primarily or as well. (p. 101)

Dunn uses the theory of oral transmission to explain a number of other passages in the Gospels. From the media ecology perspective, it provides an insight into how oral cultures retain important information before the account becomes locked into a written text. An oral culture, like any other, must engage in some kind of information management. This pattern shows the beginning of theology: the information management indicates an attempt to understand belief by the choice of materials it preserves. Kelber (2013a) makes the role of theology stronger by calling attention to the narratives themselves. Narrative analysis highlights that each Gospel has its own internal dynamic, drawing different "theologies" of the role of Jesus, often connected to the memory of Jesus refracted in the needs of the communities. In Kelber's (2013g) view, the media ecology includes not just the oral and scribal interactions, but also those of memory.

The Gospels show various signs of information management, both in terms of small elements and in terms of rhetorical structures. Mark's Gospel, usually accepted as the earliest, has an additive storytelling structure with repeated use of "and," a framing of episodes through the use of *inclusio* as an oral marking of sections, and dramatic literary style. Havelock (1963) identified several features characteristic of oral composition. Reid offers this summary:

> Havelock maintains that narrative structure is one of the identifying compositional conventions typical of oral technique because semantic rhythm and the balancing of "notions" are central to a theory of primary orality.... He also maintains that parataxis, the stringing together of one idea syntactically after another, is essentially an oral construction, as opposed to the hypotactic balance of subordinated clauses indicative of literate syntactical construction (Havelock, 1963, pp. 76–77). (Reid, 1994, p. 429)

Although Reid does not accept all of Havelock's conclusions, he recognizes some and goes on to provide a detailed analysis of the *inclusio* and parallelism that holds the Gospel of Mark together. Such a structure gives the hearers (or possibly readers when the text was written down) a sense of expectation, a way to anticipate the elements still to come.

• • •

But the structure of the oral performance does more than keep the hearer attentive. It must also involve the hearer. Each instance of the spoken word took place in a given context; for the Gospels, that context had a connection to the growing Christian community. Hearon (2004) describes this as a "social construction":

> If the spoken word is intended to lend support to particular "social postures" it must, at one and the same time, reflect the context in a way that hearers will recognize and with which they will identify, and engage the hearers to a degree sufficient to create in them the capacity to entertain new social boundaries (Robbins 1993: 146, Horsley and Draper 1999: 295). Our "oral and aural written remains," then, belong to an act of social construction, an act that is undertaken through performance. (Hearon, 2004, p. 99).

Reid (1994) offers an example of how this invitation to "entertain new social boundaries" might work. He points out that the Gospel of Mark somewhat unexpectedly leaves out a final balancing element at several points, resulting in the necessity of the audience's filling in the missing element. The Gospel of Mark does this twice: at the call of the disciples (p. 439) and the proclamation of the resurrection (p. 440). In both instances, these elements function as interaction invitations to the hearers. "By creating functional lacunae in the denouement of selected narrative complexes he [Mark] indicates his unwillingness to allow an audience simply to experience his story passively. He demands that they respond, that they choose" (p. 440).

Such immediacy characterizes the oral world, even one in which people eventually move from oral memory to writing. Working not from the Gospels, but from studies of predominantly oral cultures—the work of Havelock on the pre-Socratic Greeks (1963) of Parry on the Homeric epics (1971), of Lord on Yugoslavian bards (1960)—Walter Ong (1982) summarizes characteristics of oral composition and of oral cultures more generally. Some of these details come from what texts preserve. Ong and the others argue that the written texts of ancient materials indirectly record a key media ecology—the development of human thinking adjusting itself to the tool of writing. Older texts exhibit features quite different from newer or later ones; the oldest consist of lists and inventories or summaries of laws and achievements. Later ones contain narratives, drama, poetry, history, and so on. And the narratives and drama, written down in a culture predominantly oral, provide a window onto how oral cultures work to preserve and manage information. In the instance of the Christian tradition, early texts open that window onto how people understood and explained their faith.

Early texts, Ong argues, show thought patterns closer to the purely oral life world (1982, pp. 15, 16). The world of these ancient texts reflects a culture where, even though some could read, most could not, so the human mind retained its oral habits. The key aspect of such a culture was the absolute necessity to remember. An oral culture can only know what it can remember. That also means that a great deal of the collective energy of every oral culture is focused on memory: remembering how to do important things (hunt, make tools, grow food) and remembering who they are (stories of ancestors, God, creation, the land or sea) and remembering how to act (codes of behavior), and so on. Oral cultures, however, do not lack technologies, and they invested energy in technologies of remembering. Over the centuries human cultures developed all kinds of memory aids, so that the cultures could remember things. As Ong points out in *Orality and Literacy*, these aids shape not only the ways that people remembered but also the ways that people thought. What better way to help memory than to think memorable thoughts (Ong, 1982, p. 34)? These "memorable thoughts" acted as prebuilt packages that helped both to store and to recall ideas and information. Without the tools to store knowledge, forgetting something meant the permanent loss of that knowledge or information. And so oral cultures developed in such prebuilt processes a technology of information storage—a set of organizational patterns and social practices to promote recall and memory. These tools of memory "must always to some extent involve the psyche as a whole" (Yates, 1966, p. xi). In other words, the memory techniques, many of them developed in quite sophisticated ways over the centuries, affect human thought and signal key values. Such tools lasted well into the fifth century and beyond: "Extending a thesis introduced by Francis Yates (1966), King's study, which ranges widely over classical rhetoric up to and including Augustine's *Confessions*, adduces ample evidence of what was a fundamental strategy of the ancient art of persuasion: to bring auditors to see what was being said, so that the images they visualized were vivid to the point of being indistinguishable from actuality" (Kelber, 1994, p. 205). This applies not only to persuasion, but to memory in general. The more vivid the image, the more memorable. Yates shows how the pattern of visual memory, first developed in oral presentation, still influenced information management in the Renaissance. The "tool set" of oral memory stood in contrast to the tools of writing but still informed early writing practice. As writing became more and more widespread, it developed its own patterns of knowledge and arrangement in the psyche.

Because they lose any knowledge that they cannot remember, members of oral cultures develop memory techniques and do not abandon them until writing has a firm foundation in a culture. This becomes absolutely essential, Ong argues, on the principle that "you know what you can recall" (Ong, 1982, p. 33). In addition to visualizing things, primary oral cultures developed all kinds of habits of thought, from dialogues (two minds do better than one) to mnemonic patterns. Ong explains:

> Your thought must come into being in heavily rhythmic, balanced patterns, in repetitions or antitheses, in alliterations and assonances, in epithetic and other formulary expressions, in standard thematic settings (the assembly, the meal, the duel, the hero's "helper," and so on), in proverbs which are constantly heard by everyone so that they come to mind readily and which themselves are patterned for retention and ready recall, or in other menemonic form. Serious thought is intertwined with memory systems. (p. 34)

Based on his reading of the studies of primary oral cultures, Ong concludes that thinking apart from the memory systems "would be a waste of time" since the culture could not remember it and would lose the thought, no matter how important (p. 35).

These patterns of memory do have limits, so the members of primary oral cultures must choose what to remember. Many cultures also divide the labor of remembering, with religious figures, elders, tribal leaders, bards, and others focused on particular aspects of the group's knowledge. For theology, this cultural background shapes what people remember, the relative importance of those elements, and their interpretation.

From recorded material that reflects primary oral cultures, Ong develops an inventory of patterns that "set off orally based thought and expression from chirographically and typographically based thought and expression" (p. 36). These include formulaic patterns, rhetorical forms, narrative types, and character preferences. Each contributes to the ecology of the medium of spoken word and memory. People retain a familiarity with some of these patterns today, since preliterate children depend on memory rather than writing and much of children's culture (Knapp and Knapp, 1978) maintains an oral dimension. However, today's children also learn literate patterns early, because culturally valuable things have a literate structure that they learn from literate parents and even from entertainment media. Among the still recognizable patterns, for example, oral cultures make use of all parts of the body to help them remember: singing, dancing, acting out rituals, moving in certain ways, keeping rhythms. Oral cultures use every aspect of language: rhymes, metrical patterns, and repetition through synonyms. Oral cultures put things into narrative forms: stories with their plots are easier to remember than are abstract formulations. Oral cultures draw on the whole community to help remember: they tell the same stories over and again. Ong refers to this as the "noetic economy" of the culture, the set of ways in which the culture governs and regulates thought (Ong, 1982, p. 70).

Primarily oral cultures use an additive style rather than a subordinative one. Though not addressing theology, Ong notes the pattern in theological materials: Genesis 1:1–5 contains nine links using "and" (1982, p. 37). Similarly, as noted above, the Gospel of Mark features repetitive use of "and" as a link in its presentation of the life of Jesus. Oral style aggregates ideas, partly for formulaic or metrical reasons (that is, for the ease of memory). So, orally based narratives have "not the soldier, but the brave soldier; not the princess, but the beautiful princess" (Ong, p. 38) and so on. The thought may reflect clichés, but clichés both bind thought units together and provide a certain obviousness that helps memory. A writing culture more readily breaks these clichés apart through analysis, but an oral culture runs the risk of forgetting the unit unless it keeps it together. Not surprisingly, oral cultures feature a great deal of redundancy—if the speaker or "rememberer" forgets one part, he or she has a backup. If a hearer does not make out a phrase, the redundant copy supplies the lack. The more or less easy-to-remember redundant expression gives the speaker time to recall the next part of the performance. A culture of writing does not need such aids. Writing itself supplies them.

A culture threatened with total loss should its members forget key things becomes quite traditional or conservative, in the root meaning of "preserving." Such cultures honor those who best remember the ways of the culture and continually enact performances to enhance such knowledge.

As Yates has pointed out, remembering involves the human psyche and has an impact on it. One such impact occurs as oral cultures keep everything that people know close to the human life world (Ong, 1982, pp. 42–43). Because people in primary oral cultures cannot write things down, they aid recall by connecting important information to daily life (a variant on the visualization technique mentioned earlier). Genealogical lists store information in terms of family relationships; most people already can recall their family members, so attaching added information about tribe or history or obligations makes sense (Goody and Watt, 1968, p. 32). Instruction or information about work or activity comes through apprenticeship, through repetitive practice. Where people must store such information apart from the doing, they often include it in stories. A seafaring culture, like that of ancient Greece, recounts Odysseus' building of boats multiple times in the *Odyssey*—the shipwrecks not only provide dramatic tales, they also give an excuse for instructions on boatbuilding (as well as on behavior in strange places, puzzling out challenges posed by unexpected dangers and storms, and other things). The psychic organization keeps things close to how people live; in so doing, it provides a kind of handy reference—when in such and such a situation, recall the story. The pattern remains in Christian reflection as people apply events in the life of Jesus or words from his teaching to solve a problem or to explain why they act as they do. The theological content of the Gospels retains close ties to proper behavior, a theological pattern also evident in the letters of St. Paul.

A related characteristic of primary oral cultures and another that keeps things close to daily human life features what Ong terms "agonistic" behavior (1982, pp. 43–45).

> By keeping knowledge embedded in the human life world, orality situates knowledge within a context of struggle. Proverbs and riddles are not used simply to store knowledge but to engage others in verbal and intellectual combat: utterance of one proverb or riddle challenges hearers to top it with a more apposite or a contradictory one. (1982, p. 44)

The contest at the heart of such agonistic displays sharpens the mind and the memory, and helps people to remember. Similarly, stories of battles and feats of physical strength capture people's imagination—indeed these kinds of stories seem easier to remember—so that even entertainment becomes a teaching tool. Typically, even violent encounters begin with the exchange of insults, a verbal violence. For example, the contest of David and Goliath narrated in 1 Samuel 17 begins precisely in this way. The initial conflict of Jesus with the devil and the ongoing debates with the Pharisees and other religious leaders structure the Gospels, serving to highlight what the Christian community believes through the creating of oppositions. Meier (2001) provides important background on the lack of history about the Pharisees and other groups opposed to Jesus, as support for the theological role of these conflicts. The agonistic form serves as an information management tool in early Christian theology.

The "close to the human life world" pattern that aids recall also draws people into a story through a kind of empathy. Narratives that connect the knower and the hearer with what they hear become more memorable. They also foster situational knowledge rather than abstract knowledge. Havelock (1978) argues, for example, that the pre-Socratic Greeks thought of justice as justice in a particular situation—how one should act in regard to given circumstance or event—rather than as the abstraction that appears in Plato or Aristotle. The same applies to other virtues: wisdom does not exist apart from the wise woman or wise man, something that appears in the Hebrew Bible as well. Even collections of wisdom sayings, when written down, needed someone to apply them to a situation. Ong provides other examples of such situational thinking (1982, pp. 51–55), reporting on the work of A. R. Luria who found that nonliterates did not use abstract geometric terms (circle, square, etc.) but identified them by reference to a concrete object like the moon or a door.

The more people participate in knowledge or information, the more easily they recall it. Oral cultures make use of stories, whose characters then become familiar examples of applied information, from polite behavior to valor in adversity to solving problems to genealogy. Such "heavy characters" (pp. 69–70) both promote identification with the character and provide an information storage function. These characters also draw in a chain of more stories or heroic adventures. Apart from Odysseus or Achilles in the Homeric epics, we see the practice at work in the biblical characters of Moses, Samuel, David, Elijah, Job, and Jesus. Just the name evokes the memory of their deeds, their virtues, their failings, and their trials—a virtual narrative encyclopedia. The narratives do aid recall, but do so in particular ways, fostering one kind of thinking but working against another that developed later with literacy.

In addition to such larger patterns, the oral memory makes use of every bodily resource to help people to remember. People often combine oral recitation with gestures, bodily movement, playing musical instruments, and dance (p. 67). A musical setting for stories and sayings increases their ease of recall, as does a set of linguistic helps: rhyme, alliteration, metrical rhythm. A rhyme pattern and a rhythm reduce uncertainty in terms of what sounds fit the pattern, making memory more reliable. Even the arrangement of material helps the memory. Formulaic verse forms both store information and help to recall it (p. 35). How well we still recall oral forms from our (unlettered) childhood: "thirty days has September, April, June, and November . . ." That formula, like so many others, makes use of rhythm and rhyme. Storing information in formulas proves very efficient, if somewhat narrow.

The oral form also involves repetition: information appears more than once, often in different patterns. Effectively, this increases the odds of its preservation: should one version disappear, the other will remain. Various kinds of word play also increase the information storage capacity of oral discourse.

The linguistic form comes to mind and, along with it, the information stored within it.

The biblical tradition and the New Testament develop in this kind of oral world. And the kind of theology that flourishes in this ecology will do so through oral means—key stories and sayings as well as commentary. In a world that combined oral memory with writing, the New Testament follows that pattern, containing written material in addition to that which seems to have originated orally. The letters of Saint Paul were written, or more properly, dictated to a scribe who wrote them; the letters in turn were read out to the various groups who received them. Saint Paul's reasoning reflects some aspects of writing but his organizational patterns still show oral roots. For example, 1 Corinthians 5–12 is organized around a series of questions, introduced in a kind of conversational style and then addressed in the oral ordering. Paul also makes use of memory groupings, as for example, in his lists of vices and virtues in the fifth chapter of the Letter to the Galatians.

However, the Gospels reflect more strongly an oral beginning and reflect how the medium shapes the theology. As noted above, Dunn (2001) presents a great deal of material to show how the Gospels could have developed from an oral core. An example different from those listed earlier indicates how such oral forms reflect theological concerns; this example comes from the Gospels of Matthew, Luke, and John: the healing of a member of an official's household at a distance (Matt 8, Luke 7, John 4). In the account a distraught father comes to Jesus to ask for healing but, when Jesus offers to accompany the man home, the father replies that he is not worthy for Jesus to enter his home; Jesus need only to say the word. Dunn explains:

> The episode is clearly the same: it is the story of the healing at a distance of the seriously ill servant of a centurion who lived in Capernaum. Within that framework we find the same striking features: (1) a core of the story where the agreement is almost word for word (Matt. 8:8–10/ Luke 7:6–9); (2) details that vary on either side of the core, to such an extent that the two versions seem to contradict each other (in Matthew the centurion comes to plead with Jesus personally; in Luke he makes a point of not coming).
>
> Evidently the exchange between Jesus and the centurion made a considerable impression on the disciples of Jesus: the combination of humility and confidence in Jesus on the part of such a figure, and Jesus' surprise at its strength would have been striking enough. Equally noticeable is the way in which Matthew and Luke have both taken the story in their own way: Matthew emphasizes the theme of the centurion's faith, by inserting the saying (Matt. 8:11–12) that Luke records in Luke 13:28–29 (the

centurion as precedent for Gentile faith), and by rounding off his telling with a further commendation by Jesus of the centurion's faith (Matt. 8:13); Luke emphasizes the theme of the centurion's worthiness, by having the elders testify to his worthiness (*axios*) (7:4–5) in counterpoise to the centurion's expression of unworthiness (*exiosa*) (7:7a). (2001, p. 98)

Dunn continues to show how the Johannine account shares key characteristics but also diverges, evidence for him of a common oral account rather than of a written dependence of the Gospels upon one another: "The two versions (Matt/Luke and John) provide good evidence of stories of Jesus being kept alive in oral tradition. And either way we can see something of both the retentiveness of the oral traditioning process and its flexibility in allowing traditions to be adapted to bring out differing emphases" (p. 99). This account and the others that Dunn adduces highlight both the pattern of oral memory and the ways in which it interacts with the community which hears the stories. Each makes it a story of faith and each constructs a theology of the meaning of the life of Jesus from the materials.

The media ecology of the New Testament also includes another way that the New Testament interacted with its hearers: as a performance text. This refers to the ways that people did not necessarily read these texts as people think of reading today (silently, individually, etc.). The audiences who experienced the New Testament text experience it as read to them by a reader who prepared—most likely by memorizing—the text and then performed it for the community. The Gospels came to birth in a mixed communication environment of oral discourse and writing, with even writing dependent on speaking. Kelber summarizes this:

> Achtemeier, echoing the views of others, has reminded us that ancient texts were composed by dictation and with the aim of catching the attention of the ear (1990). There is impressive evidence that dictation, whether to oneself or to others, was the preeminent mode of writing. It may be assumed, therefore, that ancient texts, originating in speech and lacking in visual codes of punctuation, were perforce organized in conformity with a phenomenology of sound rather than of sight. So pervasive was the oral environment, Achtemeier states, that "*no* writing occurred that was not vocalized" (p. 15). Indeed, not only drama and poetry, but historical writings as well, were reactivated in public readings (Graham, 1987, p. 35). (1994, p. 206)

The world of writing by dictation ran in parallel to the world of reading by hearing. Even those who could read would listen to public performances. In

Rome and Greece at the time of Jesus and well into the time of Augustine, public contests of oral performance occurred regularly (Ward and Trobisch, 2010, pp. 25–28). It seems reasonable that the Christian community also had public oral performances of their religious texts: "When Christians came together they probably expected the same [stylized reading] from their performers as they read out literature generated by memories of Jesus' life and ministry, apostolic letters, wisdom writings and prophecy, and of course the sacred writings of the Hebrews" (p. 29).

Such public reading predates Christianity. Early Christianity follows a pattern in Jewish life and worship. Second Kings 23:1–3 describes an event in the seventh century BCE in which King Josiah has the book of Deuteronomy, recently discovered during a renovation of the Temple in Jerusalem, read out to the people. The reading occurs in a ritual setting and the scribes read the scroll so that all may know and remember its contents. Nehemiah 8:1–3 recounts a similar episode from after the exile, when the governor commands the priest Ezra to read the book of the law of Moses to the people. When Jesus reads from the scrolls of Isaiah in the synagogue at Nazareth (Luke 4:16–22), the New Testament records a similar oral performance (Ward and Trobisch, 2010, pp. 30–32). St. Paul tells the Christian communities to read his letters aloud (1 Thess 5:27, Col 4:16). Ward and Trobisch provide any number of examples from early Christianity of the oral performance of the Scriptures as part of community worship and gatherings, from accounts in the *Apology* of Justin Martyr in the second century to the writings of Eusebius of Caesarea in the fourth (p. 32).

The theology of the Gospels depends not only on the narratives of the life and teachings of Jesus, but also, as Reid (1994) argues, on the involvement of the audience in the narration, through filling in the gaps or, as King (1991) suggests, through visualizing the images. Ward and Trobisch also note another level of participation: "Audiences might sing along or audibly quarrel with the teller, hum or harrumph, or perhaps accompany performers with musical instrumentation" (2010, p. 38). They also propose another possibility, based on a custom in imperial Rome of private performances. They suggest that Mark's Gospel seems designed for oral performance as a "closet drama":

> "Closet" dramas were performed either by solo performers or small ensembles. This innovation would provide a compelling model for a Christian writer who looked for ways to express controversial views about the meaning of Jesus' ministry; it allowed the composer of the gospel to employ literary elements that others would recognize. Gilbert Bilizekian establishes a plausible case that tragedy, in accordance with

the conventions of the "closet" drama, was a significant influence on the composition of the Gospel of Mark. "The gospel of Mark could be the product of the skillful combination of elements as disparate as the evangelical narrative on the one hand, and on the other, compatible literary devices borrowed piecemeal from an established classical paradigm, specifically that of Greek tragedy." (Ward and Trobisch, 2013, p. 39)

The New Testament material, particularly the Gospels, seem designed for this kind of oral performance based on a written text.

One kind of theological reflection or method emerging from the oral patterning of the Hebrew and Christian Scriptures goes under the general title of "narrative theology" (Navone and Cooper, 1981; Navone 1984; Shea, 1980, see ch. 2.). The term refers to reflection on faith through stories—much as the Christian Gospels provide an understanding of Jesus through narratives of his life—or through audience involvement, whether in the narrative or in wrestling with parables or puzzles. Narrative theology moves through several steps: choosing what to remember, deciding how to arrange it, highlighting key questions, involving the audience, and inviting the audience to make a choice.

• • •

The second main oral source of theological reflection in the early Christian era came from preaching. The evidence of preaching that we have, mostly from homilies recorded by scribes or later dictated to scribes (the practice of Saint Augustine in the fifth century) shows a pattern of Christian preaching consisting of commentary upon the Scriptures. Like the Scriptures themselves, this reflects a combination of oral and written. The Scriptures would be first performed or recited before the congregation and then the preacher would offer commentary on those particular scriptural texts. The Gospel of Luke presents Jesus as doing exactly this in Luke 4:16-27 when Jesus recites a passage from the prophet Isaiah and then comments upon it. This practice emerges as well in the rhetorical performances of classical Rome (Kaster, 1988; Kennedy, 1999), where the rhetor mastered key texts and interpreted them for his hearers. The form of this classical training encouraged the writer to both find topics (in the Christian case, those drawn from the Scriptures themselves) and then the best method of proposing those topics in ways that people could both understand and remember. Sometimes these involved the embellishments and methods drawn from the Roman schools of rhetoric, since audiences would already know and expect those kinds of information management tools.

Early Christian preaching shows the same patterns of oral memory taught in the schools. This reflects a noetic economy geared towards preserving information and aimed towards persuading the audience. Initial preaching explicated texts of the Hebrew Bible, applying them to Jesus (this occurs as early as the New Testament Letter to the Hebrews and, to a lesser extent, in the letters of Saint Paul and the Gospels themselves). Some of the Christian preaching focused reflection upon the mysteries of Christianity (the rite of baptism, the celebration of the Eucharist), as in, for example, the fourth-century-CE preaching of Cyril of Jerusalem in his instruction to the newly baptized candidates. Other Christian preachers developed a kind of guide towards religious or holy living, based on various texts from the Hebrew Bible, as Gregory of Nyssa (also in the fourth century) did with the life of Moses as a model of Christian living. Others used examples closer to their own period, such as the acts of the various martyrs and witnesses to the Christian gospel under persecution.

The format of early Christian theology grew out of an oral tradition that combined orality with the possibility of writing. The writing prepared a record of that instruction for later generations. We see this most clearly in the work of Augustine, the rhetorician, who employed scribes to record his homilies as well as the books that he dictated. One reason for the later influence of Augustine lies precisely in this—the preservation of so much of his thought in writing.

Two main kinds of Christian theology appear in this early period. The first comes in what becomes the New Testament Scriptures, the recording of the life of Jesus and the various kinds of writings offering initial commentary, whether the letters of the New Testament or other narratives of Christian life. The retellings involve the participation in the events themselves. The narrative structure of this Christian theology offered meaning to life as it held up patterns of imitation. Another aspect of that kind of oral theology in the narratives of the Gospels included wisdom literature or puzzles that required an active pondering by the hearers. In either case the hearers would be drawn into the mysteries that they would listen to or participate in through the performance of the Gospels on the Scriptures. This acting out of the religious material allowed people to incorporate it into their own lives through imitation.

The second major approach to early Christian theology also comes from hearing, but in this case the homilies appeared as ways to encourage both understanding and behavior. The preacher provided an analysis of the materials presented to the congregation. Here, as we see in the writings of Augustine, the preachers drew upon the canons of interpretation found in classical rhetoric. The Hebrew and Christian materials appear as having different levels of meaning, from literal to allegorical, concepts fully developed and locked in during the medieval era with its greater dependence on writing (see ch. 3).

Theology in this early Christian era appears less as an analytical process than as a guide for living. Such oral theology takes on a form much more fluid than later theology. Having texts based on writings—of the Bible or of the recorded speaking of the early Church Fathers—led to an ever-growing canon of reflection. Presumably those spoken materials found most helpful would then be copied out and shared with more groups as well. While oral theology has not gone away (and often appears in homiletics), by the sixth or seventh century of Christian thought it moves from a theology that is purely oral or oral reflection on written text to more of a written set of materials.

The media ecology analysis shows a combination of spoken word and written word, with aspects of both kinds of noetic organization. The oral tradition begins with an emphasis upon narrative and the highlighting of personal involvement. In such cases, faith-seeking-understanding becomes a way of living. Only later, as a body of written texts emerged and as a class educated in writing grew, does theology take on the role of a more abstract analysis, where faith seeks understanding in abstract concepts.

2
THE STORIES OF FAITH
Narrative and Theological Meaning

> But because he wished to justify himself, he said to Jesus, "And who is my neighbor?" Jesus replied, "A man fell victim to robbers as he went down from Jerusalem to Jericho. They stripped and beat him and went off leaving him half-dead. . . ." (Luke 10:29–30 NABRE)

Several communication forms typically appearing in oral cultures exemplify the forms of thought of those cultures. People and cultures think with the communication available to them, and their reflection on their beliefs shows the marks of those tools. Theological media do not differ much from regular communication media as both exist as parts of an ecology in which people interact with each other, as well as with the important aspects of their common living, their history, and the existential questions that face all humans. Their thinking appears in wisdom sayings, stories, rituals, and patterns of behavior. Oral cultures, like all cultures, need both to think and to recall the results of that thinking. To do that, they employ all kinds of tools to maintain what they know, to manage the information vital to their living.

Oral cultures are not without technologies, though these tools do not consist of machines or implements but rather of other artificial ways to extend the human senses (McLuhan, 1964, p. 7). People need to amplify their thinking and supplement their memories. Over the centuries human cultures developed all kinds of memory aids, so that their cultures could remember things. As Ong (1982) points out, these aids shaped not only the ways that people remembered but also the ways that people thought. What better way to help memory than to "think memorable thoughts" (p. 34)? These "memorable thoughts" acted as prebuilt packages. Even centuries later, we are still familiar with some of them, since all of us began life without the technology of writing (though we learn that technology early on). For example, oral cultures make use of all parts of the body to help people remember: singing, dancing, acting out rituals, moving in certain ways, keeping rhythms. Oral cultures use every aspect of language: rhymes, metrical patterns, and repetition through synonyms. All this, of course, describes poetry, a communication form beloved of oral cultures. Oral cultures also put things they know into narrative forms: the plots of stories are easier to remember than abstract formulations. The narratives of oral cultures draw on the whole community to help remember: groups tell the same stories over and again and everyone learns them—the stories become part of who people are. Ong refers to this as the "noetic economy" of the culture, the thought patterns or the information management techniques of the culture. The noetic economy describes the set of ways in which a culture governs and regulates thought. In other words, these characteristics of oral cultures provide the affordances with which the cultures think—and think theologically.

This chapter will focus on narrative or storytelling because the inheritance of oral cultures remains active with us today and affects how people reflect on their faith. People still tell stories, still use stories, and still follow the structure of stories for their faith-seeking-understanding.

Stories or narratives—accounts of related events or, in the words of Scholes and Kellogg (1966) "all those literary works which are distinguished by two characteristics: the presence of a story and a storyteller" (p. 4)—appear throughout human history and in every human culture (Kelber, 2013a, p. 34). Much of the theological material of oral cultures takes the form of narratives. While we might examine the religious stories of any culture (and all of them have them), the reference point here remains the Judeo-Christian tradition. The earliest stories about belief in this tradition come from the Hebrew Bible (or Old Testament). Typically, the things that most people remember of the Bible come from the stories: the books of Genesis and Exodus, Judges, and 1 Samuel provide stories of creation; the story of Abraham sacrificing his son, Isaac; stories of the plagues in Egypt; stories of crossing the Red Sea; stories of David and Goliath; stories of the other adventures of David; stories of the prophets Elijah and Elisha. That tradition continues in the New Testament (Christian Bible) with the Gospel narratives about Jesus.

Scholes and Kellogg's "presence of a story and a storyteller" directs our focus for the moment to the oral or performed story. Narratives serve simultaneously as entertainment, as instruction, as memory devices, as ways of thinking, and as community builders. Each of these functions contributes to the media ecology of storytelling in general and more particularly as theology. In thinking about the media ecology of narratives and stories, this chapter begins with the media ecology within narrative, then turns to the media ecology that situates narrative in the world of its hearers, then continues with the media ecology of narrative in the theological world, and ends with the media ecology of our more common thinking about what we believe, of faith-seeking-understanding.

Media Ecology within Narratives

A good narrative entertains. It demands and holds our attention; we become not simply hearers but participants. To do that, narratives combine the parts of their own created ecosystems in various ways, mixing character, plot, point of view, meaning (Scholes and Kellogg, 1966), and even medium together with the hearer to create new worlds.

Narratives create a "storytime," the temporal realm within the story, ranging from the "once upon a time" to the "in the spring, at the times when kings go off to war" (2 Sam 11:1) to any other moment that hearers can imagine. But whatever that time, narratives live in the present tense, always making the past present, connecting times in the spoken word. "In oral or oral-aural communication [the world of the story], both speaker and hearer must be alive. Without the speaker's living action, there are no real words. Without a living hearer, the words are ineffective, uneventful, inoperative, a movement toward nothing" (Ong, 1992, p. 130). Narrative time becomes timeless, and good stories speak truths across time. More than this, the oral or performance quality means that every telling is a first telling, an original telling (Kelber, 2013f, p. 458). Stories deal with "someone who speaks" (Navone and Cooper, 1981, p. xv). And that speaking is always present: "The telling of the stories of that time, *illius temporis*, brings them into the here and now of my time" (p. 37). The timeless enters the time of the hearer, creating a memory in which it dwells. Ong (1992) puts it slightly differently: "There is no narrative set down in the past once and for all, to survive in the present as a monument. The oral story actually exists only when it is being performed" (p. 144).

And so, stories forge a bond between hearer and teller, a bond of trust, expectation, and even suspense. That bond rests both on what Ong terms "interiority" (1967, p. 117) and on other parts of the narrative. The communication medium for oral storytelling—sound—connects the interior being of the teller with the interior of the hearer. That aspect of the narrative increases the sense of presence, of immediacy, and of truth in the telling. The other parts of the narrative play their roles, too. Stories invite relationships with characters—the characters interacting among themselves in the "storyspace" in ways that both mimic and model the relationships that story hearers know. But the stories also invite relationships between the characters and the hearers.

Communication study, considering later media (film, radio, and television), terms these relationships with characters "parasocial relationships" (Horton and Wohl, 1956), things similar to face-to-face relationships but based on a fiction of some kind—a fictional character; a television, radio, or online "personality"; a construction onto which people project their desires and hopes. In a good story, the hearer cares about the characters and lives her life along with the characters.

Narratives and stories also bring their hearers into contact with action, with a plot of some kind. In oral storytelling, the plot usually unfolds chronologically, though its past may mimic the past in the lives of its hearers: the past appears only as a character "remembers" something past (God's reminding Moses of the divine promise to the patriarchs of Israel, Homer's explaining the anger of Achilles), allowing explanation for the present. Despite the resemblance with lived experience, plot carries a sense of its construction within it, as a story's truth depends on something false: "Plot is paradoxical. On the one hand, it makes a story seem real and gives it its psychological appeal or bite. . . . On the other hand, plot is what differentiates art from real life. Plotting is highly artificial, a contrived arrangement" (Ong, 1992, p. 142). Put differently, "for life, after all, does not narrate, and narrative is always artificial" (Kelber, 2013a, p. 34). Plot arranges life events so that meaning appears, leaving out the more random qualities of day-to-day living.

The constructed plot both allows the storyteller's point of view and compels the hearers to take that point of view. In the entertainment of a story, one cannot peek around the corner or behind a wall, as neither corners nor walls exist in the storyteller's construction. That interaction between present tense, character, action, point of view, listener attention, and immersion in the sound of the story creates meaning. At the moment of the story, it creates and sustains the world: such is the basis of a "willing suspension of disbelief" (Safire, 2007). In contrast, questioning or analyzing stories comes with literacy and the distance provided by the written word. Any interpretation comes not during the story's telling but perhaps in our remembering.

As already suggested, the ecology of narratives includes both storyteller and storyhearer, both storytime and storyspace. The next level of the ecosystem, moving from the elements of the story to its relationship with the hearers, highlights several other aspects of narrative and moves closer to showing how narratives can serve as means to reflect on faith.

The very structure of stories—narrated action—makes them easy to remember. Ong (1982) describes many other memorable features of the story: "heavy" characters anchoring the action, sequences of events, visual images, emotional impact, dramatic tension and resolution, and imaginable locations.

The immersive world of story and the ease of remembering a story help to account for narrative's power to teach. People learn from their environments, including the imagined environments of stories. And so, oral cultures rely on narratives for education (Ong, 1982, pp. 33–36), as appears, for example, in the *Odyssey*, where Odysseus' frequent shipwrecks allow the story to instruct a seafaring people on how to build a ship. Something similar occurs in Exodus 25–31, where God instructs Moses, who in turn chooses Bezalel and Oholiab, to build the altar and sanctuary. From their stories, people of oral cultures also learn their histories, genealogies of ancestors, dealings with God, religious rituals, practices of farming, methods of animal husbandry, ways of conducting trade, and other things. (To be thorough, oral cultures also draw on other methods and sources of memory and teaching such as apprenticeship, maxims, drawings, rituals, and so forth.)

The media ecology approach also suggests that in considering the power of stories to teach, we focus on the form of the story as well as the content. As noted earlier, stories have character, plot, setting, and action, but also genre. Some stories tell of adventures or wars; some stories, of growing up and coming to maturity; some stories, of deliverance; some stories, of tricksters; and so on. But story form also includes the media in which the hearer connects to the teller. Although everything so far has focused on oral storytelling, stories from the earliest times also lived on in performances. Later, as people mastered different media, storyteller and hearer met in the oral performance of inscribed stories (that is, in performances based on texts), in written stories, and in the scripted stories of films, television, and so on. The change in media form imposes its own constraints, which later chapters will address. Each of the story forms offers frameworks for telling the story and remembering it. On the one hand, Ong argues that the form limits the content—the structure of the story has affordances: that is, it offers the opportunity to do some things but not others, though it leaves people free to choose among the options. The form does not dictate choices, but it does narrow them. So, if you are going to tell a story of a hero, then the story can only have one hero and a certain number of characters that work with or oppose the hero; it must have action; it must have a limited time span; it must end with the hero's triumph; and so on. On the other hand, the form facilitates things like remembering through the affordances of a limited set of story patterns as well as through linguistic aids ranging from rhyme to alliteration to rhythm.

Stories facilitate both remembering and learning. Again, Ong (1992) highlights the importance of narrative to a culture:

> The paradigmatic situation out of which narrative arises in an oral culture is caught in the invitation, "Tell us a story of the days of old." In literate cultures, such a story may well be a luxury. In an oral culture, it is a matter of life and death. Without such stories, the culture would disappear, the personality structures in which it consists and which constitute it would disintegrate. Narrative about the past encapsulates most of the lore of an oral culture; that is to say, it stores the culture's verbalized knowledge. (p. 144)

The corollary to this process is that the members of oral cultures learn to think in stories. The medium shapes the message (McLuhan, 1964). Members of an oral culture will not analyze nature but will tell a story of how to live in it or of how it came to be through God's creating actions: "In the beginning, when God created the heavens and the earth—and the earth was without form or shape, with darkness over the abyss and a mighty wind sweeping over the waters—Then God said: Let there be light, and there was light" (Gen 1:1–3). In this instance, the storytime places the hearers in God's time while the story explains the world around them. As sources of learning and as memory devices, stories help people to remember by adding a structure to their experiences.

The stories people tell do more than help people to think. They also provide categories for thinking, for managing the information available to them: "In this sense, narrative is the primal way in which the human lifeworld is organized verbally and intellectually" (Ong, 1992, p. 140). Stories both make sense of the world and create the tools that people use as they encounter new things. Because the stories foster thinking based on memory and form an educational system, stories also create and shape community. Stories build community by providing common memories, problem solutions, and explanations that help define how people see and understand themselves. Examples from contemporary communication study illustrate this. Prosecutors have complained that jurors now expect detailed forensic evidence in trials because they have watched a steady stream of fictional police stories where such evidence regularly appears (Shelton, 2008). Political communication scholars note that the stories in news accounts or social media tell people what issues to think about, setting an agenda for public action (McCombs and Shaw, 1972). Teens draw on popular narratives in film and television to make religious sense of the world (Clark, 2005). Groups of people form fan clubs based on the films or stories they follow: one need look no farther than *Star Trek*, *Star Wars*, or *Game of Thrones* fans. The narratives create communities, as they did for the ancient Greeks or Hebrews. In each instance, narratives play a role in how people think, what they think about, what they remember, and how they define themselves.

A media ecology perspective calls attention to one final thing: narratives are themselves ecosystems. Narratives create worlds, with roles, rules of behavior, laws of physics, gods and goddesses, power relations, ideas, and all other aspects of human life. In this sense, the stories people tell create worlds where anything can occur; in other words, they offer a place to test out various "what if" scenarios. What happens if the hero makes one choice rather than another? What is the proper or moral thing to do in a given situation? If a group does not know what to do in a given situation, stories can allow them to seek something new without risk to the old.

Media Ecology and the Theological World

As hinted at earlier, narratives stand among the first communication media in and by which people expressed the understanding of their beliefs, not by analyzing beliefs or faith but by letting it live in stories. The faith-seeking-understanding that forms a part of living simply happens. Narratives that illustrate how people live a relationship with God, and the process of telling stories that reflect on that belief, appear in every culture, from the stories of the classical Greek pantheon to the *Ramayana* and *Mahābhārata* in the Hindu tradition, as well as to the narratives of the Jewish people in the Hebrew Bible: "The need to make scraps of life cohere in the imagination and to plot events so as to give them a semblance of coherence and sequentiality may thus reasonably be counted among the human universals" (Kelber, 2013a, p. 34). For all of the reasons listed above, these narratives provide the ecosystems in which people both attempt to record their experience with God and to make sense of their beliefs, as well as to explain who God is or how God acts.

Stories originating in the Hebrew Bible have become well-known, not only in Judaism but also in Christianity and in Islam. Early stories tell of Abraham's obedience—of his willingness to sacrifice Isaac, the child of God's promise, until he is stopped by the voice of the angel. Others tell of Jacob stealing his brother's birthright and wrestling with an angel on his journey to reconciliation; still others, of Jacob's children selling their brother into slavery in Egypt and God turning that betrayal into a deliverance from famine. Narratives tell of God's call to Moses, of the deliverance of Israel from Egypt, and of the reception of the commandments. Much later stories tell of Job (a what-if story to explore why the good suffer), of Daniel saved from the lions, and of God's providential care of Tobiah. Each story of God's involvement with humanity tells of how the storyteller and the story community seek to understand what they believe and to make (religious) sense of their world.

The use of narrative does not disappear as cultures acquire writing. Religious or meaning-making narratives come to us today as among the first materials preserved in writing. Later generations continued to use the media form of storytelling to reflect on their belief, as a well-established research tradition illustrates in early Christianity. Among New Testament scholars, Kelber (2013a, 2013b) explores "the narrative impulse" (2013a, p. 34), spelling out, among other things, the interactions of oral and scribal media forms (2013d). He also offers a wider context for Christian narrative:

> In the context of ancient literary history, the canonical Gospels can hardly claim uniqueness as far as narrativity is concerned. The golden age of Hebrew narrative extended roughly from the tenth to the seventh century B.C.E. Prose narratives, especially in the form of biographies, were a standard feature of Hellenistic culture. In part at least they owed their existence to the desire to keep alive the memory of extraordinary deeds and powers that were associated with famous poets, philosophers, and rulers. . . . But it remains questionable whether the Gospels are fully assimilable too, and explicable by, Hellenistic narrative models, if only because the narration of a crucified Son of God was a moral, aesthetic, and literary monstrosity, contradicting Jewish, Hellenistic, Roman, and Barbarian sensibilities. (2013a, pp. 34–25)

The Gospels, even as their subject goes beyond the received traditions, do come from those traditions of narrative. Though Kelber's concern focuses on narrative as formative in the development of the Gospels, he calls attention to the cultural dominance of narrative in both community identity and categories of thought as well as its role in structuring the theology of the Gospels. In his view the Gospels act as complex narratives that simultaneously create a theology of redemption and invite people into that redemption through various narrative techniques such as concealing and revealing (Kelber, 2013b). Kelber and others studying early Christianity also highlight another ecological aspect: the very nature of narrative changes over time and across cultures. People expect certain kinds of story and story patterns, but those shifted, either in response to interactions with other groups (as with the Christian Gospels) (Schillebeeckx, 1979, pp. 77) or interactions with different media.

Though not the only oral form used in early Christianity (Kelber mentions sayings; the fathers of the church regularly used sermons, many of which they transcribed and preserved), narrative continued as a theological form for centuries, even as writing played an ever-greater role in the mix of communication media. St. Athanasius (fourth century CE) wrote a life of St. Anthony of the Desert as a theological guide on how to live a Christian life. Other lives of the saints, particularly the acts of the martyrs—gripping stories of courage, betrayal, suffering, and triumph through death—circulated widely in the church and become a distinct narrative style, though one that interacted with scribal cultures. These stories, based on historical people and events, typically show how the storyteller understands living out faith in ways that encourage the belief of the community.

The later Christian tradition continued to use narratives to reflect on belief and even to teach more systematic understandings of faith. Perhaps the mostly widely known example appears in Dante's *Divine Comedy* (fourteenth century) in which the narrator journeys through hell, purgatory, and heaven. The structure of the poem mirrors a kind of "theological geography," with sins and sinners, virtues and saints arranged in a kind of moral order from least to most serious. Dante's long narrative, like epic poems of the classical era, can serve as a kind of encyclopedia or memory system for the culture, but in this instance for theology. Theologians like Albert and Aquinas both taught memory systems that incorporated places (Yates, 1966, p. 72); they systematically arranged theology in ways that could suggest similar principles. Dante's use of place to guide the journey through vices and virtues suggests a similar didactic ordering. By remembering the order of the journey through hell, for example, one easily remembers a lengthy list of sins, presumably to avoid them. At the same time, Dante's story freely incorporates liturgical and ritual elements easily recognizable to his hearers (Nayar, 2014, p. 102). Nayar develops in greater detail the theology of the Eucharist that runs through the poem as a whole. Aided by writing or by artificial memory systems, this and other later Christian narratives explicitly teach theology.

A similar, though less theologically complex, example shows the incorporation of art and music into the religious narratives. In the sixteenth and seventeenth centuries, the stations of the cross—ritualized narratives of the death of Jesus—grew in popularity in the Catholic churches in Europe (Jensen, 2017, pp. 195–97). The stations became multimedia experiences, with the narrative illustrated by fourteen images (the trial of Jesus, Jesus taking up his cross, Jesus meeting the women of Jerusalem, and so on) and accompanied by congregational singing. These stories presented a theology of the cross, a participation in the story, and an invitation to feel sorrow for sins. In the stations, the place, the imagined movement through the place via images, the sounds, the story plot,

42 | A Media Ecology of Theology

The 3rd and 4th Stations of the Cross in St. Joseph's R.C. Church, Cardiff, Wales
Wikimedia Commons

and the characters all invite a participation in a theology of death and deliverance. That theology became rooted in the interiority of all who participated.

Parallel accounts of the importance of narrative to both reflect on belief and to teach theology occur in other religious traditions. Oster (1999) calls attention to the ways that theological narrative has dominated rabbinic literature in Central European Judaism from the sixteenth century on and entered into the storytelling of contemporary writers like Weisel, Singer, and Sholom Aleichem. She explains:

> For even the most fanciful narratives were at bottom didactic in that interpreting them was not seen simply as an amusing intellectual game; neither were even the most poetic tales seen as art for art's sake, but rather a way, through metaphor and narrative, to convey moral and ethical teachings, to use narrative style designed to touch the human heart "so that one should recognize Him who created the world, and so cling to His ways," "To bring down Heaven to earth and to elevate man to Heaven." One studied Aggadah ["that which is told"] in order to get to

know God ("Aggadah" 355–356). . . . In one rabbinic reference to Aggadah, the Biblical description of manna (Exod. 16:31) is invoked as a comparison: "Some sages say that, like manna [which drew the heart of a hungry man], Aggadah draws a man's heart [to Torah], even as water [draws the heart of a thirsty man]." (Stern, 1992, p. xviii). . . . In the 12th century Abraham, the son of Moses Maimonides, wrote an introduction to Aggadah in which he elevated Aggadah as a serious medium by calling on its readers to be interpreters of its "real meaning"; in so doing he was elevating as well his ideal listeners and readers, expecting them to be capable of finding meanings hidden from those who could understand only those more obvious meanings open to any interpreter. (¶4)

Here the Jewish tradition shows the same logic of narrative as appears in the Christian tradition. Moreover, narrative serves to accomplish an understanding of belief, a function that characterizes narrative itself. The rabbinical tradition makes it clear that narrative's role in theology is not limited to Christian theology, though the stories told highlight different theological conclusions. Oster concludes with a rabbinic story that explains the theological efficacy of narrative, in which, "according to Eli Weisel, God created man because He loves stories—a conclusion Weisel reaches based on the Chasidic tale of the Baal Shem Tov:

> When the great Rabbi Israel Bal Shem-Tov saw misfortune threatening the Jews it was his custom to go into a certain part of the forest to meditate. There he would light a fire, say a special prayer, and the miracle would be accomplished and the misfortune averted. Later, when his disciple, the celebrated Magid of Mezritch, had occasion for the same reason, to intercede with heaven, he would go to the same place in the forest and say: "Master of the Universe, listen! I do not know how to light the fire, but I am still able to say the prayer." And again the miracle would be accomplished. Still later, Rabbi Moshe-Leib of Sasov, in order to save his people once more, would go into the forest and say: "I do not know how to light the fire, I do not know the prayer, but I know the place and this must be sufficient." It was sufficient and the miracle was accomplished. Then it fell to Rabbi Israel of Rizhyn to overcome misfortune. Sitting in his armchair, his head in his hands, he spoke to God: "I am unable to light the fire and I do not know the prayer; I cannot even find the place in the forest. All I can do is to tell the story, and this must be sufficient." And it was sufficient.

Only the last, Rabbi Israel, is said to speak to God. Only he has the privilege, it might seem, but in fact, he does so because he has no other means of getting God's attention. Nothing is left to him but words—his own words—and the faith that God will listen, for to speak implies a listener. (¶20–21)

New generations continue to use stories as ways to reflect on their belief, that is, to do theology. As with the rabbinic tradition, some tell (or write) stories with an ear to faith: Isaac Bashevis Singer, Graham Greene, Evelyn Waugh, Annie Proulx, Annie Dillard, Ron Hanson, Denise Levertov, and others. As with the stations of the cross, others use different media forms, particularly film and television (as discussed in ch. 10). Whether biblical stories or contemporary narratives, the media ecology stays the same: a storyteller, a story, and a listener; a story world; characters that call to the listener; a captivating plot; the opening of an interiority; a structure of memory; and an experience of someone beyond ourselves.

The Case of Narrative Theology

While narrative has never disappeared from the media through which people reflect on their belief, it did fall out of favor with those studying theology as an academic endeavor. But this group began to more seriously attend to narrative in the late twentieth century under the title "narrative theology." Mostly, this referred not to narratives but studying narrative. Comstock (1987) notes, "narrative theology, reflection on religious claims embedded in stories, is one of the most significant currents of late twentieth century thought" (p. 687). In his review of the key thinkers, Comstock sees two general approaches: a group who "believe narrative is an autonomous literary form particularly suited to the work of theology. They oppose the excessive use of discursive prose and abstract reason, insisting that Christian faith is best understood by grasping the grammatical rules and concepts of its texts and practices"; and a group who "deny narrative unique theological status. Believing that Christian sacred narratives are irreducibly infected with historical, philosophical, and psychological concerns, they seek to apply the methods of those disciplines to their interpretation" (p. 688). Both apply narrative to analyzing the biblical material at the heart of Christianity. And both groups seek to accomplish three points: "the description, explanation, and justification of the Christian religion" (p. 689). While important, the work of these groups of scholars remains at a fairly abstract level. In other words, they do not create narratives but analyze them.

Taking a different approach from the media ecology of narrative, the narrative theology group examines specific characteristics of narrative, noting that, following Crites (1971), humans spontaneously think of their experience in narrative form. That is, they acknowledge that the medium has shaped how people think and that such shaping has endured. Shea (1978), somewhat like Ong, speaks of stories as a "structure of consciousness." Shea (1980) also suggests that key aspects of narrative or story make it almost inherently theological: story puts one into a tradition or community (pp. 77–80); demands an intrinsic appreciation (or an interiority) (p. 78); acts on people as a group, forming a community (p. 79); leads to an interaction or a dialogue that results in the creation of new stories—which can share in divine creativity (p. 84); and creates an engrossing nontheoretical experience that is accessible to all (pp. 86–87). Shea concludes, "storytelling has a specific religious dimension. Sam Keen (1970) has remarked that 'telling stories is functionally equivalent to belief in God' (p. 86). The very act of storytelling is an implicit affirmation of ultimate meaning" (Shea, 1980, p. 88). Shea concludes by listing seven elements that show the progression of storytelling into theology:

> (1) People relate stories of coming to faith. These are tales in which the initiative of God is stressed. (2) Within these stories the reality of God is acknowledged and God language enters into the conversation. (3) A felt-perception of how the reality of God relates to us is expressed and conveyed in images. (4) The images generate further stories which explore the relationship. (5) These stories yield insights and values. (6) The insights and values have implications. They push toward strategy and action. (7) The faith-motivated behavior yields another set of stories, the stories of enacted faith. Within each element of this basic storytelling process which creates the event of church, experience and tradition are simultaneously at work. (p. 90)

Similarly, Navone and Cooper (1981) explore the aspects of narratives that allow their theological usefulness, developing a series of theses drawn from anthropology, sociology, and theology and then, like Shea, applying them to the analysis of specific stories. Navone and Cooper, like most of those following "narrative theology," give a priority to the text, demonstrating what Kelber (2013e) criticizes in studies of biblical narrative as a bias to print culture.

Tilley and Zukowski (2001) build on Tilley's earlier work on story (1985) by moving their discussion of narrative theology into the media ecology world. Using Ong's (1978b) comments on how electronic technologies have changed the human noetic economy as a starting point, they ask how narrative will affect theology in a world of secondary orality—that is, narratives experienced in film, on radio, on television, and through social media. They acknowledge that the story world of communication teaches people how to

46 | A Media Ecology of Theology

live, creates social (or public) selves, and makes things happen (the "performative" role of communication). Tilley and Zukowski find in narratives the main way that cultures communicate meaning and they see television (their main focus in 2001) as the most important narrative system in contemporary culture. In addressing theology, they argue three important points:

> First and foremost for us, not only must the central vehicle of communication not be conceived as "doctrines" or "morals" or "rules," but as stories which contextualize images which shape our perceptions, our imaginations, even our very desires. Narratives, not bare propositions, carry images and thus effectively communicate meaning. Narratives form us as much as we form them. Whether considered as *fides quae creditur* or *fides qua creditur*, the Christian faith has a narrative structure. . . .
>
> Second, the media in and through which the narrative is communicated shapes the meaning of the narrative and, hence, of the social selves who hear, respond to, and dwell in those narratives. . . . That culture is not separable from the narratives that constitute it, but clearly is a culture, even a "virtual community," constituted powerfully by "an electronic technology" that is as much in us as around us. . . .
>
> Third, we need to note the theological and religious significance of the point that the same words or gestures placed in different contexts, different narratives, different discourse systems do not have the same meaning—and, we would argue, but cannot do so here—cannot have the same meaning. The many meanings of "redemption" and the varying soteriologies of the New Testament and subapostolic eras provide a case in point. The conundra we face when trying to explicate soteriology as ransom, as at-one-ment, as redemption, as satisfaction, as substitution suggest to us that the context in which these stories are told or doctrines proclaimed control their meaning. (pp. 6–7)

Moving even closer to the media ecology tradition, Tilley and Zukowski speculate on how the world of cyberspace and social media will affect the contexts in which narratives shape belief. As the technology of communication changes, they expect that how people experience and create narratives will change. They end with a challenge for Christianity: "The praxis is not the delivery of information; rather it is always, wittingly or not, the shaping and reshaping of lives in communication and communion" (p. 10).

• • •

The ecosystem of narrative, even as it interacts with other communication systems (whether oral, scribal, written, or multimedia) provides a look at one way in which people think theologically. The affordances of narrative and the ways in which the different parts of the ecosystem (story, storyteller, hearer, storytime, character, plot, memory, culture, media, and so forth) interact shape a long-standing theological practice. As many of the scholars proposing a narrative theology suggest, the narratives are, in fact, a theology, one that works by creating and describing worlds and showing how God acts in people's lives and histories. Media ecology can help people understand the communication forms and their affordances—what people can and cannot do with the media. Those affordances—and their limitations—might also remind us that not all theology (faith-seeking-understanding) is good theology or orthodox theology, particularly if we evaluate one medium by the criteria of some other medium.

3
EDUCATIONAL SYSTEMS
Managing the Content of Faith

In the fourteenth century, prospective lawyers studied the *Processus Sathane infernalis contra genus humanum*, an account of a trial in which the ever-enterprising devil brought a lawsuit against God, arguing that he had been unjustly deprived of his property—the human race—in the redemption. Attributed to Bartolo of Sassoferrato in the 1330s, the processus (a kind of moot court proceeding), features a legally well-versed demon arguing a case before Christ in the heavenly court. In the course of the trial, the devilish lawyer and the court exchange arguments and receive and appeal rulings, all conforming to the then-current reforms of legal procedures and guarantees of due process promulgated by Pope Clement V after 1315. Not without humor, the *Processus Sathane* at one point has Mary, the mother of Jesus, step forward as the only one willing to take on the representation of the human race; here, the lawyer representing the interests of hell objects to her role in the trial because she is related to the judge. In the midst of both theological debate—medieval theologians still argued various theories of the redemption, with Anselm's *Cur Deus Homo* a recent entry that held that the Redemption was satisfaction owed to God, not paying a debt to the devil—and legal procedure, the document manages to present key legal practices to the novice lawyer in memorable detail (Taylor, 2005).

As a teaching document the *Processus Sathane* highlights a media ecology perspective on theology, but more particularly on education in a mixed-media world. Its method shows information management tools suited to both oral cultures and increasingly literate ones. The document incorporates the key aspects of oral memory: a strong narrative, dominant characters, information tied to places and actions, and so on. At the same time, it appears as a written text based on other written texts—the court precedents and practices. And it teaches oral performance, since legal arguments, then as now, occurred orally before a judge. Here is a document with a foot in both the oral and literate worlds.

This media ecology matters because it forms a bridge between a theology grounded in oral cultures and narratives—supported in church settings and rituals—and the soon-dominant theology expressed in the written word. Against a background of theology as commentary, particularly in sermons—an ever-expanding body of work—this period evolved a new educational system that aimed to improve the management of information, so that the teacher and student could summon evidence for argument and proofs from precedent.

Fourteenth-century educational practice combined oral and literate techniques; it foreshadowed later changes in education and society. It also shows how writing came to "restructure consciousness" (Ong, 1982, pp. 78–116). The impact of the communication technology of writing (and later printing) on theology and the wider society emerged slowly—literally over centuries, in what Raymond Williams (1961) calls "the long revolution" in the context of English life:

> Yet there remains a third revolution, perhaps the most difficult of all to interpret. We speak of a cultural revolution, and we must certainly see the aspiration to extend the active process of learning, with the skills of literacy and other advanced communication, to all people rather than to limited groups, as comparable in importance to the growth of democracy and the rise of scientific industry. (p. xi)

Literacy in its various forms, of course, existed since the time of the Babylonians, Egyptians, ancient Greeks, and classical Romans. But, as Williams suggests, those who could use that technology belonged only to a small, elite group. The vast majority of the ancient populations had neither literacy nor any opportunity to become literate (Kaster, 1988, p. 24). The habits of thought now associated with literacy emerged slowly, as the larger society became literate, in that long revolution. The connecting point between orality and literacy occurs with education, as students first learn to use the information management tools presented by writing and, second, to take full advantage of them.

It should come as no surprise that the Christian Church manifests the oral/literate pattern in its theology, because the theology developed both among an elite educated class and among the wider community. The former left texts while the latter turned to other means of expression, such as art, narrative, church designs, or other communication modes. To see the gradual triumph of literacy in theology necessitates taking a long view, one of centuries. Several key theological figures—from Augustine to Aquinas to the modern period—represent the changes.

Augustine

Augustine (354–430) came to Christianity after a young adulthood spent searching for God. Earning his living as a teacher of rhetoric, he had grown up in a household that gave him the best, though conventional, education of his day. Like young boys before him, he first studied grammar and then rhetoric.

The grammar curriculum consisted of a program to learn one's letters through mastering the alphabet and then the syllables (phonology and morphology), the parts of speech, and then various texts. The Roman system followed the Greek pattern, with the students studying texts, recitation, and writing (Marrou, 1956, pp. 150–55). Even at this first stage, the education was partly literary. The young scholar would have practiced writing through imitation and, from the *grammaticus* (his teacher), learned ways to interpret texts. Following on this, the student would begin more advanced study with a rhetorician: "Typically that schooling was purely literary. . . . [There were] three goals, pursued first in a grammarian's school, then in a rhetorician's: mastery of correct language, command of a fairly small number of classical texts, and an ability to turn the knowledge of language and literature to a facility in composition and speech" (Kaster, 1988, p. 11). Such education took place in towns and, in the Christian era, often in towns associated with an episcopal see (p. 20), leading to the formation of an elite class, usually the children of the wellborn (p. 15). Such education formed a prerequisite for the civil service or for any kind of advancement. To teach as a rhetorician, particularly in a major city, put one on the path of advancement. From his autobiography, we know that this kind of motivation figured in Augustine's moves to Rome and Milan.

In the East, much of the church education followed Origen (185–254) who, with his classical training as a *grammaticus* (Van den Broek, 1995, p. 44), established—not without some misgivings about the value of classical literature—a school of theology and biblical interpretation (Kennedy, 1999, pp. 157–58). Origen's school taught grammar, geometry, arithmetic, moral purification, dialectics, physics, ethics, and theology. He more or less followed the Stoics in dividing philosophy into logic, ethics, and physics (Van den Broek, 1995, p. 45). The pattern was classical and, even with a Christian flavor, it still retained the "information processing" and storage techniques of the classical education: the arrangement of materials, the patterns of ideas, and so on.

By the fourth and fifth centuries, more and more educated men (given the Roman Empire's practice, only boys received this kind of education) brought their learning to the Church, along with its focus on the literary classics, their interpretation, and the arrangement of knowledge. Even a partial list of these converts suggests the scope of rhetorical literacy (that is, the ability to read and write, focused on the oral performance and interpretation of texts) coming into the Church:

> Consider, for instance, the men from the mid-third to the end of the fourth century who we know taught in the schools of grammar or rhetoric and (usually later) held some position in the Church hierarchy, who might therefore most conspicuously represent the mingling of the traditionally educated classes and local Christian leaders: in the West, Cyprian at Carthage, Victor, the grammarian and lector at Cirta/Constantina, Marculus, a rhetorician who became a bishop and Donatist martyr, and Augustine; in the East, Malchion, rhetorician and later presbyter at Antioch, the two Apollinarii at Laodicea (the elder a grammarian and presbyter, the son a rhetorician and later a bishop), and other rhetorician-bishops—Gregory of Nyssa, Amphilochius of Iconium, Optimus of Phrygian Agdamia and Pisidian Antioch, and Ablabius, the Novatian bishop of Nicaea. (Kaster, 1988, p. 73)

Another, who shared the educational background but not the teaching profession, was Jerome, Augustine's contemporary and a translator of the Bible into Latin. He, for one, admitted the hesitations of Origen and Tertullian about the value of the classical texts, which he loved, recounting a dream in which he was accused before the judgment of God as being "a Ciceronian, not a Christian" (Kaster, 1988, p. 81).

Though the advanced rhetorical education admitted other subjects (such as mathematics, music, and astronomy), it overwhelmingly trained students in literary interpretation and provided a framework for finding ideas (Marrou, 1956, pp. 160, 198). By the third century in the West, most educational systems would have followed the *Institutio oratoria* of Quintilian (1856), which set out a complete pattern for education. Predominantly rhetorical, it guided the rhetor in finding arguments and arranging them—that is, in information handling. The educational system as a whole not only trained children for good citizenship, civic life, and a life of virtue, but also in the use of communication media, in storing and manipulating information—the body of knowledge and procedure that defined society. Rhetors learned, for example, systems to search for relevant things to say in a variety of circumstances, using a set of *topoi* (the Greek word for place), as for example: person, time, place, number, cause, act, manner, and opportunity (Quintilian, 1856, III.6). In other kinds of speaking, such as forensic or legal cases, they might call upon a system of different kinds of arguments: from definition, division, commencement, increase, event, dissimilitude, opposition, consequentiality, cause and effect, comparison, or supposition (V.10).

These, coupled with a memory system for remembering what they had assembled, gave them a kind of universal information-handling system.

This system, along with the study and interpretation of the texts of classical literature, is what so many theologians from the fourth to seventh centuries brought to their work. However, rather than interpreting Virgil, they looked to the Bible. From a media ecology perspective, the important things are: the educational system, the methods of interpretation, the methods of finding and storing information, and the method (often oral) for passing it along.

Educated in this system and a teacher within it, Augustine of Hippo represents an interesting range of communication expertise in both his practice and in his later reception by the church. After embracing Christianity, he prepared for a new teaching role:

> When Augustine is ordained a priest in 391, he immediately asked his elderly bishop Valerius for time to study Christian scripture. As one possessed of a literary education in the Roman classics, the request is natural. Communities, after all, are formed by reading and interpreting authoritative sets of texts, and literate Catholic teachers of scripture like Ambrose and Jerome are becoming increasingly important to a church on the rise. Now, charged with the duties of his new office, Augustine would have to know these texts as well as he had learned Virgil, Cicero, and Terence. (McCarthy, 2007, p. 328)

Augustine learned these well. His writings, especially his commentaries on the Christian Scriptures, present a look at the development of his thinking during his long years as bishop and teacher of the Christian community in Hippo. As one would expect, his ideas change over time. But without the written copies of his sermons, we would not know this. Apparently, he employed scribes who took down his sermons and recorded his dictated books. A careful teacher, Augustine revised these works later in life.

Throughout his work, Augustine is quite conscious of the differences among media forms. Hence, the written Scriptures carry a different authority from the oral commentary or exposition (McCarthy, 2007, p. 330). Ironically, this also applies to his own work. During his lifetime, Augustine seemingly had little influence in the church. Living in fifth-century north Africa, he corresponded with many, but the bishop of Constantinople, for example, ignored his letters and many of his contemporaries felt he had little authority (p. 326). Centuries later, and filtered through the scholarship carried out during the Middle Ages, we see him as much more important because the body of his writings survived. As McCarthy notes, "Failure to observe important differences between written and verbal communication patterns yields a view of Augustine's authority as univocally magisterial rather than reflecting an 'intricately interrelated world of social power'" (p. 327). What authority he had in his lifetime stemmed from his face-to-face interaction with his church community, from his interpersonal connections to other churches through letters, and from the week-to-week commentaries on the Scriptures (p. 346). During his lifetime, when he depended on oral communication, he reached a much smaller audience. After his death, the multitude of his writings (and no doubt the abundance of cheap papyrus, which made copies plentiful and inexpensive) and their rhetorical polish and style extended his influence.

Augustine appreciated the difference between oral and written: "He himself is aware of key differences in the dynamics of the written and spoken word. The former is stable and requires a learned expert to teach others its steadfast meaning across time; the latter is fluid, demands an active community to make it a living voice of present, personal appeal" (McCarthy, 2007, p. 327). But Augustine proposes an interesting reversal when he applies this to the Word of God incarnate. In his commentary on Psalm 45:2 ("My heart overflows with a noble word; . . . my tongue as nimble as the pen of a scribe"), he like many commentators attributes this to God the Father and the generation of the Word. McCarthy explains Augustine's thinking:

> Augustine here adopts his master's [Ambrose] strategy by explaining the "spirit of the letter." The begetting of the Word (unlike human begetting) is ineffable, conceived in the most interior space of the Father's heart. Augustine explains that the verb [*dico*] in "*I speak* of my words to the king" means to "put forth a word" [*profero*], but that God does not put forth words the way humans do. God's speech is without beginning or end and so constitutes only one Word. In precisely this respect, Augustine argues, God's Word is more like the script on a page than like sounds issuing forth from the human tongue, and so Augustine explains the line "My tongue is the pen of a scribe writing swiftly":
>
>> What the tongue says, makes sound and passes away. What is written, though, remains. When therefore God speaks the Word, and the Word spoken does not make a sound and pass away but is spoken and remains, God prefers to compare this to written words [*scriptis*] than to sounds. . . .
>
> What is of interest here is the way Augustine assesses the difference between two "technologies" of the human word, spoken and written, such that the analogy of divine generation with the spoken word is less appropriate than analogy with the written word. Although Augustine does not deny

the temporal, material quality of the script on a page, written words seem closer to the "real thing" than the words that sound in our ears. (p. 330)

Because the written word remains, it better describes the Incarnate Word. However, Augustine could just as easily have described the Incarnate Word as oral, as living, as interactive—as addressing individuals in a dialogue of salvation. But here, the importance lies in the permanence of the Word. True to his education, Augustine combines both oral and written culture and does so in a way that suggests that even the nonliterate in his congregation at least knew how written texts worked.

McCarthy also indicates that Augustine changed his views about his congregation's literacy: "If especially early on Augustine stresses the grammatical virtues of the educated elite of late antiquity, over his episcopacy he increasingly insists that those who are not initiated into literary culture are no less capable of understanding the Bible. The 'uneducated' still engage in biblical exegesis, but not that of a lone grammarian sitting before a text in the study. . . . [Instead, such a one] intentionally participates in the prayer, worship, and reflection of the whole community and is challenged to live out one's life within that 'school'" (2007, p. 333). The view seems consistent with Augustine's *De Doctrina Christiana*, a work in which he explains his later approach to rhetoric. Opting for a simple style rather than the Ciceronian approaches he knew so well, Augustine equates a Christian rhetoric with the popular rhetoric or common speech, not that of the grammarian (Kennedy, 1999, p. 180).

In the first several books of the *De Doctrina Christiana*, Augustine explains how to discover the meaning of the Scriptures, with guidelines for "interpretation required by ignorance of the meaning of signs" (book 1) and "interpretation required by the ambiguity of signs" (book 3). In book 4, he treats of the Christian orator, explaining how one should explain the meaning discovered through the methods taught in the other books (Kennedy, 1999, pp. 180–81). In doing so, Augustine does not deny the need for style or elegance, but commends the style of the Scriptures, which, like the popular style, is simple. While the ordering of the treatise is not unlike classical rhetorical instruction, the examples come from the Scriptures or the Church Fathers. Following the classical authors Augustine studied, he demands that his ideal orator live as a model of virtue. However, with the concern for common speech, Augustine broke with the tradition of classical rhetoric.

> His central heresy, from an ancient point of view, was his insistence that communication is more important than elegance. To be intelligible is a greater thing than to be stylish. "What is the use of a perfect speech," he

asks, "that the audience cannot follow, when there is no reason for speaking at all if the people we are talking to do not understand us?" (4.10.24) (O'Donnell, n.d.a, ¶79)

For Augustine, the chief thing for the people to understand remains the Scriptures. With this, then, Augustine shifts Christian education to a rhetoric focused on the Scriptures and on understanding.

But Augustine has another, profound but indirect, impact on education. Augustine's theology, of which we have over five million words (O'Donnell, n.d.b, ¶1), comes to us in books addressing theological topics, like *The City of God* or the *De Trinitate*, and in multiple series of sermons. His theology of oral commentary enters history as written text and, along with the works of a number of other Fathers of the Church, becomes the books studied by generations of future students of theology. The popular theology of narratives, images, icons, architecture, and liturgy recedes in the face of this written tradition. The others do not disappear but the ecological mix shifts.

Aquinas

Thomas Aquinas (1225–1274), one of the great, if not the greatest, of medieval philosophers and theologians, lived "at a critical juncture of western culture when the arrival of the Aristotelian corpus in Latin translation reopened the question of the relation between faith and reason, calling into question the modus vivendi that had obtained for centuries" (McInerny and O'Callaghan, 2010, ¶1). The thirteenth century also saw the further development of universities as educational systems with the revision of the Dominican *studium generale* by Albert the Great (Kennedy, 1912, ¶7). In other words, Aquinas lived at another time when the ecology of communication shifted. Aristotle's learning and works had reached the West through contact with the Islamic culture coming from the East via Spain, as Greek manuscripts and translations accompanied traders. The trading network brought the recovered learning into contact with a network of monasteries. These, established in previous centuries, ensured enough copyists to circulate the texts and the stability of an educational system to foster an understanding of them. Other factors, beginning in the twelfth century, make up a wider ecology that enabled this: the growth of cities (Morris, 1972, pp. 38–39), political stability (p. 41), and the patronage of nobility (p. 43). The thirteenth century saw the initial rise of the great European universities; not only centers of learning, they also helped establish in their cities all the supporting communication structures to encourage the circulation of ideas. In addition, the great orders like the Franciscans and Dominicans indirectly promoted travel from place to place (monastery to monastery, university to university), as Aquinas' own life shows: born in Italy, he studied with the Benedictine monks at Monte Cassino, then at the University of Naples, then with the Dominicans (whose community he joined) at Rome, Cologne, and Paris (Kennedy, 1912, ¶3–7).

His education reflects the times. As the son of a noble family, he began grammar school at around age five at the Benedictine monastery of Monte Cassino; showing promise, he went to the University of Naples at 11 years old, where he studied Latin grammar, logic, and the natural sciences—that is, the Trivium (grammar, logic, rhetoric) and the Quadrivium (music, mathematics, geometry, astronomy). In his later teens, he became familiar with Aristotle's *Metaphysics* and the *Sentences* of Peter Lombard (Kennedy, 1912, ¶3, 5).

By the time Aquinas came to studies in the 1230s, the emphasis in education had shifted from the classical focus on rhetoric as a means to find and organize knowledge to grammar and logic as classification systems (Yates, 1966, p. 66).

The influence of Aristotle's logic—filtered through and revised a bit later, for example, in Peter of Spain's summary of dialectics (c. 1245), a work that equated dialectic and logic—played a great role. Peter's opening definition gives a sense of what had happened in displacing rhetoric: "The work opens with what is probably, after the definition of man himself, the most repeated definition in all scholastic philosophy: 'Dialectic is the art of arts, and the science of sciences, possessing the way to the principles of all curriculum subjects'" (Ong, 1958, p. 56). Such was its influence that logic superceded rhetoric as *the* information management system for learning. Aquinas' own work gives another sense of the sweep of logic: "Taking reason in its broadest sense, so as to include all the operations of the mind which are strictly cognitive, namely, the formation of mental images, judgment, and ratiocination, we may expand St. Thomas' definition and define logic as 'the science and art which so directs the mind in the process of reasoning and subsidiary processes as to enable it to attain clearness (or order), consistency, and validity in those processes'" (Turner, 1910, ¶6). Information management had changed from a system based on finding arguments to one of finding clarity or locating information (Ong, 1958, pp. 83–91). The necessity of such a shift had emerged with the greater store of knowledge passed from one generation to the next—another consequence of written sources. Peter Abelard (1079–1142) had noticed a problem in the twelfth century in the opening of *Sic et Non*: "Within so great a volume of material, some of the opinions of even the saints appear, not only to differ from one another, but actually to be in conflict" (quoted in Morris, 1972, p. 60). One task facing education, then, was to teach how to manage such material.

Part of Aquinas' initial study consisted of his mastery of the *Sentences* of Peter Lombard, a twelfth-century handbook of theology, made up of a listing of key theological topics and citations of church authorities to support its opinions. This handbook also reflects an educational shift that progressed slowly from the time of Augustine to the time of Aquinas. By the time of Peter Lombard, education consisted not only of attending lectures but also of reading. In his magisterial exposition of the educational reforms of the sixteenth-century scholar Peter Ramus, Ong refers to "the scholastic, scientific passion for fixity and exactitude, associated with dependence on written documents" (p. 92). The turn to writing became evident in the centuries previous to Aquinas and Peter Lombard. In his educational guide, the *Didascalicon*, Hugh of St. Victor (1096–1141) commends two kinds of knowledge: reading and meditation, focused respectively on the arts and sciences and on the Scriptures (van Zwieten, 1995, p. 177). Clearly, meditation as practiced in the monasteries, depended in some ways on a prior reading of the Scriptures and the literacy necessary for that (p. 183). And so, among other things, monastic education included learning how to read. Richard of St. Victor (d. 1173), a monk of the next generation at Hugh's monastery of St. Victor, who composed a book to instruct the junior monks in monastic reading, teaching them how to read for benefit by exploring the meaning of the words through their own experiences (van 't Spijker, 1995, p. 210). Richard's method of reading the Scriptures involved the various kinds of interpretation used by the Fathers. Among other things, he encourages the novice monks to use the images that occur in the Bible as symbols of the interior life. He demonstrates the method with a reading of the book of Joshua, where each image mentioned in the text connects to some interior experience of the monks: "Again, Richard plays with his images, by attaching yet another cluster of meanings to these stones" (in reference to the memorials Joshua erects on entering the Promised Land, connecting them to yet other meanings) (pp. 204–5). As van 't Spijker explains, "Learning by experience, by introspection, turns out to be linked to a literary enterprise" (p. 206). And, it seems that this kind of reading connects as well to the kind of memory techniques and use of images that characterize oral cultures, oral memory, and a more oral type of information management.

Aquinas would have also studied artificial memory systems: "Early biographers of Thomas Aquinas say that he had a phenomenal memory. As a boy at school in Naples he committed to memory all that the master said, and later he trained his memory under Albertus Magnus at Cologne" (Yates, 1966, p. 70).

Such memory systems originated with the Greek rhetoricians and came to the Middle Ages through the works of Cicero. They made use of visual imagery to retain almost any kind of knowledge. Like his teacher, Albert, Aquinas wrote a treatise on memory systems; for Aquinas, images acted as a part of this theory of knowledge, despite a contemporary suspicion of images as being false to dialectic: "It is as a concession to human weakness, to the nature of the soul, which will take easily and remember the images of gross and sensible things but which cannot remember 'subtle and spiritual things' without an image. Therefore we should do as Tullius [Cicero] advises and link such 'things' with images if we wish to remember them" (quoted in Yates, 1966, p. 71). Though Aquinas gives his own rules for memory, the artificial memory system has for him (as for Cicero) a twofold function: an aid for memory, certainly, and a filing system, a way of managing the increasingly large amount of information available to the teacher, scholar, speaker, or clerk (pp. 64–65, 74–77).

Formed in this kind of an educational environment, Aquinas came to teaching through an apprenticeship system, offering his own commentaries on key texts and incorporating the "new" Aristotelian philosophy. Dissatisfied perhaps with the arrangement of Peter's *Sentences*, Aquinas prepared his own summary of theology in which he both arranged the topics and sorted through the authorities. Johnson (2005) argues that Aquinas developed the *Summa Theologiae* as text for the teachers of theology in the Dominican convents, so that they could have a reference guide to their teaching. Various Dominicans copied the text and brought it to other monasteries; they also arranged for its publication by the stationers of Paris (p. 140). Comparing versions of the *Summa*, one based on lecture notes of the students and the other based on the published text, Johnson adds a detail interesting from the media ecology perspective: "Whatever differences there are between the two—the texts from the *Summa* tend to be ever-so-slightly longer and to quote authorities more fully—can be explained by the fact that in writing more than in lecturing Thomas's text would be clearer, tighter, and more detailed" (p. 139). Three noteworthy things emerge here. First, the *Summa*, though perhaps delivered orally as lectures, is a product of writing. Unlike Augustine's theology, transcribed during an oral delivery, Aquinas' theology is a written text presented orally. Second, it confirms a shift in the nature of theology "from exegesis to dogmatics" under the influence of the educational shift to dialectics (van 't Spijker, 1995, p. 197). Third, the mode or arrangement—questions logically arranged to build on each other, objections based on previous opinions and sources, the responses to the questions, and replies or rebuttals to the objections—indicates both an information management system and the availability of library resources. The very sophistication of the work indicates a complex network of communication interaction: from writing's manuscripts, ink, and paper to publishing and sales, to libraries, to an educational system, to schools and universities, to roads, and so on. Many of these things did exist at the time of Augustine, but the mix had changed, as had the human consciousness that employed it. Theology, too, had changed, now with an emphasis on dialectic, with the use of texts as evidence, rather than as sources for commentary, with the sense of a body of doctrine or faith to defend (Pelikan, 1978, pp. 9–23)

Education, Printing, and Information Management

In its long revolution, education shifted again several centuries later, after the invention of printing from moveable type. Eisenstein (1979) has catalogued many of the consequences that invention afforded for education: more and cheaper books, the faster spread of ideas, an increase of literacy (more access to books, especially outside of the monastic schools and universities, meant more readers), independent study from books, textbooks and practice books for students, new systems for managing information, and new gatekeepers (see ch. 4). Not surprisingly, the sixteenth century saw different attempts to adopt this new communication technology in education. Ong (1958) has provided in great detail the account of one such reform, that of Peter Ramus. A professor at the University of Paris in the mid-sixteenth century, Ramus set about recasting dialectics in order to make the subject more accessible to schoolboys. This had serious consequences for the educational system and for how people managed information: "The structure of Ramist dialectic is responsible for the liquidation of several items commonly present in other dialectics and/or rhetorics: notably the four parts of the oration, the search after facility in expression or 'copie' of words, ... amplification, and decorum" (Ong, 1958, pp. 210–11). To aid his teaching, Ramus turned to the printed book. Using the visual space, as well as the ease of producing identical pages that printing afforded, he presented dialectic as a series of dichotomized outlines. The students could refer to these tables to find appropriate arguments and proofs. While such outlines may well have existed before, their presentation in books helped to disseminate them across Europe and led to their adoption in schools from Paris to Prague, Cambridge, and Harvard. In effect, Ramus had proposed a new, more efficient means of information handling.

The system also replaced the memory systems that helped to classify information from the classical era: "For the Erasmian type of humanist the art of memory was dying out, killed by the printed book, unfashionable because of its mediaeval associations, a cumbrous art which modern educators are dropping" (Yates, 1966, p. 158). Though Ramus did not oppose memorizing, he did oppose the old information management system.

> One of the chief aims of the Ramist movement for the reform and simplification of education was to provide a new and better way of memorizing all subjects. This was to be done by a new method whereby every subject was to be arranged in "dialectical order." This order was set out in schematic form in which the "general" or inclusive aspects of the subject came first, descending thence through a series of dichotomized classifications to the "specials" or individual aspects. Once a subject was set out in its dialectical order it was memorized in this order from the schematic presentation—the famous Ramist epitome. (Yates, 1966, p. 232)

Ramus did not need the old system because he had created a simpler, more "logical" dialectical system for organizing information. Ramus' system appealed to Protestants because it did away with the images used to remember concepts. The rejection of images "places Ramus as sympathetic to the iconoclastic movements which raged during his lifetime in France, England, and the Low Countries; and I would suggest that it is relevant to his attitude to images in the art of memory" (237). For whatever reason they may have left images behind, though, Ramus and his contemporaries did not abandon the need to classify and sort the information multiplying around them. They found other ways. One—not at all attributed to Ramus—came with the ability to create an index for printed books. The identical nature of each copy printed justified the work involved in creating an index (Ong, 1982, pp. 123–26). This and other reference systems gradually replaced the older memory systems.

Another educational reform developed later in the sixteenth century, one associated with the schools of the then-new Society of Jesus (Jesuits). Conforming both to Renaissance humanism and to the new teaching tools available, the Jesuits had students focus on the classics, on learning through reading, debate, discussion, and writing. The *Ratio Studiorum* (or plan of studies) of 1599 provides a series of rules for teachers of various subjects. Though not addressing memory systems, it does promote a culture of citation of sources, the use of books, student written compositions and examinations (as well as oral examinations), and the organization of knowledge, often based on Aquinas (Society of Jesus, 1599). The *Ratio* pays particular attention to theological education, quite aware of the religious controversies of the Reformation and Counter-Reformation. With it, education has become a system, with a universal method, set down in writing, distributed in printed books, and used at schools around the world.

The sixteenth century saw not only these changes in education, but, as the ecology changed, in the performance of theology as well. From the time of Abelard, theology in schools had taken on the oral performance of disputations, when individuals would debate given or disputed questions. The very arrangement of the *Summa Theologiae* of Aquinas reflects a written manifestation of the method. When Johann Grünenberg of Wittenberg printed Luther's Ninety-Five Theses, he dramatically changed a long-standing theological custom of professors announcing debates of disputed questions to the local community. The local debate became a best seller in central Europe. Even Luther himself found it somewhat mysterious how the announcement spread so far and wide (Eisenstein, 1979, p. 306–7). One answer comes from Luther's preexisting popularity as an author, something an enterprising printer would have known and tried to capitalize upon with a "new" work (Edwards, 1994, pp. 156–57).

From that time on, theological debate took place more and more in print, before a wide public, and in a kind of slowed motion, with exchanges of printed works rather than oral disputation. Debates in the vernacular languages sold more copies, so printers and booksellers encouraged such pamphleteering. Without much forethought, theological practice passed from the domain of the church and the universities to that of the printers and booksellers. Historians have examined and debated this move, attributing it to a wide variety of cultural changes, including a media ecology (Hitchcock, 1971). In any event, the practice of theological debate through published sources continues to this day. Some churches, particularly the Catholic Church, try to regulate the publication of theological material through a process of prior review (Catholic Church, 1993, ¶890; 1983, ¶822–32). However, most theologians engage their work through regular publication in journals and books. That comes from what they learned in the contemporary educational system.

Not surprisingly, the educational practice has adjusted, with most schools publishing a reading list for students of theology. Libraries catalogue theological resources and publishers offer databases of materials, since no memory system can track their rapidly multiplying abundance. Theology occurs in writing, governed by a publishing enterprise and aided by computer-assisted database indexing systems. As the ecology of communication changed, the theological enterprise took advantage of it.

Another engine of change affected the understandings of theology, if not the methods. New education gave rise to new thinking, a thinking congenial to the theology of the Protestant reformers, something that Gay (2018) terms "the technological worldview." Partly due to his interest in theology's relationship with technology, Gay expands the ecology of the theological world beyond communication and educational practices to include economic forces, scientific methods, and philosophical currents. Gay argues that "enthusiasm for disciplined empirical reasoning in the practical reform of material life, ... one of the distinctive features of seventeenth century English Protestant culture," came indirectly as "a kind of unintended outgrowth of a distinctively Protestant understanding of religious duty" (p. 106). In some ways, the instrumentalism that led to the modern technological culture arises, he suggests, from the Puritans' understanding of Calvin's implementation of the *sola scriptura*. If "the Scriptures must be allowed to speak for themselves" (p. 115), then so too must the natural world (p. 116), opening itself to examination and manipulation, thus giving rise to a kind of separation between nature and humanity and an openness to Ramist methods. Protestant theology, which avidly adopted Ramist methods of teaching and memory management, rejected the rationalism of medieval theology and its dialogic methods of memory and debate: "Instead of preceding and preparing us to understand our experience of the world, [Protestant] theology was increasingly left to follow behind observation and experience, making sense of both as best it could" (p. 116). The new education led to a new theology, which in turn led to a new understanding of humanity—one that would in its turn reinforce an educational tradition.

4
WRITING AND PRINTING
Shifting Theological Authority

During and after the reign of Charlemagne in the ninth century, the Western Church experienced a series of theological controversies. Today, almost no nonspecialist in theology recognizes the people involved (and even some theologians might stumble on identifying their positions): Gottschalk of Orbais; Ratramnus of Corbie; Hincmar, bishop of Reims; and Radbertus of Corbie. They disagreed about the nature of the Eucharist (anticipating the disputes of the thirteenth and sixteenth century theologians), about predestination, and probably about other things as well (Pelikan, 1978, pp. 50–105). Their arguments and positions might seem strange to contemporary ears, but their methods, not altogether so. They matter from a media ecology perspective because their working habits involved a new technology of data storage and manipulation—writing—in ways that differed from earlier generations of people doing theology—that is, reflecting on faith.

The use of writing in theology had, of course, existed in Christianity from its beginnings. The Letters of Paul, a part of the New Testament, provide its earliest examples, dating to the early second half of the first century of the Common Era. Those whom theology regards as its founders—the Fathers of the Church—left written records; if not, the contemporary world would not know them. Similarly, the later Christian world knows the work of some early heretics, or rather those parts of their works that others (usually opponents) quoted in their own written works, since the orthodox believers saw no reason to preserve such heterodox writings. In these instances writing served, as it had for centuries, as a data storage technology. Writing supplemented memory; writing allowed people separated by distance or time to "hear" the "voices" of those whose words the texts encoded. However, writing at this stage of theology remained linked to oral expression. Paul dictated his letters to a scribe (Rom 16:22) as custom demanded. The same held true for centuries; even so prolific an author as Augustine of Hippo created his theology in sermons transcribed as he spoke, in treatises dictated to scribes, and in letters, also dictated. Writing proved useful to record what the orally-based educational system trained people to do: to find arguments, think memorable thoughts, and order information for oral recall.

Even the written Scriptures functioned more as performance texts, with reciters proclaiming God's word to assembled Christians (Ward and Trobisch, 2013). The engagement with the Scriptures remained primarily oral for most people; in fact, lectionaries—collections of biblical readings for liturgical use—outnumber manuscript Bibles in the early Church. Those reflecting on belief—bishops, monks, and teachers—followed oral practices of commentary.

By the ninth century, things had changed. The monks of Corbie and Orbais, living in communities dedicated to prayer, theology, and copying manuscripts—that is, to preserving the written record—began to use writing differently. Most likely they were not the first, but their disputes show them doing different things with writing. In their theology, writing became more than a data storage mechanism; it also functioned as a data manipulation tool and as a tool that shaped their thinking. Gottschalk, for example, worked with concordances, a technique impossible without writing. This marks a change in the handling of theological and scriptural evidence, one connected to the changing media environment. Later theology followed this pattern and extended it. Peter Abelard's famous twelfth-century work, *Sic et Non*, juxtaposed seemingly contradictory texts and set out rules for resolving the differences. While the rules may have derived from oral dialectics, the arrangement of the texts depends completely on writing.

Media Ecology and Writing

As a technology, writing (and later, its amplification in printing) changed both how people reflected on belief and who those people were. While many people continued to engage in faith-seeking-understanding through many other forms of expression, the alliance between educational systems, monasteries, church authorities, civil bureaucracy, and, later, the book trade (all combining into an ecosystem) reinforced the primacy of writing and the authority of written texts. In dealing with religious data or information, writing became the primary tool. Thus, it privileged those who used it and eventually erected entry criteria for doing theology. As seen with education (in ch. 3), the shift took time and only slowly spread through Western Christianity. But in the centuries after the printing press, theology definitely took on a written form, to the point where many overlooked all other forms of reflecting on faith.

What did writing do? How did it come to such a privileged position? Many, particularly Ong (1958, 1969, 1982) and Eisenstein (1979), have described the impact of writing and printing on Western thought and so offer hints to its power. Ong and others exploring the effects of writing begin with the reminder that writing is a human technology—an artificial activity that makes use of tools and materials (pens, ink, paper, parchment, bindings, and so on) developed for the purpose of writing; it demands that its users learn specific skills both for creating and decoding texts. They do not mention but imply the social structures supporting this work: the manufacture of writing surfaces, the teaching of the requisite skills, the storage and preservation of written texts, systems of study to teach writing and reading, and so on. Such skills, though restricted to a minority, are ancient: Archeologists have found in Acadian and Egyptian sites practice tablets and even texts of schoolboys chronicling their learning to write (Wolf, 2007, see ch. 2). The technology and the social group using it shape each other. To offer a contemporary example, a similar change occurs as younger users grow up with new communication technologies—these "digital natives" interact with the new technologies in ways that differ significantly from older users. The same most likely occurred with writing: the longer people employed that technology, the differently they used it. And the evidence from earlier and later texts—like the change in information management at Corbie and Orbais—shows how writing changes human thinking.

This fits the media ecology model. With all human communication interacting, the human senses form a "sensorium" (Ong, 1968, pp. 3–8)—the constant interaction of sight, hearing, smell, touch, and taste, all of the means of human interaction with the world. Changing any part of the mix affects all the other parts. When one attends more to what one sees, one pays less attention to what comes by hearing. Lessening what people perceive by hearing and increasing visual information shifts the balance in the sensorium. Over a long enough period in a person's life, this can retrain the brain. Using the evidence from CT scans and neurobiological studies, Wolf (2007) points out how learning to read changes neural pathways in the brain: the link between the visual cortex and the auditory processing area becomes reinforced in specific ways. Terming the overall process "neuronal recycling," she argues that the pattern recognition tied to reading and its connection to verbal recognition make use of neural pathways between the eye and cortex originally evolved to recognize prey (pp. 11–14).

Ong (1982) sketches some of the affordances that writing provides for thinking, drawing a contrast with oral cultures. As he puts it, quite dramatically, "writing restructures consciousness" (p. 77). One of the more obvious consequences of writing involves changing the human world from an oral space into a visual space or—in the concepts used here—from managing information in the fleetingness of sound to managing information in visual recording. While people without writing systems depended upon hearing, upon knowing the world by its surrounding sound and by a live connection with what they knew, people who store knowledge in writing focus more on the visual, upon what they write, upon a kind of detached world. This change affects people by disconnecting them in some ways from the world and offering them new ways to see the world. Some of the effects include allowing people to expand their knowledge both in time and in space. Ong writes that, in an oral culture, "you know what you can recall" (p. 33). But writing extends human recall and in that way extends what people can know. Writing leads people to manage information differently, setting it apart from themselves and their "live" world. Writing also extends knowledge beyond the local and beyond the present by sending messages to distant places and by letting information pass between generations.

Second, writing allows for an economy of expression. The spoken expressions of oral cultures demand the inclusion of aids to memory, such as repetition, rhyme, alliteration, and narrative. Writing dispenses with these and offers a concise form of expression. Since words remain on the page, the reader can always turn back and see what came before; a listener lacks that luxury and must depend on the speaker to repeat and rephrase and reinforce. Third, writing need not defend memory, that is, need not seek to conserve knowledge in the fear that adding something new would cause one to forget the old. Instead, writing abandons a conservative approach to the world in favor of allowing experimentation, since the written texts safely preserve the existing body of knowledge. Writing allows intellectual risks. Fourth, the visual space of writing allows a different kind of analysis and scrutiny of ideas. One can go back and evaluate what one has written and make changes to it in ways unavailable to a speaker. This affordance of writing leads to different kinds of critical and analytical thinking. The written word on a page lends itself to a kind of objectivity, to comparison of side-by-side texts, to a dissection of ideas. Further, Ong points out that the spoken word's connection to the identity with the speaker makes it that much more difficult to separate the idea from the thinker. However, the written word, because it is written, has an identity separate from the writer. This objectivity extends to human groups, too. Ong (1982) notes, "Because in its physical constitution as sound, the spoken word proceeds from the human interior and manifests human beings to one another as conscious interiors, as persons, the spoken word forms human beings into close-knit groups. When a speaker is addressing an audience, the members of the audience normally become a unity, with themselves and with the speaker" (p. 74). Existing independently, the written text separates people, who each encounter it individually.

Fifth, writing offers human thinking the ability to subordinate concepts one to another in different ways. The studies of oral cultures that Ong cites indicate that people without writing have more difficulty in this kind of thinking. While not impossible, subordinated thought occurs less frequently in the oral world, thus obscuring some kinds of relationships among ideas. Sixth, as suggested by the very nature of writing, the written word does not change. Once written, unlike the spoken word that vanishes after the speaker pronounces it, the written word remains. All of these qualities together allow new possibilities for human thinking. They not only allow humans to think about more things but also to think about them in different ways. Seventh, writing presents itself as "context-free" discourse (p. 78), a discourse without a respondent. As Plato first points out, a written text cannot be directly questioned—it remains silent on the page. The text represents an (absent) other. This, too, restructures human thinking as people learn to manipulate ideas separately from any human connection. Ong (1975) carries this a step further when he points out that, in a writing world, communicators have no interlocutors—no face-to-face interaction—and must create an image of a hearer or, in his words, "the writer's audience is always a fiction." Writing, then, as a technology, depends on tools and introduces an artificiality into communication and thinking; it requires planning, depends on artificial rules, and fosters consciously learned behavior.

In another treatment of writing, Ong (1982) notes that the printed version of writing far surpasses the impact of even a written manuscript. In western Europe at least, the Middle Ages combined qualities of an oral culture with the beginnings of a writing culture. The educational information management system, while it had writing, still trusted the spoken word as more authentic: "Writing served largely to recycle knowledge back into the oral world, as in medieval university disputations, in the reading of literary and other texts to groups" (p. 119). The printed book itself offered new affordances for human thinking: first and undeniably, the huge increase in books cheap enough for personal possession and thus for assisting a vastly greater number of people to learn to read. Beyond that, the identical copies coming off the printing press made the creation of an index financially feasible. As an information management system, an index to a book greatly expands people's ability to find information easily (p. 123). Third, both this ability to index and the unchanging nature of the book led to a different conception of knowledge. The book now served as a container to store knowledge and this too changes the way that people interact with what they know (p. 126). Further, considering the book as a container led to an idea of ownership of information. Where the spoken word belongs to everyone within earshot, the printed word belongs to the person who possesses the book or perhaps to the person who wrote the book. Fourth, the printed book offered new possibilities—stopping something in motion or establishing fixed equivalences, for example—for books and for language. Dictionaries begin to roll off the printing presses. Spoken languages became fixed; written works suggested new words to languages as people became accustomed to see the speech they had stored (see ch. 5). Fifth, the printed page is easier to read than a handwritten one, no matter how fine the penmanship. This affordance of print led to another: "The effects of the greater legibility of print are massive. The greater legibility ultimately makes for rapid, silent reading. Such reading in turn makes for a different relationship between the reader and the authorial voice in the text and calls for different styles of writing" (p. 122). Sixth, as both writer and reading adjusted to the new style of the printed page, they also learned to use visual space differently for even more effective information management through diagrams, illustrations, and juxtaposition. For some areas, such as science, the ability to exactly reproduce and arrange drawings vastly increased the availability of accurate knowledge.

Where Ong primarily focuses on how the individual or the culture took advantage of the affordances of writing and print, Eisenstein focuses on structural changes. In her comprehensive study of how the printing press changed Europe, Eisenstein (1979) highlights a number of the consequences of printing on intellectual life. Important aspects of printing include a rapid dissemination of printed works, the standardization of the printed page, a reorganization of knowledge, new means for data collection and publishing, the increased preservation of knowledge, and the amplification and reinforcement of knowledge (pp. 71–130). In Eisenstein's view, the printing press particularly affected rationality and science, two key ways of managing information, observing the world, classifying material, and providing theoretical explanation (p. 379). Like Ong, Eisenstein also points out the shift from hearing to reading (p. 129). But she reminds us that all of these things also point to the non-determinative affordances of printing. She mentions "members of the same reading public, who confronted the same innovation in the same region at the same time, were nonetheless affected by it in markedly different ways" (p. 130). For some, the reading printed material reinforced their current situation while for others it led to a radical reorganization. For example, part of the changing ecosystem included the dissemination of news; as more people could read, they took on a greater ownership of their community and decision-making. The widespread reading resulting from printing split private life from public life, whereas in an earlier cultural reality when people formed a hearing community they made no distinction between the two as all information remained public. Reading led to a sense of privacy. But in other regions, reading aloud still dominated, and printed texts reinforced a public community.

Eisenstein also sketches some other cultural changes that afforded printing its influence, not the least of which was the book trade. More so than printing and selling, the book trade represented groups of workers collaborating with authors to produce printed works. The various key printing houses in Europe "point to the formation of 'polyglot' households in scattered urban centers throughout the continent. In the age of the religious wars, such print shops represented miniature 'international houses'" (p. 139). These printing houses, by drawing together a range of scholars as well as craft workers, reorganized the traditional knowledge economy, which shifted from monasteries and scriptoria to universities and publishing houses. The system of knowledge included more individuals from a greater variety of backgrounds (Christians, Jews, Arabs, and Greeks, as well as religious conformists and dissidents) in one place and under less rigid control.

The Shifting Media Ecology and Theology

Applying the effects and affordances of writing and printing more specifically to theology highlights how the changing ecosystem had deep consequences for how people reflected on faith. Ironically, the new ecosystem shifted theology to specialists but away from religious specialists. A notable example of the shift of authority comes in the person of Robert Estienne, who created the still-used system of numbering biblical verses; Estienne included commentaries in his editions of the Vulgate Bible. However as a layperson, he worked without ecclesiastical supervision (Eisenstein, 1979, p. 328). Estienne's scholarship offers just one look at how the printing ecosystem clearly affected the study of the Bible. Other examples of new interactions with the Bible come from the history of the Reformation, and the Reformation itself manifested many differences of interpretation and showed the use of printed materials to support various positions. Biblical studies certainly benefitted from printing, even in the simplest of ways. The study of biblical languages, the creation of dictionaries of Greek and Hebrew, and the abundance of copies in the original languages allowed scholars to compare manuscripts and to correct errors. But printing undermined the old order of biblical interpretation. While much interpretation remained, printing complicated it by making disagreements evident. The very publicity resulting from printed texts made it impossible to blur the lines between positions: "Doctrines that could coexist more or less peacefully because full implementation was lacking, thus came into sharp conflict after printers had set to work . . . With typographical fixity, moreover, positions once taken were more difficult to reverse" (p. 326). As reformers encouraged the population to read the Bible, this theological work of interpretation and commentary moved away from ecclesiastical control into the general population and into the hands of specialists in language.

In Eisenstein's telling, the Reformation was as much a work of publicists as it was of theologians (1979, pp. 308–12). Even before the work of Luther, religious groups had already made extensive use of the printed book. Preachers published sermons and devotional works to instruct believers, foster devotion, and extend religious influence. For example, Eisenstein writes about one particular priest: "When the Carthusian prior, Werner Rolevinck, wrote that he was having a sermon printed to 'communicate' with more people, he was simply providing a model for many priests, not comparing a hearing to a reading public." Eisenstein continues, "Ultimately, gifted boys who might have become preachers simply became publicists instead. 'The preaching of sermons is speaking to a few of mankind,' remarked Daniel Defoe, 'printing books is talking to the whole world'" (p. 316). In this world of shifting careers, people more and more saw theology as something occurring in printed works and not so much in art, music, and storytelling.

In theology, writing and printing changed the mindset and the method. Ong (1969) suggests five major changes, many linked to one underlying shift. That shift—appearing slowly, over centuries—arose from the nexus of writing and, later, typography's influence on education, the growth of vernacular languages, and the involvement of the state in education: all worked to change the language of education from Latin to the vernacular languages, a shift largely accomplished by the mid-nineteenth century. The same change occurs in theology, though it took longer, with Latin lasting in the theology of the Catholic Church into the mid-twentieth century. The loss of what Ong calls "learned Latin" (that is, Latin as a "dead" language with no native speakers) led to a move away from formulas, dogmatic statements, specialized or limited vocabularies, and polemics. The introduction of vernaculars also introduced greater variety of meaning and interpretation as writers developed vernacular vocabularies for their work. The first major change to the mindset and method of theology accelerated with a theology freed from Latin. What occurred in all learning had an impact on theology. And so, a theology assisted by writing depended less on memory and memory systems (and formulaic Latin phrases). Writing allowed access to a greater abundance of material, making use of its ability to store great quantities of data; it freed the theologian from the organizational patterns and constraints imposed by the memory systems (see ch. 3; see also Yates, 1966). While those trained in the artificial memory systems could recall prodigious amounts of material, the systems were limited both in scope and by the structure they imposed. In Ong's view, writing's freedom from memory systems made theology non-formulaic. Without having to memorize fixed theological expressions, the theologian could find a greater freedom in writing and a degree of originality.

Second, writing's introduction of a storage medium (page and ink) removed the framework of disputations or face-to-face oral combat between the theologians themselves. In this, at least, writing led to a more peaceable style, one focused more on ideas and less on debating points. The interposed medium also separated the theologian's thought from his or her own consciousness. It introduced a time delay for both reflection and review of rough drafts, making theology more analytic and reflective. Freed from the pressures of dictation or disputation, theology took on a more abstract quality. Because writing also promotes independence (freeing people from the shared identity of hearing another's interiority), writing encouraged a more individualistic theology, a theology less likely to imagine a congregation or community. Third, along with the later advent of printed books, mechanized writing vastly increased the material available to those studying theology, well beyond any memory system or monastery manuscript library. Here, as noted above, other layers of technology shaped the ecosystem of theology just as they did all learning: printers, editors, marketing, booksellers, trade routes—everything that enabled a manuscript to become a book and to travel around academic centers. Indirectly, the presence of books provided more time for theology, as a scholar no longer had to travel from place to place to find a copy of a given work. The increase of sources led to an increase of new ideas, but at a cost, as writing and print imposed their own organizational systems, something Ong (1958) points out as he describes the systems of Peter Ramus in the sixteenth century. In fact, it took several centuries of familiarity with printed writing for scholars and publishers to settle on standard organizational patterns in books and to determine the best ways to address unseen readers (Eisenstein, 1979, p. 230–32).

Fourth, Ong (1969) like Eisenstein (1979, pp. 303–450) recognizes a profound change in how theology dealt with the Bible. Ong asserts that an awareness of writing (even an unconscious awareness) allowed scholars of theology to understand the Bible—the great source for faith-seeking-understanding—as a book, separate from themselves and their consciousness and open to critical evaluation. In addition to the flood of linguistic materials noted earlier, biblical theology changed after the Reformation. The Reformation focus on the Bible (the *sola scriptura* that emerged as a theological principle) comes with a consciousness of the Bible as different, as separate from other Christian sources. But the changing understanding of the role of the Bible, the shifting locus of authority over the Bible, and the theological debates about interpretation took a toll. Eisenstein (1979) explains:

> Between Protestant attacks on church authority and unwritten tradition, and Catholic efforts to undermine sole reliance on scripture, little was left. Efforts to restore or to preserve the traditional faith thus only sharpened tools of analysis that helped, in the end, to subvert it.
>
> That a clash of warring faiths eventually dethroned theology and undermined confidence in Christianity itself has often been noted. My point is not that disputes between rival churches paved the way for later views but rather that printing (by revolutionizing all processes of transmission) made it necessary for churchmen to depart from earlier views and set them at odds with each other. Given the shift from script to print, it was quite impossible to preserve the status quo, and hence some kind of disruption was inevitable. (p. 327)

The impact of writing and printing on the Bible and on Christianity itself did not end there and continued to affect theology for centuries. By the nineteenth century, scholars recognized the Bible's forms of expression as different from their own ones and, imagining the Bible as a written text, sought to apply the critical tools honed by print to what today's contemporary scholarship describes as the oral culture behind the text. Kelber (2013c) traces the development of the modern biblical studies movement and the quest for the historical Jesus to that application of print-based written tools to the biblical content. While no doubt extremely fruitful for theology, the sense of the Bible as a text had its drawbacks. Kelber argues that an indirect consequence of writing and printing appears in the loss of the multiple senses of interpretation familiar to oral communities, in the loss of a sense of the Bible as a "living" (that is, spoken) word, and in the tendency to literally see the Bible as separate and separable parts.

Fifth, and much later in the interaction between writing and theology but foreshadowed in both the abundance of written materials and the application of scholarly tools to theological materials, Ong (1969) points out that theology adopted interdisciplinary tools, interacting with analytic tools created for psychology, anthropology, literary studies, the sciences, and so on. In one way or another, all modern learning treats its subject matter as a text—an unmistakable and unavoidable consequence of writing.

Definite traces of the effects of writing and printing upon theology appear in several other contemporary characteristics of the academic faith-seeking-understanding. The study of theology has emerged as an academic discipline, one among a wide range of others, with no particular claim to preeminence. As a discipline, theology remains subject to the strictures imposed by the writing culture of the university: a recognition as an academic area with its own literature; a required knowledge of the written tradition and a demonstrated mastery of the recognized analytic methods and information management techniques required for a license (PhD) to teach and publish; approved journals; an expectation of publication by its practitioners; independence from outside authorities; and so on. Writing has also narrowed the scope of theology to the point that only written expressions gain recognition. While people may reflect on their belief in art, music, film, television, and other media, these gain academic traction only when someone describes them in writing. The print-based nature of managing knowledge has also changed what counts as evidence in theological argument, as it has also changed the nature of argument.

Examples of these changes appear in the guidelines that those training others in academic theology typically impose on the characteristic written form of theology. For example, one typical graduate program in theology identifies the following kinds of "academic writing used in theological study": case study, critique (review), essay, and exegesis paper. Each requires a third-person writing style, citations, and clear organizational points (Reisinger, Scalia, and Hicks, n.d., pp. 1–2). Published articles in journals typically begin with a review of other published materials, the identification of a problem, and its resolution. Each of these emerged from the path set out by writing and print.

In retrospect, writing and its extension in print have had a profound effect on theology, not only in its method but in its subject matter.

5
TRANSLATION

Experiencing Scripture as Applied Communication

As far as material objects go, a personal or family Bible differs from most:[1] "Even though it is an important spiritual text, it is also an object of mass production with a vast circulation. At odds with the status of a sacred text, a bible originates from nowhere special, essentially having the same qualities as any other mass-produced textbook or magazine" (Woodward, 2007, p. 11). Of course, the content, not the properties of the object is what matters most, but as an object, the Bible was not always the mass-produced object familiar to contemporary culture. It existed and exists in oral memory; written upon skins, papyrus rolls, or vellum; bound in carefully illuminated and preserved manuscripts; and among the first products of the printing press. And it existed and exists in ancient Hebrew and Greek. Apart from its material condition, the Bible provides both a record of theology (that is, faith reflecting on its meaning) and a source for further theology. As a combination of the spiritual and material, the Bible offers another glimpse into media ecology, particularly at the moment that transformed the Bible into a mass-produced object: the translation into a vernacular destined for publication as an "authorized" version for a national church.

As a communication phenomenon, the Bible as an object in this sense holds interest for study and opens communication study to alternative means of examining it. Rather than addressing environments per se, communication theory or communication study historically begins with messages and audiences. Another approach examines the ecology of the media systems: the media themselves, the people, the context—the things people mostly take for granted. This focus on the often unseen aspects furthers understandings of the ecology of communication intertwined with Christian theology—the translation and dissemination of its texts. Almost from its beginnings, Christianity depended on translation: the Aramaic stories of Jesus quickly spread in the

---

[1] This chapter previously appeared as Soukup (2013).

Greek-speaking Jewish diaspora (who themselves used the Septuagint Greek translation of the Hebrew Scriptures). Then, as Christianity spread both farther west and farther east, its adherents and missionaries rendered the sacred texts from Greek into Latin, Coptic, Syriac (Pelikan, 1974, p. 41), and other languages with, as Pelikan points out, doctrinal significance found in word choices and linguistic differences. These texts, and the debates flowing from them, offer yet another opportunity to think about how communication and theology interact. And while they do suggest places to examine persuasion and audience effects, they also even more strongly suggest the fruitfulness of a media ecology approach that expands the scope of communication studies.

Like any other aspect of communication, translation in general, as well as any particular translation, does not exist in a vacuum, lying open to examination separate from a wider context. As the media ecology metaphor suggests, each communication act or artifact exists in an ongoing and living set of relationships both with other communication acts, tools, or products and with things that coexist with them in the human environment. As the biological metaphor of media ecology makes clear, all of these interact: change one and all the others adjust. The introduction of a new means of communication will affect everything else.

The sixteenth- and seventeenth-century context of the King James Bible offers precisely this situation of a changing environment, where communication technologies and social practices interact to create a new balance. Here a revised English translation of the Bible emerged in the midst of major shifts in communication practices, which in turn fed the ferment of religious debate. And the theological world took advantage of the affordances provided by the new communication infrastructure. The most immediate of these communication tools is, of course, the printing press. But the "printing press" entails a much larger world of social practices. People had to find ways to use the printing press before it could have an effect on everyday life, religious practice, and theological understanding. Those uses fit into a number of contexts.

The shifting media and religious environments of the period turn the experience of Bible translation into an interesting window on theology (the experience of faith-seeking-understanding), on how a variety of people and forces affect theology, on how elements in the ecosystems interact, and on just how complex these systems can become.

A media ecology of the King James Bible involves at least eleven contexts: those of Gutenberg's invention, the book trade, the scholarly world, practices of translation, libraries, politics, language, rhetoric, the media, theology, and reception. Each of these involves some aspect of communication and the social practices that developed along with it. Silverstone's (1994) remark about the analysis of television as a communication technology applies here as well as to television: "It involves a consideration of technology as being a part of, and not separated from, the social institutions that produce and consume it" (p. 80). The King James Bible, arriving in 1611 in the relative early maturity of the printing press, offers a privileged look at the social institutions surrounding this mass medium of the pre-Enlightenment era.

The Gutenberg Context

Johannes Gutenberg introduced printing from moveable type in the West in the middle of the fifteenth century; in 1455 he printed the forty-two-line Latin Bible. Though popularly identified with that edition of the Bible, the Gutenberg press issued many other texts. In so doing, the invention dramatically transformed learning and life in Europe by, if for no other reason, making books widely available. Before Gutenberg, copyists produced books in multiple copies, but even the best scriptoria could only produce a limited number of books each year (Bobrick, 2001, p. 82). Increasing the speed of making copies meant not only that more copies of a given book circulated, but also that a greater variety of books circulated. The time saved in copying meant that those producing books could print more things—that is, a greater selection of things (Eisenstein, 1979, pp. 169). And at that time, there was no shortage of things to print. Bobrick notes that Gutenberg's invention "was launched on a rising tide" of demand for material. In the century before him, the wealthy, who could afford manuscripts and had the education to read them, drove the market. With the printing press, the market expanded: "Books of all sorts—cookbooks, medical manuals, educational treatises, tales of courtly love, and so on—appeared, variously illustrated and in a number of different calligraphic styles" (Bobrick, 2001, p. 82).

The making of multiple copies from a single master set in type also meant that workers could more easily find errors and correct them—an important aspect of quality control and one that helped establish the reputation of printers. On the other hand, making multiple copies from a single master also meant that when errors occurred they became widely circulated, as several well-known instances attest, even in the first editions of the King James Bible (the "he" and the "she" Bibles, after an error in gender in the book of Ruth; or the "wicked Bible" after an edition that omitted "not" in the commandment regarding adultery).

The timing of the invention of the Gutenberg press also meant that it became a tool for the Renaissance and served the humanist rediscovery of Greek and other language texts from the East. Among other things, the early printers issued the texts of Greek philosophy, drama, and poetry; commentaries on language and learning; dictionaries; and, of course, the Hebrew and Greek texts of the Bible, along with translations into vernacular languages. The Gutenberg context meant that the King James Version translators had not only the original language editions before them but also several English-language translations as well as French, Spanish, German, and other language translations to consult.

The Book Trade Context

Printers built on an existing network of a book trade, a trade that had existed at least since the stationers in thirteenth-century Paris, merchants who sold and traded manuscript copies. The sixteenth-century printers increased that trade dramatically, with more editions and copies for the market. Clearly, printers published texts in order to sell them, something they did both locally and through traveling sellers. Italy alone produced ten thousand printed works in the fifteenth century; the printers of Venice alone, some twenty-seven thousand editions in the sixteenth century. These ranged from devotional works to educational texts to poetry and popular stories, anything to satisfy the tastes of the buyers. During the course of the sixteenth century, the proportion of books printed in Latin to those printed in the vernacular shifted, with a decided preference for vernacular material (Nuovo, 2010). Similar things occurred in other cities and regions, with centers of printing well known in Venice, Paris, Mainz, Strasbourg, Nuremberg, Zurich, Augsburg, Cologne, London, Oxford, Cambridge, Basle, and Geneva (Hoffmann, 1999). Even today scholars still recognize the names of the leading sixteenth-century printers Aldus Manutius, Johann Froben, William Caxton, and Robert Estienne.

The Renaissance printers combined business and scholarship, though in different degrees. Some focused more on quickly issuing editions to capture the market; only later did printers recognize that their sales depended on the quality of their books. Printing also grew with governments fostering the print trade through various licensing schemes in which traders organized book fairs to promote the exchange of books and create a kind of European market. The book fairs also benefitted from the Reformation, with works by key reformers like Martin Luther selling widely—"between 1517 and 1520,

Luther's 30 publications probably sold well over 300,000 copies" (Dickens, 1968, p. 51, quoted in Eisenstein, 1979, p. 303). The competing religious groups quickly took to printing to spread their respective ideas, something that increased the book trade itself (Eisenstein, 1979, p. 407). Of course, the printers' output ranged far beyond the religious or the Scriptural or even the classical languages. The mix of texts led to a vibrant business, with printers setting up in every major city and selling books even in remote areas through the services of book peddlers (p. 376).

Depending on the country, the printing and book trade business also depended on government patronage, permission, or licensing. In England, the crown could seize illegal copies and destroy the presses that produced them. During the century prior to the King James or authorized version, English translations of the Bible took place mostly outside of England and depended on smugglers to reach their intended audience. The sixteenth-century book trade became a huge business, spurred on by profits, of course, but also, when it came to the Bible, by religious conviction, and by imaginative ways to deliver finished or partly-finished texts to the market. The history of the translations includes the accounts of numerous smugglers, secret agents, spies, and scholars.

Later, with a change of monarch and an authorized version, printers and the printing business had a strong commercial motivation to promote that version. Norton (2000) comments:

> In spite of the later perception of the KJB's superiority, this publishing triumph owed nothing to its merits (or [the] Geneva [Bible]'s demerits) as a scholarly or literary rendering of the originals: economics and politics were the key factors. It was in the very substantial commercial interest of the King's Printer, who had a monopoly on the text, and the Cambridge University Press, which also claimed the right to print the text, that the KJB should succeed. (p. 90)

Like the text, the relatively new communication medium of printing succeeded less on its own merits than on those of the industry of which printing formed a part.

In the end, this context and the competition among printers and traders led to an environment that increased the availability of books, improved the quality of those printed, promoted sales, and lined up alliances with state and trade. This provides a good example of Silverstone's idea that communication technology, like any successful technology, must become part of social institutions for it to succeed. For the printing press and the printing of vernacular Bible translations, the social institutions included business, both legal and illegal.

The Scholarly Context

Having readily accessible texts in sufficient numbers led to an explosion of study and of language skills. Some of the printers mentioned already produced dictionaries and lexicons. Henri Estienne II "carried on the pioneering lexicographical work that his father had begun in the *Thesaurus linguae latinae* of 1531 and the Latin-French and French-Latin dictionaries of 1538 and 1539–40, with his own monumental *Thesaurus linguae graecae* in 1572–73" (Hoffmann, 1999, p. 390). These dictionaries provided one foundation for general and translation education. Another foundation appeared in the educational system itself. No longer did students have to travel to find a text, because the sixteenth-century printers increased the availability of school texts. Hoffmann recounts the innovation of the Parisian printer Thomas Brumen, "three-quarters of whose production consisted of interfoliated and double-spaced quarto editions in which the student copied the translation between lines and their teacher's literary and grammatical commentaries in the margins and extra leaves" (p. 386).

The printers aided scholarship in two other ways, one of which would have great significance. The lesser contribution came first from Aldus Manutius, who introduced Greek fonts; a Venetian type-cutter, Francesco Griffo "surmounted the technical problems associated with designing Greek fonts which included all the necessary diacritics" (Hoffmann, 1999, p. 387). Even more valuable was the practice of producing corrected critical editions of the Greek and Latin texts. Erasmus led the way: "The publication of an emended Greek text of the New Testament with a parallel Latin translation in 1516 established Erasmus as the premier evangelical humanist" (Boyle, 1999, p. 44). Not only did he provide a text but he corrected it in subsequent editions. Hoffman (1999) explains a key point:

> Printing in fact boasted an undeniable advantage over manuscripts: if one proofread early enough, one could reset type, whereas a scribe enjoyed fewer options with regard to a pen stroke already indelibly committed the page. In other words, although the initial typesetting could easily prove inferior to scribal work, movable type afforded the opportunity to achieve a level of correction unattainable even in the best scriptorium. (p. 388)

Such scholarly collaboration between humanists like Erasmus and his successors and the best printers (particularly Manutius, Froben, and Estienne) led to the establishment of accurate texts. Hoffman gives the example of Estienne, whose careful work led to the situation "that his editions remained standard references centuries afterwards. He introduced innovations such as verse numbering still in practice today, and for his 1550 edition of the Greek New Testament, he collated no fewer than 15 manuscripts—demonstrating just how far the quality of printed editions had come in the hundred years since Gutenberg's 42-line Bible" (p. 390).

But as in any social practice, the collaboration between scholars and printers amplified the importance of the communication technology and spilled over into other areas as well. The availability of the materials to study language and texts went hand in hand with the expectation—indeed, the demand, at least by Erasmus—that theologians know the Scriptures. Boyle (1999) explains:

> Although grammatical knowledge did not make a theologian, neither did its ignorance. Erasmus corrected the scholastic neglect and abuse of grammar by requiring a classical trilingual education and by commending its utility. The comprehension of the mysteries of Scripture often depended on knowing the nature of the thing designated. Knowledge was double: of things and of words. (p. 46)

The renaissance of texts and of classical languages also influenced the great educational institutions, which promoted the study of these new materials. Such educational reform in the sixteenth century prepared the way for a later generation of Bible translators, giving them the social practices of education, textual emendation, and ongoing correction that have come to define learning. By the time King James authorized the work on the Bible, he could draw translators from Oxford and Cambridge and entrust the work to these universities.

The Translation Context

The scholarly context of "biblical humanism, which received a new impetus after typefonts could be cast" (Eisenstein, 1979, p. 331), and of critical editions, opened the way for translations. Key elements came together: the increased study of classical languages, the availability of corrected texts, interlinear editions, a willingness to revise existing translations (as seen, for example, in Erasmus' work on the Vulgate), and a market for comparing translations. By the early sixteenth century, scholars had two critical editions, the works of Erasmus and of Cardinal Ximenes. In addition, they had wider access to a number of vernacular language translations. In the period of the Reformation, many groups published translations of the Bible, since the reformers encouraged Bible-reading among the people, most of whom did not read Latin.

In the English-speaking world, translations or partial translations had existed for centuries, with texts first prepared in Old English. By the fourteenth century, the English-speaking world had the translation of Wycliffe in manuscript form, and in the sixteenth century, William Tyndale began work on a complete English translation (with the English New Testament printed in 1526). Others soon followed: the Coverdale Bible (1537), the Matthew Bible (1537), the Great Bible (1539), the Geneva Bible (1560), the Bishop's Bible (1568), the Rheims New Testament (1582), and the Douay full Bible (1610). In addition, revisions and new editions appeared regularly, with or without crown approval (Metzger, 2001, pp. 56–67).

The translators and revisers working on the King James Version drew on all these translations and more. Bobrick (2001) points out some of the translation resources:

> They pored over all previous English versions; consulted the Complutensian Polyglot of 1517; the Antwerp Polyglot of 1572 (which included a fresh interlinear Latin translation of the Hebrew by Arias Montanus); the Tremellius-Junius Bible of 1579 (which contained a Latin translation of the Old Testament from the Hebrew and the New Testament from Syriac); Sebastian Munster's Latin translation of the Old Testament; Theodore Beza's Latin translation of the New; Latin translations of the whole Bible by Sanctus Pagninus, Leo Juda, and Castalio; the Zurich Bible; Luther's Bible; the French translations of Lefevre (1534) and Olivetan (1535); the Spanish translations of Cassiodoro de Reyna and Cypriano de Valera (1602); and Giovanni Diodati's Italian Bible (1607). (p. 238)

The translators themselves clearly understood that they acted in a long tradition of Bible translation. In the preface, "The Translators to the Reader," of the 1611 edition, one section "The Translating of the Scripture into the Vulgar Tongues" provides a brief history of translation from Jerome to at least the fourteenth century.

The media context for the King James Version translators consists, then, of a variety of printed books in the original biblical languages, Latin, and the key languages of Europe, as well as an interpersonal network of scholars and translators. Indirectly, the communication ecology also includes the expectation that people should have the Bible in translation and that some, at least, should develop the language skills for translation.

Libraries

Libraries provide another element in the media ecology of the King James Version. While libraries had long existed in monasteries and cathedral schools, they had limited and noncirculating collections. Printing and the book trade led not only to an increase of books but to an increase of private libraries.

Printers, scholars, and noble families kept collections of books, thus making reference easier. James I, who authorized the translation, "was a true bibliophile. He built up a considerable private library in the classics; owned a host of theological works (including those by Calvin, which he read in Latin); was especially well read in the French poets, such as Ronsard, Du Bellay, and Marot; and of course had many writings in English and Scots" (Bobrick, 2001, p. 206). Such collections add another dimension to the communication background of the King James Version: the habit of having books in many languages available increases the likelihood or the expectation of people's knowing those languages and being prepared to translate them. Private libraries also made it more likely that the translators themselves had access to a fairly broad spectrum of sources in a number of languages.

The Political Context

The existing English translations raised a number of theological and political issues, another circumstance that constitutes the larger environment of the King James Version. These extend beyond the specific communication contexts, but they do affect the communication. Some of the areas of contact illustrate how media ecology works.

The religious and political elite recognized that the Bible formed a teaching tool and that it communicated particular expectations to the people. King James himself objected to glosses in the Geneva Bible that implied a limitation on the power of the monarch. He also recognized the problem of keeping both the established church group and the Puritan group aligned with the monarchy and the church. At the Hampton Court conference in 1604, most of the decisions supported the Anglican group. Some commentators (Maltby and Moore, 2011) suggest that one reason James commanded a revised translation was to offer something to the Puritan group. When John Rainolds, the Puritan head of Corpus Christi College, asked for a new translation, the King quickly agreed. This group process model suggests that a political communication influenced the King's actions.

Another political factor also played a role: the fact that the King "authorized" the revision meant that the translators could both work freely and draw on royal support. This has at least two consequences for the work. On the one hand, in contrast to the sixteenth century, the translators did not need to work outside of England, in places free from persecution or other external constraints (Ellingworth, 2007, p. 108). On the other hand, the royal authorization of the work implied a possible interference or at least a subtle influence on the work. James already had reservations about the Geneva Bible—when Rainolds requested a new translation, the King replied that he "could never yet see a Bible well translated in English; but I think that, of all, that of Geneva is the worst" (Bruce, 1978, p. 96). The translation/revision teams working under royal command would have understood the political limits to their charge. The guidelines for their work included instructions about lexical items and about the use of marginal notes, including "3. The old ecclesiastical words to be kept; as the word church, not to be translated congregation, &c. . . . 6. No marginal notes at all to be affixed, but only for the explanation of the Hebrew or Greek words, which cannot, without some circumlocution, so briefly and fitly be expressed in the text" (Campbell, 2011, pp. 36–37).

In addition to royal politics, ecclesiastical politics played a role. The Anglican and Puritan groups differed theologically and each used a Bible to support their position. The more radical reformers, those influenced by Calvin and Knox, rejected church hierarchy and translated key terms differently: "elder" rather than "priest" for the Greek "presbyteros"; "overseer/manager" rather than "bishop" for "episcopos"; "assembly" rather than "church" for "ekklesia"; and so on (Ellingworth, 2007, p. 109). The choice both supported an ecclesiology and presumed one. "The decision to retain 'bishop' (instead of 'elder' or 'senior') reflects a decision to favor episcopacy rather than presbyterianism as a model of church government; as disagreement about the form of government was a gaping fault line between the church hierarchy and the puritan minority, this decision was critically important" (Campbell, 2011, p. 82). The Roman Catholics, in their Douay translation, often chose Latinate terms, opting to maintain a continuity with accepted theological usages (Norton, 2000, pp. 45–47). Each transmitted its position in the word choices of their translations. Here, ecclesiastical politics guided linguistic choices in the King James Version.

A final aspect of the political context emerges only after the translators completed their work. Done at royal command and funded by the crown, the translators produced an "authorized version," commanded to the churches and commended to the people. But it took time for the authorized version to gain favor. "It is one thing to be the Bible of the official Church, another to be the Bible of the people. In 1611 the people had their Bible, the Geneva, and the KJB was simply the Church's third attempt to produce its own Bible" (Norton, 2000, p. 90). Within 40 years the situation changed. "The last regular edition of the Geneva Bible was published in 1644. Thereafter, to buy a Bible meant to buy a King James Bible" (p. 90). Norton acknowledges that the eventual triumph of the King James Version arose not from any sense of its superiority, but from "economics and politics." The "authorized" certification made it attractive and profitable to printers.

Linguistic Context

The translators' wrestling with word choices in their work—something of concern for English Bible translators from Tyndale in the 1520s to Gregory Martin working on the Catholic Rheims New Testament published in 1582 (Norton, 2000, pp. 41–45)—serves as a reminder that the English language itself was still developing and evolving as a language in the sixteenth and seventeenth centuries. Unlike many languages, English has freely adopted (and adapted) words from other languages (Crystal, 2010), leading to its huge vocabulary today. Largely German and Celtic, English received an influx of French words at the Norman conquest in 1066, with the upper classes bringing their French across the English Channel. The tradition of Latin in academic, learned, legal, and administrative circles added yet another set of (often specialized) vocabulary. Trade across the English Channel brought renewed contact with German and Dutch peoples and words. Regional dialects added more variation. William Caxton, the first English printer, "was keenly aware of the impact of his work on English diction, then in considerable flux, and in his own translations tried not to overemphasize unusual words (or 'curious terms,' as he called them) while not wanting his language to seem too plain" (Bobrick, 2001, p. 83).

The Bible translators could choose from a variety of words and themselves introduced both words and phrasing. The English penchant for importing words and the resemblance of Anglo-Saxon's stress rhythms to Hebrew patterns in some ways made the translators' work easier. Bobrick (2001) comments on both as he discusses the work of Tyndale. First, the Anglo-Saxon patterns enabled

> Tyndale to draw on traditions of native expression to give the Hebrew an English feel. His fidelity to the original also gave rise to the quintessential "noun + of + noun" construction of English biblical prose. Instead of "Moses' book" we have "the book of Moses"; instead of "a strong man," "a man of strength." This extended to the way superlatives were expressed: instead of "the holiest place" or "the best song," Hebrew had "the holy of holies" and "the song of songs." This imparted to English a certain rhythmic sonority it had not formerly possessed. (p. 119)

He continues, addressing the easy ability to bring new words into English:

> Tyndale also boldly adopted a number of Hebrew words and compounds, such as "scapegoat," "passover" and "mercy seat," which English has kept, as well as various Hebraic turns of phrase—among them, "to die the death," "the Lord's anointed," "the gate of heaven," "a man after his own heart," "the living God," "sick unto death," "flowing with milk and honey," "to fall by the sword," "as the Lord liveth," "a stranger in a strange land,"

"to bring the head down to the grave," and "apple of his eye." It is said that he also introduced into English the adjective "beautiful." (p. 119)

Later translators, including both the King James Version and Douay-Rheims teams did the same, though not all their choices successfully entered the language. Many of Martin's terms in the Rheims New Testament (especially the Latinate ones) come into English through the King James Version, which took them over. However, other terms like "exinanited" were not accepted into English (Norton, 2000, p. 46).

The freedom and the necessity with which the translators imported words comes as a heritage of Elizabethan England. Ebel (1969) notes that an earlier generation *had* to import a vocabulary.

> But it is useful to recall here that at the outset of English printing, and well into the early years of Elizabeth's reign, translators were apologetic and uneasy about their "inadequate" language; that their embarrassment was justified by the real poverty of the English vocabulary; and that in the course of the century, as vocabulary and idiom seeped into English from the continental vernaculars (partly by means of translations), English actually experienced a resplendent triumph. (p. 596)

Motivated by a desire to make learning available in English and not restricted to universities and Latin speakers (p. 598), Elizabethan translators extended Tyndale's and the Reformers' desire to make the Bible available in common English to a desire to make everything available in English. But it required a linguistic flexibility: "Florio prefaces his translation of Montaigne with a list of neologisms which includes 'conscientious, endeare, tarnish, comporte, efface, facilitate, ammusing, debauching, regret, effort, emotion'" (p. 596, n. 17; *sic*). That practice of listing new words in prefaces appears in tables at the end of Tyndale's work as well as at the end of Martin's Rheims New Testament (Norton, 2000, p. 45).

Rhetorical Context

The religious, political, and linguistics contexts of language choice highlight yet another part of the media ecology of the King James Version: the rhetorical context. "Rhetoric" here refers to the sixteenth-century usage, indicating the decoration of language, belles lettres, the arrangement of words, the use of imagery, and other stylistic things, rather than to the classical Greek and Latin understanding of rhetoric as the finding of available arguments or the use of probable proofs.

Every language has its canons of style. For a translator, a key question emerges as to how to render such aspects of language simultaneously with the verbal meaning of a given text. This challenge for Bible translators dates back at least to Jerome's work on the Vulgate: how much of the style of the Hebrew or Greek should become a part of the translation (into Latin, in Jerome's case), particularly when style itself differs from one language to another? That is, a given turn of phrase or word arrangement (or alliteration, assonance, etc.) may prove elegant and meaningful in one language but not in the other. A given word arrangement, alliteration, or assonance may prove impossible to recreate in another language. Bible translators face a choice between translating words in the word order of Greek or Hebrew, or translating the high (or low) style into Latin or English, even though that means that they have to abandon a literal approach. Jerome, who translated both classical Greek texts as well as the Bible, followed different principles at different times: "In his letter to Pammachius, he says that while translating literary works he followed the classical idea of a 'free translation,' with one exception, the Bible. He saw 'mystery even in the word order of the Bible'" (Jinbachian, 2007, p. 33). At the same time, Jerome was not slavish, recognizing with Cicero, Horace, and Boethius that a word-for-word correspondence could betray the original text (p. 32). As justification for this, he cites the Scriptures themselves:

> The Apostles and the Evangelists in quoting from the Old Testament sources have tried to communicate the meaning rather than the literal words, and that they have not cared greatly to preserve exact phrases and sentence constructions, so long as they could clearly present the substance of their subject to men's understanding. . . . In dealing with the Bible one must consider the substance and not the literal words. (Quoted in Jinbachian, 2007, p. 33)

The situation takes on greater complexity with the variety of material in the Bible: "The contrasting forms of the Bible made it necessary to render it 'word-for-word' (*verbum e verbo*) where it was a legal document, and to translate 'sense-for-sense' (*sensus de sensu*) where it was a literary work" (Jinbachian, 2007, p. 34; cf. Burke, 2007, pp. 88–89). This marked a change from the Old Latin (that is pre-Jerome) translations, which are "largely 'word-for-word,' probably because that was understood to have been the Septuagint approach, and because it was, after all, the word of God being translated" (Burke, 2007, p. 84).

Resembling in some ways those two classical approaches, though drawing on contemporary social science (anthropology, ethnology), later generations of translators would further distinguish between formal correspondence translation and dynamic equivalence translation, as Pym points out in regards to the work of Eugene Nida (Pym, 2007, p. 202). While informative, Pym's substantive criticism of these approaches as following a "representational epistemology"—that there exists a meaningful source text with an existence independent of language such that its meaning can be separated and reinserted into another language—raises more questions than it settles about the role of rhetoric. It does, however, support the wider media ecology approach, which indicates that all factors play a role. While not taking sides, media ecology does affirm that the translation choice itself is meaningful. The communication event or experience consists of all aspects of the ecology.

The rhetorical choices taken by the various translators leave their marks. Tyndale's identification of Hebrew poetic structure with that of Middle English led him to translate the Psalms, for example, with a more literal dependency on the Hebrew texts (Bobrick, 2001, p. 119). The use of the Psalms in the daily prayer of the church in turn established a preference for this style of poetic translation, which itself influenced the later development of English stylistics. The King James Version similarly cultivated a growing preference for Elizabethan expression and vocabulary among subsequent generations of English speakers, long after Elizabethan and Jacobean English had passed from popular usage.

The Form of the Media

The King James Version, like the earlier English versions since Tyndale's, appears as a printed book rather than a manuscript or other form of communication. That matters for media ecology. The book form itself also involves any number of communicative choices: the page size, the type face(s), decorative capitals, the use of images, the quality of the paper, the quality of the editing, the use of white space (that is, the arrangement of type on the page, with or without marginal notes), the binding, and so on. Each of these contribute to the look and to the cost of the book. And each of these things communicates something about the book itself. For example, the Great Bible, intended as a pulpit Bible, had a size too large for personal use. The King James Version appeared first as a pulpit Bible "of great volume" or size and only later in smaller sizes for individual use. Bobrick (2001) describes the first editions:

> The text itself, printed Gothic type and folio format (16 inches by 10½ inches), was laid out in double columns enclosed within rules. Ornamental capitals adorned the beginnings of chapters, but the chapter summaries, headings, and marginal notes were set in roman type. Also

in roman were those words not in the original but inserted to make the meaning clear. (p. 253)

This latter usage led to the unintended consequence in later editions of people misinterpreting the change of typeface to signal importance rather than addition.

During the early years of its publication, though, the King James Version appeared as one among several other Bible translations, with the most popular alternative the Geneva Bible favored by the Puritans. Anglican Bishops commended the King James Version to the people, using phrases referring to the book's appearance. Norton (2000) comments on an interesting consequence of this: "It may have gone without saying that Bibles 'of the largest volume' and Bibles without notes meant the KJB, but such phrases do suggest that people found it difficult to distinguish the KJB from the Geneva Bible as a version, but relatively easy to distinguish it as an artefact" (p. 92). The physical appearance of the text acted as a carrier of meaning or identity. The printer and the translators may have deliberately used the physical appearance to signal other things as well: "In keeping with the idea that the new version was but a revision of the old, there were emblems of continuity; for example, some of the general ornamentation of the title page had been borrowed from the Geneva Bible, while the Bishops' Bible supplied a figure or two as well" (Bobrick, 2001, p. 253).

The Theological Context

The King James Version came during a period of intense theological dispute, starting with the Reformation debates about Catholic practices in the early sixteenth century and continuing throughout Europe and England. Those debates became increasingly public, with controversialists on every side publishing tracts and books that became best sellers for both private and public reading: "Under the aegis of patrons like the Earl of Leicester, corps of translators labored to convert useful and edifying works of every kind into the mother tongue. The missionary zeal of lay evangelists, who objected to withholding Gospel truths from any man, was completely compatible with the new movement" (Eisenstein, 1979, p. 360). Not only did the Reformers want the Scriptures translated, they wanted to highlight passages that supported their positions. Thus, as noted already, they and their Catholic opponents debated over how to translate words—for example, was *ecclesia* better rendered as "church" or "assembly"? But they also fought a war over marginal notes, with the Geneva Bible, among others, taking a strident tone against the papacy. The same theological urgency marked out the parties in England, the Puritans arguing for a position more compatible with that of Continental reformers and the Anglicans remaining closer to Roman positions. The theological competition most likely improved the overall translation enterprise as more and more individuals undertook translation. Whatever the particulars, this heated theological atmosphere spurred translators on. King James, as we have seen, approved the translation and revision project for theological as well as political reasons.

The translations became part of a virtuous theological circle, since those trained in theology undertook more education in Scripture. Moreover, since even the untrained could read the Bible, more people engaged in the reflection on faith that defines theology itself.

The Reception of the King James Version

Communication study often concerns itself with audiences and with audience reaction to and interpretation of messages—Aristotle's *pathos*. Lacking survey research for the seventeenth-century publication of the King James Version, we must turn to proxy measures in the publication history and contemporary discussion. Even here, the evidence remains slim. From the perspective of four hundred years later, we see the success of the King James Version. However, this did not happen immediately. Norton (2000) comments, "To become the Bible of the people it had to dominate the field of Bible production and to be the form of words habitually used when a text is quoted, for that is the hallmark of acceptance and the key to specific literary appreciation" (p. 90). The eventual successful reception of the King James Version depended on its authorization. Exclusive contracts with the king made it very much in the commercial interests of the printer and Cambridge University for the authorized version to succeed. In effect, they stopped printing the Geneva Bible "for 'private lucre, not by virtue of any public restraint, [and so] they were usually imported from beyond the seas'" (Norton, 2000, p. 91), usually through Amsterdam. Although it took time, "rhe ultimate success of the new Bible would owe much to the enthusiasm of James. Published by royal authority, it 'swept forward with a majestic stream of editions'—in folio, quarto, and octavo—which eventually left all its rivals behind" (Bobrick, 2001, p. 253). And it had time, with editions regularly coming off the presses.

Popular opinion about the King James Version is difficult to determine. Norton (2000) offers an interesting observation: "If there was instant acclaim for the KJB, all evidence of it has been lost, whereas evidence of dissatisfaction has survived" (p. 90). The latter evidence consists of critiques by contemporaries like Hugh Broughton and Ambrose Ussher. Broughton, a scholar omitted from the translation teams—some say because of his difficult personality—published a *Censure of the Late Translation for Our Churches*. In it he writes that "the 'ill done' translation should be burned" and that he would not recommend the King James Bible (Hamlin, Maltby, and Moore, 2011, p. 123). He goes on to criticize everything from word choices to the translation of proper names. Given his personality and perhaps resentment at his exclusion, it is hard to know how much to credit his critique. Ussher, writing around 1620, sought to revise the translation: "He offers a large number of new interpretations not to be found in any other translations, and . . . he implies that he is offering a more elegant translation. Unlike the translators so far discussed, he suggests that elegance of style is to be found in the originals and preserved in the translation" (Norton, 2000, p. 94). As Norton noted, little else remains in the record.

The eventual reception success of the King James Version comes partly from its monopoly position and, as a consequence of that, from its familiarity in the language of the church. As people heard it and prayed with it, its phrases and cadences helped shaped the linguistic practices of English speakers throughout the world. But that took time and appears more varied than many suppose. David Crystal (2010), the eminent English linguist and historian of the language, specifically addresses the question of the influence of the King James Version on the language, noting that "if there is an influence on our present-day written language, it has to appear in grammar, vocabulary, spelling, punctuation, or the broader patterns of usage that we impressionistically refer to as matters of 'idiom' or 'style'" (p. 4). He discounts any influence on grammar, spelling, and punctuation, as these do not show any appreciable influence of the King James Version. Conducting a careful review of the text, Crystal concludes that he finds "only 257" stylistic influences, though he acknowledges that these far outnumber the idiomatic influences of the next-ranking sources, the plays of Shakespeare (p. 258). However, this inheritance as well as that of vocabulary comes from the set of translations that the King James Version team drew on. The greater impact, Crystal thinks, comes from an influence on spoken and written English—the result of people's hearing and reading the text in church or in school. Here he credits the King James Version as creating preferences for rhetorical expressions (bathos, chiasmus, hyperbole, irony, oxymoron, personification, and satire), language play, phonetic properties (iambic rhythms, alliteration, assonance, euphony, monosyllabicity, and rhyme), and brevity of expression (p. 261).

From a publishing perspective and from a communication perspective, the King James Version eventually had a most impressive reception. Other measures of influence show a substantial impact on the English language, but one measured more in perceived influence than grammatical or graphological characteristics.

• • •

The media ecology of the King James Version gives some idea of the complex interaction of communication and other factors that affected the translation and, indirectly, of how people reflected on their belief both in the seventeenth century and long after. As with any human project, things did not have to turn out as they did, but the new communication technology and its associated social practices allowed them to take the path that they took. Without these communication technologies, that path would not have opened in the same way and the King James Version's production and subsequent history would not have been the same. The story also becomes a story of theology. While theological concerns did lead translation choices, the translation itself, once established, influenced subsequent theology, both of the academy and of the ordinary believer whose faith-seeking-understanding often began with a translation that many people regarded not as a translation but as the original word of God.

Just as the study of the King James Version highlights many supporting structures for the printed word in theology, the wider media ecology of theology encompasses other media as well. Up to now, this study has examined the ecologies of speaking and writing. The world of theological expression goes beyond these forms as Christians also make use of art, music, architecture, ritual, film, and now social media. The subsequent chapters address these.

6
ART

Shaping the Sacramental Imagination

Sometime in the second century in the catacombs of Rome, an unknown Christian sketched an image of a shepherd holding a sheep over his shoulders, an image that appears about 120 times overall in the catacombs (Milburn, 1988, p. 30). The Christians appropriated this image—one well known in art for one thousand years and adapted by the Greeks to represent Hermes the compassionate as a representation of Christ, the good shepherd, the descendant of David (the shepherd king of Israel), the new king who would shepherd his people and preserve them in the face of death. Catacomb artists joined this and other images into a theology of hope: "The subjects chosen for representation in the catacombs naturally tend to be those appropriate to private tombs, with an emphasis on scenes of deliverance illustrating the power of God to save those who put their trust in Him" (p. 27). Other common images there and in other burial sites (for example, on sarcophagi from the later centuries) include the orant figure—a person praying with hands uplifted—as well as representations of biblical scenes of deliverance: Daniel in the lions' den, the people of Israel crossing the Red Sea, and so on. Such art grew out of the contemporary culture and extended it: "Art historians have contrasted the sepulchral representations of the catacombs to traditional didactic religious art, interpreting images of exhortation and encouragement. They can also be viewed as a confessional art" (Goethals, 1990, p. 18). As confessional art, all of these images express a Christian theology of deliverance from danger and death, of hope in God.

Such images serve to remind us, if we needed reminding, that words, whether spoken or written or recorded in whatever medium, do not exhaust the communication potential for Christianity. Within the first centuries of Christian history, artists began a theology by visual expression, by image—that is, a theology expressed in images. That movement eventually led through cultural clashes and biblical debates to (in the ninth century

CE) a theology of image—that is, a theological reflection upon images themselves and a justification of the use of images in Christian life and thought. Throughout the following centuries, Christians have employed images in even more sophisticated ways, creating a complex ecology of image, one that has unconsciously influenced theology even as theology has shaped it.

Jensen (2000) describes the interaction in this way: "Visual art often serves as a highly sophisticated and even eloquent mode of theological expression" that cannot be separated from "the biblical narratives, liturgical practices, and the common traditions of scriptural interpretation" (p. 3). To understand the theological impact of art requires an understanding of the different roles of art in the Christian tradition:

> Among these are the decorative, illustrative, and didactic uses of art, but added to these are functions that might be characterized as exegetical, symbolic, liturgical, and iconic. The former are not to be denigrated. Beauty offers glory, and education brings illumination. However, the latter four functions assume that visual art is capable of mediating or even manifesting more complex theological ideas—including the incarnation and the presence of the divine in creation without necessarily being straight-jacketed by the prevailing (authorized) dogma or catechesis. (p. 6)

These roles or functions of religious art give a sense of the ecosystem in which art takes on theological meaning. The ecosystem also includes the art's "content," the audience, the locations of the art (buildings, manuscripts, and homes, but also the geographic differences between Eastern and Western Christianity), time periods, and the thought worlds of the believers. The story spans Christian forms, places, and times.

Hints from the Media Ecology of Ancient Christianity

Symbols stand among the earliest forms of expression to appear as images. Clement of Alexandria, writing in the early third century CE, refers to a number of symbols, suitable for the signet rings of Christians: "Now our seals ought to be a dove or a fish or a ship running before the breeze or a tuneful harp or a ship's anchor. And if there should happen to be a fisherman, he will call to mind the apostle and the children drawn up from the water" (quoted in Milburn, 1988, p. 2). Earlier, according to the testimony of Justin Martyr (mid-second century CE), Christians had incorporated the symbol of the cross and adapted the symbol of a ship from Egyptian, Roman, and Greek practices.

Other symbols indirectly hinted at the cross: the tree of life, a plough, a ship's mast, an axe—each incorporated a cross shape and each also appeared in various biblical accounts (Milburn, 1988, pp. 2–3). The *chi rho*, made of the first two Greek letters of the word "Christ," and which includes a cross shape, also appears early on materials found in Christian burials from the beginning of the second century (p. 5). And, of course, Christians used the symbol of a fish, the word in Greek making an acrostic for "Jesus Christ, Son of God and savior." Milburn (1988) explains further:

> This, when taken in connection with references to fish in the Gospel story of the miraculous feeding of the multitude, made it easy for Christians who partook of the Eucharistic bread and wine to think of themselves as receiving through faith the body of Christ, described allusively as the fish. The epitaph of Abercius, bishop of Hieropolis in Phrygia, contains the words "Faith has provided for us as our food a Fish from the fountain, mighty, pure, one whom a virgin brought forth," and a gravestone from Autun retains this Eucharistic reference in the words "Eat when you are hungry, receiving the Fish in your hands." (p. 30)

Each of these already marks a media ecology, where a symbol draws on a letter, image, or word to form a code for Christian belief.

Across the Mediterranean from the Roman catacombs, the synagogue and church at Dura-Europos (by the Euphrates River in modern-day Syria) also featured images from the second or third century; the construction of the church dates from the period of Roman rule between 165 and 256 CE, most likely 241 (Silver, 2011, ¶14–23). The discovery provided a significant insight into both Jewish and early Christian practices since it showed how Hellenistic Judaism incorporated human images in decorating their places of worship, despite the ban on "graven images" in Exodus 20:4. The Christian site, a house church with a baptistery, seems modest enough to have remained hidden, as befits a religious group facing persecution. However, that site also made use of images: "The paintings, all found in the baptistery, depict common biblical scenes of both the Old and New Testaments: Jesus walking on water, the Good Shepherd, David and Goliath, and others" (Silver, 2011, ¶23). Goethals describes the others: "One of these is a sketchy representation of Christ's healing of the paralytic, showing only the figure of Christ and the healed man as he takes up his bed and walks. Other vignettes depict . . . Jesus reaching out to a sinking Peter as the disciples watch from a boat; Jesus with a woman at the well . . ." (Goethals, 1999, p. 137). The images, collectively, invoke a theology. As with the images in the catacombs, the matter of these images focuses on deliverance, where the physical and mental deliverance (from external foes, from the natural threats of the sea, from illness, from ignorance) signifies a spiritual deliverance: "In his report on the Christian building at Dura-Europos, historian Carl Kraeling concludes that this selective grouping of biblical vignettes symbolize the victory over sin and death achieved through the savior figure, Jesus" (p. 137).

In reporting the opinions of art historians and archeologists, Goethals notes that any interpretation of these images and their theology must include three aspects: the context of the city (that is, of the images in the synagogue and temples), the liturgical role of the baptistery, and the Christian literary sources of the third century. Goethals then offers this conclusion:

> To more completely understand the images, we would need to study the texts recited during particular rites, the oral or written Scriptures, the cultural context in which artistic styles mingled, and the sociopolitical circumstances of a local community. Moreover, . . . we need to remember that even the static images of the early Christians were experienced in a dynamic context of ritual words and actions. Enlivened by the movement and sounds of liturgy, visual images were integrated into a vital composite of religious meaning. (Goethals, 1999, p. 137)

In effect, Goethals suggests that we can understand not just Dura Europos but all Christian art and its theology only through a media ecology. Jensen (2000) adds another opinion from art historians that plays into the mix: "Certain scholars have suggested that the material evidence is more reflective of the faith of the common folk than literature, which is perceived as being primarily representative of the aristocratic and educated male clergy" (p. 29). This group suggests that one need also to attend to things outside of the Christian context, both from Judaism and paganism. Each of the elements makes sense only in their interaction. The media environment provides the critical piece for us to grasp the theology.

The early centuries of Christianity show people reflecting on their belief in symbols, decoration, icons, and illustrations, either in funerary or liturgical contexts. Jensen (2000) hints at yet another aspect of the ecosystem when she notes that the simpler symbols and images "invite viewers to apply their own meanings and values, making precise interpretation [by later historians and theologians] impossible. Two of these, the shepherd and the praying figure (orant), were extremely popular and appear in early Christian art more frequently than any biblical subject" (p. 32). While we cannot know the precise theological conclusions of an earlier era, we should remember that the viewer formed an essential part of the system, one that also tied into the larger context of Christian belief. Again, Jensen adds another aspect to the visual theology: "most of these images have thematic counterparts or parallels in theological or exegetical writings of the early church" (p. 32). Illustrations of biblical stories offer another look at early theology, but again, in the larger context of Christian life: "The use of biblical themes generally underscores the prominent place scripture stories played in the faith and daily life of Christians, especially in an era when theologians were preoccupied with doctrinal formulation and refutation of heresy, and apologists attempted to give Christianity a philosophical pedigree as well as an intellectual justification" (p. 64). Christian art, then, does not exist in isolation from liturgical practice or theological interests of the communities in which artists live. This becomes even clearer when we find similar images or biblical themes appearing in different contexts:

> Like any complex symbol system, early Christian iconography cannot be served up as a catalogue of images with simple definitions. For example, a portrayal of Abraham offering his son Isaac as a sacrifice ... might be part of a simple message of deliverance in one context, particularly if it is juxtaposed to other scenes that might relay the same meaning (Daniel in the lion's den and the three youths in the fiery furnace, for example). But a nearly identical presentation of Isaac's sacrifice could also serve as an early Christian type of Jesus' sacrifice in a different programmatic context—one that might include the raising of Lazarus and the "sign" of Jonah. (Jensen, 2000, p. 67)

Sometimes the liturgical settings (baptism or Eucharist) determine the meaning, an indication that the environment of the art matters to its theological purpose (p. 72). In her consideration of a number of such settings, Jensen speculates that biblical depictions took on a kind of iconic usage and from then became symbols of specific theological ideas like "God's steadfast protection" or "prototypes of Christian heroes" (p. 75). The art moves from illustration to teaching to a representation of a theological truth. Another path from art to theological understanding passes through what Jensen calls "visual exegesis" (p. 77). The images depict a biblical scene and offer an interpretation, a kind of commentary. Jensen sees a parallel to the methods used in Judaism and in early Christian homiletics: "This guiding methodology often reasoned that scripture was not meant to be understood purely on a literal or historical level, but that its true, or higher, meaning was imparted symbolically or metaphorically. Seeking this secondary level of meaning often meant finding the figures or types in the text—symbols that referred to something hidden at the obvious or literal level" (p. 77). And that, she argues, has a visual element: the artist creates the interpretation through the portrayal and arrangement of elements.

After the emperor Constantine's Edict of Milan, which marked an end to the persecution of Christianity, the environment of Christian art changed from catacombs and house churches to public buildings. The same things apply to the aspects of theological expression in the art of the church of the first millennium as to the art of early Christianity: "Christian art has a broader message, a larger audience, and may now accommodate itself to a grander 'playing field'" (Jensen, 2000, p. 92), but the visual retained its theological importance. And the change in the cultural and legal media ecology affected the content of theology: "As the circumstances of the church changed, so did the focus of this theological reflection (e.g. from individual death and resurrection to the triumph of the Christian faith and Christ's divine realm)" (p. 92). The favor of the imperial court finds a reflection in the theological themes in the art: "This new iconography was designed to emphasize the glory, power, and majesty of this triumphant religion, perhaps subtly associating it with the power and triumph of the Roman Imperium, or (alternatively) directly contrasting it with dying aspects of Roman traditional paganism and the old gods, and maybe even the imperial cult itself" (p. 98).

The church of San Apollinare Nuovo in Ravenna provides an example. Ravenna served as the capital of the western Roman empire in the sixth and seventh centuries. This church, built at the beginning of the sixth century by Theodoric, features a series of liturgical and decorative mosaics: a series showing a procession of male and female saints towards the altar, a set of portraits of biblical figures above them, and still higher up, a series of scenes from the Gospels and passion of Christ. Goethals comments on the interpretation of such images: "In his studies of the churches at Ravenna, historian Otto von Simson has shown how these are at the same time representations of the liturgical dramas: 'the Savior's life, death, and resurrection did not happen once in the dim past . . . but take place mystically within the faithful themselves as they are enacted in the liturgy' (1948, p. 79). The biblical subjects at San Apollinare Nuovo appear to be selected and arranged to reinforce the liturgical rites that occur in the sacramental time and space" (Goethals, 1999, p. 138). Because San Apollinare Nuovo served as an imperial church, a political interpretation overlays the theological. Even the processional figures of the saints (which replaced an earlier processional depiction of the members of the imperial court) serves to remind the viewers of public processions in honor of the emperor. The heavenly court, then, bears some resemblance to the earthly one and vice versa. The church also represents Christ, not on the cross but in glory as the pantocrator or ruler of the world, as an emperor. Other common themes in churches of this period show Jesus as lawgiver and Jesus as teacher (Jensen, 2000, p. 107), images reflecting different theological understandings of the Christ, of Christ as transcendent or authoritative.

This tradition of drawing religious themes from both Christian life and secular administration continues in later Christian history and practice. The great medieval cathedrals also joined art to religious purposes, political comment, and cultural practices. Ferree (1898) points out that the statuary at one of the porches of Chartres cathedral joins these contexts through its representation of four figures:

> ... the prophet Jephthah, King Louis VIII of France, his daughter, the blessed Isabelle, and Zacharias, father of St. John the Baptist. Surely, never were personages of wider origin brought together in a single group; yet there is a real reason for just this combination. Jephthah, as the sacrificer of his daughter, is a symbol of Christ. As the prophet, though differently, Louis VIII had consecrated his daughter Isabelle to God and a holy life; she built the monastery of Longchamps near St. Cloud, of which she became abbess, and is therefore represented in her religious garb. The sister of St. Louis, king of France, under whose reign the cathedral of Chartres was dedicated, and who was one of its chief benefactors, and his father, are naturally commemorated in its decorations. And as for Zacharias, did he not, in his immortal *Benedictus*, rehearse the innumerable benefits that our Lord brought to humanity, and is not his effigy properly placed on His temple? (p. 163)

Art historians have noted similar things of all the great cathedrals. Carved with representations of biblical scenes, of moral lessons and consequences—judgment, heaven, and hell—and of political and religious ceremony, the churches themselves offered very particular theological lessons. In Ferree's term, they become "Bibles in stone." More than this, they also served as catechisms in stone, joining church practice (hearing the Mass or participating in festivals, for example) with entertainment and learning. In her history of artificial memory, Yates (1966) points out that the classic memory systems taught people to use physical places or the mental images of physical places to remember lists of things and to associate particular ideas with physical representations like statues. In the medieval period, Albert the Great "advises the use of only 'real' memory places, memorized in real buildings, not the erection of imaginary systems in memory. Since he has mentioned in the previous solution that 'solemn and rare' memory places are the most 'moving,' perhaps one can further deduce that the best kind of building in which to form memory places would be a church" (p. 75). Further, both Albert and Thomas Aquinas taught the use of artificial memory to recall moral teachings. The art of medieval cathedrals could well serve such purposes. Yates suggests similar uses of church art in Giotto's painting of virtues and vices in the Arena Capella in Padua (pp. 101–2). The art, now associated with teaching, reflects also a subtle shift in theology: not only is it a reflection on belief—a faith-seeking-understanding—but a body of ideas to be remembered.

The art of the medieval church makes full sense only in terms of the ecology of its setting. At the church of St. Mary Madeleine in Vézelay, one enters the sanctuary through one of three portals.

> [T]heir general theological symbolism is clear: these portals through which worshipers pass into the ritual space of the sanctuary dramatize the Incarnation. Over the south portal the tympanum depicts the birth of Christ, the moment when "the Word became flesh and dwelt among us," the human beginning of the mystery of the Incarnation. Above the north portal the sculpture on the tympanum portrays the appearance of Christ to his disciples on the road to Emmaus and his ascension into heaven. The large central portal is generally assumed to represent Pentecost: the manifestation of the Holy Spirit to the followers of Jesus and the beginnings of the church. (Goethals, 1990, p. 28)

Within the building, the unknown artists "did catechesis through architecture, sculptures, images." On one side of the capital of a column (a physical support for the church structure and implicitly a support for the faith of the Church), they show "Judas after he hanged himself, but on the other is the Good Shepherd lifting him onto his shoulders and taking him with him" (Pope Francis, 2018, p. 12), as though to indicate what Jesus means by forgiveness. The theology expressed in the stone matches the theology expressed in the worship.

Medieval church art also highlights a theological shift in terms of the suffering Christ. As we have seen, the late imperial churches, especially of the Greek-speaking East, pictured a glorified Christ. Where the cross did appear, Christian iconography tended to use it as a simple sign or as a symbolic component part of another image, such as an anchor. By the tenth century, images of the crucified Christ become more frequent, something that Jensen (2000, p. 151–55) connects to the fifth-century Christological debates: if Christ were truly human and truly divine, and he truly suffered death on the cross, then the divinity suffered. Medieval Western saints such as Francis Assisi, Bonaventure, and Julian of Norwich furthered a devotion to the suffering savior. The veneration of the cross had a place in the liturgy of Good Friday, opening

Chapel of the Crucifix
Santi Giovanni e Paolo
(Venice)—Crucifix,
in Carrara marble, by
Francesco Caprioli
Wikimedia Commons

a space for the cross in the lives of people. And art followed. Jensen (2017) places the art of the crucifix into a larger environment:

> [B]efore the tenth or eleventh century, both Eastern and Western depictions typically refrained from showing Jesus as suffering physical agony and death. Consistent with the earliest known crucifixion images, they tended to present Christ as vigorously alive, his eyes wide open, and often robed in the purple garments of a king. . . .
>
> Gradually, from the ninth through the 11th century, the depictions of Christ's triumph over death began to shift toward a visual representation of the suffering man-God, or *Christus patiens*. Evolving theological reflection on the significance of Christ's death, the growing emphasis on the purpose and value of Jesus's physical agony, and the development of guided meditation on Christ's Passion within certain early monastic communities all contributed to this transition. (p. 151)

The crucifix became an image of God's love and its various depictions vied for greater realism. The reason may not be hard to find. Carpenter (1972) comments, "Any technology, including language, can make reality frighteningly explicit, especially human reality" (p. 135). If this is the case with language, even more so with art. And, as people focused more on the sufferings of Christ, the art influenced the thinking of theologians in the West who articulated theologies of satisfaction, of shared suffering, and of redemption.

A Media Ecology of Smaller Canvases

The urge to decorate, to make one's faith visible, does not end with places of worship. Another media ecology combination brings art together with manuscript pages. Over time, people added illustrations to the written text of the Scriptures. The tradition did not originate with Christianity, but dates from at least the Egyptian Book of the Dead, centuries before the Christian era (Nordenfalk, 1995, p. 7). Similar illustration appears in Roman manuscripts, both pre- and post-Christian era. Nordenfalk claims that some of this decoration arose as a means to find one's place in a scroll (p. 7). Later illustrators added representational images, as in a sixth-century manuscript of the Aeneid (p. 12–13). About the same time, illustrators of biblical manuscripts began to add particular biblical scenes, which not only provided color but in some ways a visual commentary on the passage. Nordenfalk comments, "Nevertheless, by a strange paradox, this heathen art served the cause of the new religion and in fact went far to body forth the sanctity and transcendence of the Word of God" (p. 36). Like the art of the catacombs and churches, these illustrations offer a kind of theology in several ways.

The relation between text and image provides another wonderfully complex media environment, with several interacting relationships: the physical relationship between the drawing and the text (Weitzmann, 1947, p. 49–51); the relation between the illustration and the text, in terms of meaning, convention, archetype, decoration, and so on (p. 130–34); a critical relationship of interpretation and analysis (p. 182–92); a relationship of script and text, most clearly represented in the development of the Carolingian minuscule as a more legible "typeface" (Nordenfalk, 1995, pp. 54–55); and a relationship between decorative and illustrative purposes—a dichotomy which overlaps as much as it separates (Dalli Regoli, 1983, p. 65). Much of this ecology goes beyond the interest in theology here, but it provides a general background.

More specifically the theology emerges from the media ecology as we reflect on questions such as: Which images appear in the manuscripts? Which passages receive attention? Which places in the manuscript do the images occupy? What purposes do the images serve?

That the image does play a role remains beyond doubt: "One of the primary aspects of this relationship [between text and image] is that of the link between image and writing; the text is closely associated with the image not only in the meaning it expresses but also in the way it is drawn up" (Dalli Regoli, 1983, p, 63). This occurs in a number of ways. Dalli Regoli notes that, on the most basic level, illustrations "serve to support the credibility and authority of the text" (p. 68). In a more complex interaction, illustrations provide metaphorical and allegorical interpretations for the text (p. 69). Here, it seems that the artist extended the textual theology in building on the traditional four senses of the biblical text: the literal sense, the allegorical sense ("defining what Christians are to believe"), the moral sense ("defining what Christians are to do"), and the analogical sense ("defining what Christians were to hope for") (McGrath, 2011, p. 132). The manuscripts offer abundant examples of both artistic interpretations of texts and artistic commentaries.

Goethals (1999) discusses several examples. The ninth-century Utrecht Psalter uses human figures to illustrate and comment on the text of the psalms. Psalm 57 ("Have mercy on me, O Lord") has a drawing below the columns of text:

> While the text begins with the words *Miserere mei*, the psalmist quickly moves to voice confidence in God's care. The exuberant drawing at the bottom of the page is existential, expressing the terror of the psalmist's situation and, at the same time, the wonder of God's protection. Vigorous rhythmic lines crisscross each other, creating several spatial zones. God and the heavenly host visually reign above. At the center is the psalmist who is "among lions." Below him are the enemies who have fallen into a pit dug by themselves, but intended for the psalmist. To the right and left are the "attackers," armed with bows and arrows and lances. . . .
>
> Although the imagery clearly has a narrative function, the figures are not positioned in a fixed theatrical space; nor are they staged on a particular plane. Instead, dynamic, black and white vignettes range freely in a visual poetic motion that parallels the rhythm of the text. . . . In this illumination, words and drawing seem inseparable: indeed, the lines seem to perform the text rather than simply illustrate it. (Goethals, 1999, pp. 142–43)

The illustration serves to bring the viewer into the experience of the psalm. Whether literate or not, the person seeing the page shares the psalmist's confidence amid terror. It seems as though the manuscript tells us that it is not enough to recite the words of the psalm; one must also feel them, identify with them.

The Book of Kells from the late eighth or early ninth century offers another kind of textual commentary or, better, theological method. More abstract than the psalter, the style of the Book of Kells uses arrangement, color, and geometric form to invite the viewer to ponder the image, much as the hearer or reader would ponder the text. Though visual, the effect moves beyond the visual to the pragmatic or performative:

> Moreover writing itself was regarded by the Irish church with almost superstitious reverence, all the more so when its function was to propagate the message of the Scriptures. This conception found its most significant expression in the large illuminated initial letters, which in fact "held up" the reading of the script; in them the divine word was arranged in ornaments, just as shrines containing holy relics were bedecked with gold and precious stones. (Nordenfalk, 1995, p. 36)

The ecology of this illuminated text combines word, decoration, constraints on reading, and ideas for meditation and interpretation; Goethals points out examples of this in action, for both a page with illustration and a page with decoration. First, commenting on an image of the arrest of Jesus, which appears within a highly decorative field, she notes:

> More remarkable still is a visual pattern that signals the crucifixion that will soon follow . . . If one carefully studies the directional lines of Jesus' form, it is possible to detect a condensed cross shape. There are blue areas of Jesus' clothing, set off by a contrasting red color of the cloak, establishing the essential linear cross patterns. His outstretched arms extend these further. Beginning then with Jesus' extended arms, one can follow the blue shapes downward and see an implied intersection slightly above the knees that are pulled inward. Then the diagonal linear forms move downward to complete an elongated X-shaped cross. (1999, p. 145)

Here the decoration and the image merge to foreshadow the text and to call attention to the theological centrality of the event. The illustrators choose another artistic approach in the crafting of the border of the crucifixion page. Combining faces, creatures, lines, and text, the page offers something more:

> In this illumination, however, the text is more than text. The artist has shaped letters into a visual object. On this page are several words, the last ones forming an "X"-cross which fills almost half of the lower part of the page. Text is visually transformed and *becomes* image: the cross. The visual and verbal are fused into one cohesive symbol of the brutal climax

of the Incarnation. Yet, except for the three little groups tucked into the border, there are no visual references to human beings. Moreover, fantasy, even humor, continues to run wild in the playful ornamental border. At the same time, the abstraction, the imaged word of the cross, has become a stark and terrifying witness to the horror and despair of the crucifixion of Jesus. (Goethals, 1999, p. 147)

The illustration and decoration interact with the meaning of the text (*tunc crucifixerant XPI cum eo duos latrones* translates as "then they crucified Christ and with him two robbers"): the *nomina sacra* abbreviation, XPI, for "Christi" itself appears arranged with the *rho* (P) between the two letters, so that the text, the arrangement, and the placement all refer to the crucifixion as in the midst of human sinfulness but embedded into human culture—a theology of the Incarnation and death of Jesus.

A Theological Ecosystem External to Art

The tradition of artistic expression within Christianity did not go unchallenged. Not only did it foster freer theological interpretations (the picturing by individuals of their faith-seeking-understanding, but without the constraints of language), but it also required a theological reflection on the very propriety of images. This, too, forms part of the media ecology of Christian art, where the tools used for reflection and writing focus on the tools of image and icon. The fact that the church of the East, the Greek-speaking church, used *graphein* (γράφειν) to refer to both writing a text and writing/drawing an icon (Pelikan, 1974, p. 131) indicates an ecology where symbols of all kinds communicated meaning, but with different methods of interpretation.

The initial difficulties emerged in a world where a rising Islam, with a strict ban on human images, reinforced Judaism's ban on images set forth in Exodus 20:4, Leviticus 26:1, and Deuteronomy 4:16–19 (Pelikan, 1974, p. 91). Eastern Christianity, closely interacting with Islam and Judaism, faced the issue in ways that Western Christianity did not. And, in the East, the issues raised by the conflicts over images spread to include the Christological debates of the previous centuries, new debates about authority and tradition, debates about worship, and debates about the relations between theology and the arts (p. 91). Much of this goes beyond a media ecology, but some of the theology highlights the interactions of concern here. In a dramatic way, the debate about the theology of the image (named "iconoclasm," after those who opposed or destroyed icons) shows how theology follows practice.

In his magisterial history of the development of Christian doctrine, Jaroslav Pelikan notes that "the context for such a faith in search of understanding was the church's worship" (1974, p 34). And that worship included icons and other artistic representation. In the perspective here, the ecology of worship involves multiple media—word, song, bread and wine, movement, decoration, vestment, buildings, and so on. Pelikan continues, writing that "worship was, however, more than the performance of the divine liturgy, for faith in search of understanding was also engaged in worship, the worship of God by the mind" (p. 35).

The Eucharist, as central worship in the Christian Church, lies at the heart of the debate about images. Both sides to the debate accepted key theological assumptions rooted in the Eucharist:

> If, as has been suggested, there is a consensus among modern historians that "at the root of image worship lay the concept that material objects can be the seat of divine power and that this power can be secured through physical contact with a sacred object," this was in fact a concept held in common by the opponents and by the supporters of images; for it was the root of the universal belief of Christians in the East about the sacraments, or, as they were usually termed there, "mysteries." . . . [T]he question between them regarding the Eucharist was not, in the first instance, the nature of the Eucharistic presence, but its implications for the definition of "image" and for the use of images. Was the Eucharistic presence to be extended to a general principle about the sacramental mediation of divine power through material objects, or was it an exclusive principle that precluded any such extension to other means of grace, such as images? (Pelikan, 1974, pp. 93–94)

The "sacramental principle," to use a shorthand device, holds that images become a source of the encounter with God, just as the consecrated elements of the sacrament become the Body and Blood of Christ. Those who accept this principle see or, better, experience images as something holy and partaking of God's grace and therefore outside of the biblical prohibition, which in their reading refers to images used as idols. Familiarity with the sacramental principle nurtures, over time, what later writers will call the "sacramental imagination"—the expectation that the material world can mediate the experience of the divine. One way to understand this sacramental principle comes through ecology.

The relative lack of any written discussion of the image from the period of early Christianity hampered both sides (Pelikan, 1974, p. 99). They found a few references in the ancient Fathers and claimed the authority of tradition based on practice, but had to develop their own arguments. Both sides turned to the theology of essences, taken over from the Trinitarian debates. The core of the debate came down to definitions:

> The orthodox based their definition on the relation between the original or prototype [πρωτότυπος] and the copy that was derived from it [παράγωγον]; the iconoclasts also taught that "every image is known to be a copy of some original." But Constantine V developed this definition further by asserting that a genuine image was "identical in essence with that which it portrays." (p. 109)

While that identity applied to Christ and the Eucharist, it would not apply to images created by human artists. The defenders of images developed a different approach. Following a Neoplatonic view of the world, they understood images as in a hierarchy flowing from God, even though there was no shared essence. John of Damascus put it most clearly:

> In various developments of this stratification of images, John of Damascus identified several senses of the term "image" in Christian language about God: the Son of God as the image of the Father; the Father's eternal will to create images and paradigms for the visible world; the visible things that acted as physical types of the invisible prototypes; man as a creature "in the image of God" and therefore "called into being by God as an imitation"; the Old Testament "types," which foreshadowed what was to come in the New; images erected as memorials, whether in books or in pictures, in words or in objects, in commemoration of glorious deeds in the past, pointing backward as the Old Testament shadows had pointed forward. (Pelikan, 1974, p. 120)

The argument continued with an appeal to typical human behavior: mourners kissing the clothing of the departed to remember them and do them honor. Christian veneration of the icons followed this pattern—the devotion was addressed not to the image but to the person depicted.

Ultimately, the defenders of the images appealed to the human senses. The incarnate Christ, truly human, offered himself to the senses, as 1 John 1:1 states: "What we have heard, have seen with our eyes, have touched with our hands . . ." And the images appealing to the senses confirmed faith in the Incarnation. More than that, the use of images also showed how Christ made each of the senses holy:

> The icon served as a means for this hallowing of sight, combined as it was with the hearing of the word.
> When they put such an emphasis on the role of the senses in worship, the iconophiles were affirming the role of the body in salvation—of the physical

> body of Christ as the means of achieving it and of the physical body of man as a participant in it together with the soul. (Pelikan, 1974, p. 122)

The use of icons and images also affirmed the reality of the history of Christ (p. 130) and anchored Christian believers in the world. The belief provides a consistent approach to doctrine, faith in daily living, worship, and the Christian environment:

> A liturgical theology, by Byzantine definition, would be one in which the praise and worship of the church, as expressed in its liturgy, simultaneously determined and was determined by the church's doctrinal confession. . . . Clearly the word did not refer only to the reflection and systematization carried on by the erudite, but to the doctrine set forth in worship and instruction. (Pelikan, 1974, p. 135)

Images rooted in the faith of the Incarnation, whether depicting Christ or the saints, themselves expressed a theology that both the educated and the unlettered could hold and grasp. This theology of image, a development of the sacramental principle in which God uses the material of the created world as a means to communicate with people, becomes almost taken for granted in Western Christianity and Western art, at least until the Reformation.

The fact that images remained open to many interpretations sowed some seeds of confusion that would plague the Western church, as an incident in ninth-century Turin illustrates. The bishop, Claudius, objected to people venerating images in the churches, particularly that of the cross. Jensen (2017) recounts the story:

> Claudius argued that while showing reverence to a crucifix was intended to honor and venerate the Savior, it was actually a false and superstitious act: referring only to Jesus's degradation and death, it denied his resurrection and ascension. Essentially, because Christ no longer suffers in the flesh, venerating such an image was tantamount to recrucifying him. He apparently also included plain crosses in his invective, as he added that adoration of ordinary wood fashioned into a cross would be like adoring any other object associated with Jesus's earthly life: a manger, a boat, or a donkey.
>   Both Jonas and Dungalus [the court theologians] refuted Claudius's position, pointing out that the cross, a memorial of Christ's Passion, had been found worthy of honor from antiquity. Furthermore, they argued that rather than symbolizing death, the cross signified Jesus's triumph over death. Moreover, the wood was not venerated per se but only because it was the locus of Christ's crucifixion. . . . [Dungalus] even asked whether Claudius refused to make the sign of the cross when he presided

at baptisms or confirmations or when he consecrated the bread and wine of the eucharist. Comparing veneration of the cross to veneration of the Bible, Jonas asked whether, when Claudius kisses the book, he understands himself to be honoring leather, ink, and paper. (pp. 154–55)

The dispute stemmed both from confusion about how an image represents and from a confusion of material (wood) and symbolic representation. The philosophical confusion foretold some of the later theological issues in the West.

In addition to the theological defense of the images, Christian authorities in both the East and the West defended images on pragmatic grounds as well:

> "The original Christian defense of the visual arts," it has been noted, "was based on their usefulness as educational tools. Imagery was . . . a means of instruction or edification, especially for the illiterate." Images were preferable to the plain cross as symbols of the passion, because they communicated its meaning more effectively to the simple rustics. The images were "books for the illiterate," instructing them about the Christian message. As such, they could be worshiped, kissed, and embraced with the heart, instead of being read. The crude and uninstructed masses often failed to pay attention to the readings from Scripture in the public services of the church, but even they could have their attention drawn by images and could thus learn from them what was in the lessons. (Pelikan, 1974, p. 94)

This didactic tradition runs from at least Paulinus of Nola in the fifth century through Gregory the Great and the Greek Fathers already mentioned (Goethals, 1990, pp. 15, 22). Jensen (2000), the contemporary art historian, warns against the implication of this view on the pedagogic value of art that the theology expressed in art is simplistic:

> This statement may sum up one traditional Western perspective on religious art—that religious pictures are the "Bible of the Unlettered"—a good thing for those who have no better way to learn the stories of the faith. Although it sounds well-meaning, such a perspective actually views visual art as inferior or subservient to verbal expression and suggests that images are the "food" for childlike minds, whereas theological treatises, homilies, or verbal arguments contain the meat of adult intellectual formation. The function of art in religious contexts is thus seen as primarily didactic and as such dependent on and interpretive of what can be found in written form elsewhere. Not recognizing that visual art can be as deeply theological or intellectually sophisticated as literature consigns even the most refined examples of artistic production to the category of "popular culture" for a mass audience and

erroneously opposes it to "higher" forms of theological discourse carried on from pulpits, lecterns, and in the bookstacks of libraries in churches, universities, and theological schools. (p. 3)

Jensen's warning serves as a reminder to remember that the media matter; that different media—art in this instance—have their own ecosystem of production and meaning and can equally serve a faith-seeking-understanding.

In the West, the challenges to images did not have as strong an impact as in the East, at least until the Reformation when a number of reformers renewed the doubts about images, doubts rooted not so much in Exodus 20 as in the philosophical understanding of how images worked. After the Seventh Ecumenical Council supported the use of images in the eighth century, theologians in Charlemagne's court commented on the decrees and forbade "the actual destruction of religious images that have even limited pedagogical or decorative value" (Jensen, 2017, p. 153). The cross, as seen above, became a focal point of the debate. Jensen (2017) explains the thinking of a Parisian synod meeting in 825:

> The assembled bishops determined that images were permissible to a limited extent and that it was wrong to remove or destroy them, so long as they were not objects of actual worship. Yet they rejected the claim of the Eastern churches that images should be honored in the same way that the cross was venerated. Rather, they decided that the cross was altogether unique, different from other images and exclusively deserving of honor. They gave several justifications: that the cross had been revealed to Constantine as a portent of his victory; that it had clearly performed miracles when it had been discovered in Jerusalem; that making the sign of the cross was efficacious for consecrating the Eucharistic elements or administering baptism; and that the cross, unlike any other image, served as a sign of salvation. (p. 155)

In general, Western thinking allowed veneration of relics, the Eucharistic elements, the sign of the cross, and the Bible—sanctified things—but not artificial images (p. 154), as these served only as reminders. Those images had a place in churches but not as objects of veneration. The practice of using art to focus attention, as noted above in terms of the medieval cathedrals, became widely accepted. Let those who could not read have the Bible in image, stone, and art.

Running alongside these justifications for images in Christian worship and the expression of theological understanding in nonverbal forms was another, more skeptical tradition, which, particularly coupled with rising literacy, recognized the limits of images to convey theological truth. During the twelfth century, at the height of the development of the great medieval churches, St. Bernard of Clairvaux encouraged—if not commanded—that monastic churches eschew images. Ceding that images did instruct the simple, he did not see that justification in the case of monks whose worship and contemplation should focus on the word of God. For them, images only provided distraction (Goethals, 1990, pp. 90–91). As part of the Cistercian renewal, the monks issued this statute:

> 20. *Concerning sculptures, paintings, and the wooden cross*: We forbid sculptures or paintings in either our churches or in any of the rooms of the monastery, because when attention is turned to such things the advantage of good meditation or the discipline of religious gravity is often neglected. However, we do have painted crosses which are of wood. (Rudolph, 1987, p. 29, quoted in Goethals, 1990, p. 36)

But this does not put an end to the faith-seeking-understanding in the visual realm. With the ban on images, the monastic builders sought other means to express their faith. Rather than illustration, they, like the manuscript artists, turned to decoration. The Cistercians marked their churches with geometric patterns, proportionality, and light. Light has Christian theological connotations, going back to Jesus' statement, "I am the light of the world" (John 8:12). Light reveals, illumines, and symbolizes the divine (Goethals, 1990, pp. 38–40). The patterns and proportions also convey a theological stance: "One may deduce a kind of 'meaning' from the deliberate elimination of representational imagery and from the resolve to use only pure forms as ornament. These decisions can be linked to a larger, more ancient mystical tradition in which numbers, abstract forms, and relationships symbolize religious knowledge and experience; knowingly or not" (p. 39). Goethals also reminds us that the spare beauty of the Cistercian churches functioned in tandem with the monastic liturgical celebrations, as a part of a more complex ecology of worship.

Writing, Art, and Worship

Later developments in Western Christianity—the attempt to purify the Church in the Reformation, the rise of other venues for art in the Renaissance, the changing patterns of worship, the automation of bookmaking through the printing press—all served to split art from worship and other religious venues. In other words, the environment, the ecology changed. These events did not destroy art or put an end to theological reflection through art, but they did change how it took place. The increased emphasis on a theology in written form (rather than in sermons or oral disputations) lessened interest in a theology in visual form and in some ways cheapened it, much as Jensen identifies in the ways that written theology viewed the other forms as "childlike" (Jensen, 2000, p. 3). The Reformers embraced writing and the thought patterns fostered by writing as a clearer path to God. To increase attention to the Word of God in the Bible, the Protestant reformers followed the Cistercian path and removed distracting images. Carlstadt, Calvin, and Zwingli went further, and each broke the connection between the material and the devotional—first in the Eucharist and then in the arts. In various ways they rejected the sacramental principle that had consciously or unconsciously undergirded images and faith since the iconoclasm debates.

Zwingli's case makes this clear. His reforms followed two paths. He wanted to purify worship and, as part of this, regarded images as temptations to idolatry, to seducing the mind of believers by something other than God. In this, his reasoning somewhat resembled that of the ninth-century Bishop Claudius of Turin. But Zwingli also radically revisited traditional Eucharistic theology. Taking his place in a debate active since the thirteenth century, he chose to argue for a symbolic, not real, presence of Christ in the Eucharist (Smith, 1987, p. 99). J. P. Singh Uberoi summarizes Zwingli's position:

> Zwingli insisted that in the utterance "This is my body" (*Hoc est corpus meum*), the existential word "is" (*est*) was to be understood, not in a real, literal, and corporeal sense, but only in a symbolical, historical, or social sense (*significat, symbolum est*, or *figura est*) . . . Dualism or double monism was fixed in the world view and the life-world of the modern age, which was thereby ushered in. . . . By stating the issue and forcing it in terms of dualism, or more properly double monism, Zwingli had discovered or invented the modern concept of time in which every event was either spiritual and mental or corporeal and material but no event was or could be both at once. . . . Spirit, word, and sign had finally parted company for man at Marburg in 1529; and myth or ritual . . . was no longer literally and symbolically real and true (Uberoi, 1978, p. 31, quoted in Smith, 1987, p. 99).

The unlinking of the material and the spiritual, the lessening of the impact of the Incarnation in Christian worship, led to the expulsion of art. If the Eucharistic elements did not share the nature of Christ, then no created thing could give an experience of God. Goethals (1990) explains further:

An important additional factor, however, is Zwingli's sympathy toward a kind of Platonic dualism which tended to devalue the material world. Thus, unlike Luther, he rejected the cultural homage that medievalists brought to the Eucharistic mystery and so desacralized all material elements as aids to devotion. Zurich's churches became highly rationalized, functional spaces in which liturgy consisted essentially of the preaching and hearing of the word of God. . . .

[Catholic worship fostered] the concrete engagement of worshipers with material elements; [its artistic styles] confirmed mysterious connections in the sacraments between the finite and the infinite. The radical reshaping of liturgy by Zwingli, however, denied any such sacramental relationship; materiality and faith were separated. The believer was oriented to God solely by faith and Scripture. Christian worship centered not on the Eucharist but on the reading, hearing, and interpretation of the Bible. (pp. 49–50)

For Luther, the "preached word has a sacramental dimension" (Jensen, 2017, p. 183). So, while Lutherans retained images in their churches, they placed less emphasis on them. In the general Protestant view, art, along with the materiality of the Eucharist, loses its place in the ecology of worship. Art continues to express a theology but only, from the perspective of formal theology, in a lessened, nonrational way. Though the artist continued to reflect on faith, artistic expression seemed less connected to theology itself.

Artists both Catholic and Protestant, Renaissance and post-Renaissance did create a theology in their works. Catholics and Protestants differed. For Catholics, "the art that emerged from the time around and just after the Council of Trent thus focused on the centrality of the sacraments, the Passion of Christ, and the role of the saints in a style that was highly sensual, tending toward dramatic lighting and sumptuous colors. The aim was not only to communicate doctrine but also to promote the spiritual and devotional function of religious art" (Jensen, 2017, p. 192). For example, Caravaggio's religious themes, his use of light and darkness, his powerful depictions of the struggles between good and evil (and his continued access to church venues in Catholic Italy) leave him closer to the mainstream Catholic theology. Rembrandt's religious works, rooted in northern European Protestantism (his *Return of the Prodigal Son*, for example, or his portraits of biblical figures), invite a reflection on faith in a different way, a calmer, more thoughtful appreciation. The theology is still there, in the art of both south and north, but in different ways. In many Protestant denominations, church or congregational hymnody replaced art in addressing many of the key religious themes, particularly the death of

Christ (Jensen, 2017, p. 197–203). Goethals (1999) argues that in the West theological reflection in art moved out of the Protestant churches and into homes, landscapes, and biblical illustrations (pp. 149–52).

Art in the Ecology of Faith-Seeking-Understanding

Art as a form of theological reflection, as a type of faith-seeking-understanding, has figured in one way or another throughout Christian history. Unlike written expressions of theology, it combines different systems of expression: visual signs, both representational and decorative, and conceptual signs. It invites others into its reflection on faith, but typically in particular environments—churches, Bibles, tombs, and so on. Within this larger theological and media ecology, art takes on a number of roles or functions in its theological reflection. First, it serves to recall a story by depicting characters, representational types, or events, as in the *Biblia pauperum* of medieval cathedrals. Second, it tells its own story by the choices of which images the artists choose or what kind of decoration the artists employ. The juxtaposition of images into a ground potentially different from a recitation or written text allows the artist to go beyond the text into an interpretation. Third, art expresses a theology. Again, this most often occurs through the selection, positioning, and depiction of images, though the process of representational or nonrepresentational art can itself become the subject matter for faith seeking its understanding of this human experience. Fourth, art interacts with other media and media content: illuminated manuscript pages, ritual performances, other church art in windows and statues, printed books, and so on. In each of these, art can complement, illustrate, serve as a counterpoint (as in the Book of Kells), or even compete with the communication offered by the other media (the great fear of reformers like Zwingli). Finally, art creates, fosters, and develops a particular kind of religious imagination: a sacramental imagination—that is, an imagination that readily takes the sacramental principle as a way to understand the world. Jensen (2000) summarizes all of this in a slightly different way:

> And so art crystallizes, or perhaps materializes, certain points of doctrine which, while based on scripture, are sometimes more often encountered in theological arguments than in ordinary daily experience. Images can make the bridge between the material and the intellectual via an interesting kind of hypostatic union—logos and icon. Complex and sophisticated symbols that communicate on many levels and refer to different stories, ideas, and matters of faith, visual images also speak directly and clearly, even to the simplest believer. Thus "religious pictures" are not merely for the theologically untrained, or for the illiterate, or for the practitioner of

popular religion at all, even while they serve the needs of persons in those categories. By the same token, neither is the deepest value of art restricted to the elite, the intelligentsia, or to those trained in the lore or techniques of its interpretation.

But, in the end, interpretation cannot be done without reference to a community and to the many ways its central values are expressed, including texts, rituals, and artifacts. (pp. 181–82)

7
MUSIC

Hearing the Divine

Commissioned to create a musical piece for the dedication of a new Coventry Cathedral, one built to replace the fourteenth-century building destroyed by bombing during World War II, British composer Benjamin Britten offered his *War Requiem*. The piece, first performed in 1962 in the new cathedral, includes a much-expanded ensemble beyond that used for a typical requiem. It also expresses a particular theology, which emerges most clearly from the composer's changes to the musical ecosystem of liturgical expression. The work offers an entry point into a consideration of how people do theology (in the "faith-seeking-understanding" tradition) musically.

A requiem, or Mass for the dead, takes its name from the Latin of the opening antiphon, *Requiem aeternam dona eis, Domine* ("Eternal rest grant unto them, O, Lord"). The Catholic Church celebrates the Mass either as a funeral for a particular person or as a memorial for the dead. In either case, the liturgy aims to ask God's mercy for the dead and, indirectly, to comfort the mourners by reaffirming their own faith. The musical settings include the sung Mass parts: the *introit* (or entrance antiphon), the *Kyrie eleison*, the sequence before the Gospel (the *Dies irae* from the first words, "Day of wrath, that day will dissolve the world in ashes" and ending with the petition, "spare them, O God"), an offertory, the *Sanctus*, the *Agnus Dei*, a piece during communion, the *Pie Jesu* (from last words of the *Dies irae*, "merciful Lord Jesus, grant them rest"), the *Libera Me* ("deliver me"), and the *In paradisum* ("May the angels lead you into paradise") sung as the body is carried from the church.

The form has a long history, extending at least to the thirteenth century when the poem, "Dies Irae" first appeared. Originally set to various Gregorian chant tones, composers began to offer polyphonic settings by the early Renaissance. Early versions of the music for the Requiem Mass varied widely in the texts and Mass parts they included. By the eighteenth and into the twentieth century the Requiem became a common form for many composers, including

Haydn, Mozart, Berlioz, Bruckner, Brahms, Verdi, Dvořák, Fauré, Stravinsky, Britten, and Lloyd Webber. In the last one hundred years, composers have also developed a "secular" requiem—concert pieces not intended for church services. Liturgical performance of the requiem occurs in the Catholic Church, the Anglican Communion, and the Lutheran Church.

Britten's work emerges from this background. He makes significant changes to several aspects of the traditional requiem. First, by titling it *War Requiem*, he marks the composition as more than a simple requiem but as both a remembrance of those who have died and a statement about how they died. Second, Britten expands the performers to include three choirs (a female choir, a male choir, and a boy's choir), three soloists (soprano, baritone, and tenor), a full orchestra, and a chamber orchestra. Third, he adjusts the places in which the performers stand, with the musicians, singers, and two choirs in the front and the boys' choir in the choir loft. Fourth, he adds material to the usual Mass parts of the requiem, in this instance musical settings of nine (anti-)war poems by Wilfred Owen, a British soldier and poet killed in World War I (Evans, 1997). Fifth, Britten changes the theological logic. The piece itself has the structure of a conversation among choirs and soloists, between traditional commendation of the dead to God and the voice of a soldier. Rather than a purely liturgical plea for mercy on behalf of the now-voiceless dead by seemingly powerless supplicants, this requiem hears the voice of the deceased as they speak to God and challenges an order of violence and war.

The piece makes theological sense only in the context of the millennia-long tradition of praying for the dead and of the centuries-long tradition of liturgical music.

A Media Ecology for Music

Music, like art and other media, offers its own affordances for people to understand their faith. Unlike narrative and writing, it does not favor the kinds of thinking most associated with theology in the West. Music creates another kind of thinking, something that Langer (1953) terms "significant form" or "expression" (pp. 24–25). Langer continues, "music is 'significant form,' and its significance is that of a symbol, a highly articulated sensuous object, which by virtue of its dynamic structure can express the forms of vital experience which language is peculiarly unfit to convey" (p. 32). Perhaps for this reason as well as for its association with primarily oral expression, music has long had a connection with worship and with the divine. People seek a different kind of understanding of faith in and through music. Anttila (2013) points out some of the theoretical background: "According to musicologist Carl Dahlhaus the romantic view of music employed words such as 'devotion' and 'contemplation' to describe it even as religious sentimentality became more aesthetic around the year 1800. Herbert Marcuse's *The Aesthetic Dimension* gives a closer examination of art's important spiritual dimension: 'Art breaks open a dimension inaccessible to other experience, a dimension in which human beings, nature, and things no longer stand under the law of the established reality principle'" (Marcuse, 1979, p. 72, quoted in Anttila, 2013, p. 1).

Music itself presents a complex media ecosystem involving time; hearing; the human voice (of self and others); instrumental sounds and the instruments that create them; a performance space and experience; oral and acoustic performance; written texts (specifying both verbal and nonverbal aspects); audio characteristics like volume, harmony, tone, pitch, rhythm, beat, arrangement, and directionality, as well as the specific qualities of instruments; and intentionality or the purpose that the music serves. Since each element has its own affordances—allowing some things but not others—the overall musical ecology presents an extraordinarily complex set of expression. This section will examine some of these key aspects of music and then the next will explore their potential theological uses or impacts.

Like oral discourse and unlike writing, music is fleeting. Time forms an essential aspect of music as sounds follow on one another, combine with others, and move along. Langer (1957) refers to music as "time made audible" when she compares it to painting:

> Music, like painting, is purely created form not of space, but of time; its materials are tones of varying pitch, loudness, and quality, but its elements are tonal forms, moving, mingling, resolving, having direction and energy, violently active or abating toward complete rest. Its time, as well as all the great and small tonal forms (melodies, progressions) that make it up, are appearances made of sound; music is time made audible and articulated as a perceptible, dynamic form. (p. 144)

A challenge—particularly acute for literates accustomed to seeing and analyzing ideas locked onto a page—arises when people apply the wrong kind of analysis to music. Langer describes the experience for concertgoers:

> Most auditors at concerts are sure they cannot understand the way modern music is "put together." They think that in order to appreciate it they must be able to detect the structure, name the chords, recognize all its devices, and spot the instruments that are used in each passage.... What the audience should hear is *musical elements*—created moving forms, or even, with apparent immediacy, a flow of life, feeling, and emotion in audible passage. (pp. 40–41)

Stopped music is not music. Experienced music involves time. Begbie (2000) identifies some of the ways in which hearers experience music's time, pointing out that "time" in music goes beyond linear or clock time to include "tension and resolution," "rhythm as motion in the dynamic field of meter," and "melody as motion in the dynamic field of key" (pp. 37–45). Expanding on this, he calls attention to how musical time differs from quotidian senses of time:

> Pinpointing some of the differences between linear and musical temporality will serve to open up some of the main trajectories . . . First, most obviously, music is structured through layers of waves of intensification and release. . . . Closely connected with this, second, it is fair to say that much of modernity has favored a time which can be conceptualized in primarily *quantitative* terms. A time-line becomes divided up and measured in units. The propensity to speak and think in this way is encouraged by the invention of mechanical clocks (quantifying duration with precision), the advent of "standard time," the development of calendars, and so on, . . . music's temporality is not of this character. . . . Third, various brands of *progressivism* have arisen, according to which, for example, history is construed as advancing cumulatively along a timeline towards a goal which gathers the temporal process together. . . . Fourth, this last feature of linear models has in turn frequently *masked or down played the role of discontinuity* as pervasive and potentially beneficial to historical process. In much tonal music, unpredictable interruptions, "indirect routes" and ruptures are an inherent and enriching part of the process. . . . Fifth, related to this, linear metaphors have often had the effect of *minimizing the place of radical and qualitative novelty*, encouraging a view of the future as proceeding inexorably from the past through the present, governed (in at least some currents of modernity) by a deistic "God," or by the laws of Newtonian mechanics, or sometimes by both. This can have the effect of curbing due recognition of the place of contingency and intrinsic unpredictability. . . . Sixth, the stress on homogeneity and continuity in linearity can have a marked effect on the way we understand *transience*. (pp. 59–60, italics in original)

To experience music is to experience different understandings of time. But music, as audible time, can take its hearers out of time. Those absorbed in music experience what Csikszentmihalyi (1991) called "flow" or a state of complete concentration such that they have no sense of time. But even this ties people to a different quality of time. Music allows an immersion in sound, a lessened sense of sight and a heightened sense of experience through hearing. Ong never tires of reminding his readers that, of all the human senses, only hearing indicates something alive, something with a very particular relationship to time. As Ong and Altree (2002) put it, "The hunter, remember, can see, touch, smell, and taste a buffalo when the buffalo is inert, even dead. If he hears a buffalo, it's a different matter: the buffalo is doing something" (p. 378). Sound indicates life or power, both dependent on time. Music connects people to a living reality through hearing and through feeling.

Second, because it is sound, music creates a sense of space. Too often identified with what we see, space can also describe the distance dimension of what we can hear. The phrase, "in earshot," refers to a flexible space farther than what people can touch or see, something extending to the place where people live. Similarly, sound describes a three-hundred-and-sixty-degree space, whereas vision allows a sense of space only in the direction of sight. Thus, music links time with place in particular ways: both describe where people live. As with time, acoustic space implies presence, both the present tense of time and the presence of another: "In this sense acoustic space is precisely not 'pure space.' It is essentially inhabited space" (Ong, 1967, p. 164). But more than that, music delineates boundary spaces (something manipulated and made more concrete in structures for performance—concert halls but also churches). In these instances people create spaces in which music can be heard. But the boundaries also mark divisions between people and between groups. Within those physical spaces, music creates virtual spaces, something that Langer (1957) claims as a characteristic or "primary illusion" of art (p. 36). Even if not in its specific dimensions, people experience the illusion. Langer explains, "Music also presents us with an obvious illusion, which is so strong that despite its obviousness it is sometimes unrecognized because it is taken for a real, physical phenomenon: that is the appearance of *movement*. Music flows; a melody moves; a succession of tones is heard as a progression" (p. 36, italics in original). Music also reshapes the boundary aspect of space, in what Mann (2010) terms the relationship of physical and social space (p. 213–18). In her study of music in the Catholic missions of seventeenth- and eighteenth-century Mexico and California, she points out that both the indigenous peoples and the Spanish missionaries used music (as well as dance and ritual) to claim the lands and the social interactions on them. The sounds and styles of singing created the places in which people lived. Finally, in addition to auditory and social space, music also creates a performance space, with performers and instruments arranged in particular relationship to each other and to the audience. In this way music and its sounds define people through their positioning vis-à-vis each other. They offer what Meyrowitz (1985) in another contexts calls "a sense of place." We know who we are from our positions. The performance space creates various acoustic possibilities, with voices and instruments emerging from directions and spaces, taking advantage of how people hear.

Third, the human voice plays a significant role in much music, bringing with it all of the affordances of resonance and of speaking. Ong argues that voice has a primary affordance of interiority. The voice reveals something of what lies physically within people through breath and vibration and resonance—at the very least the sense of a living being. More significantly, the voice reveals interiority, the dual relationship of people's consciousness to themselves and to that of other people (Ong and Altree, 2002, p. 385). Where the voices in music articulate words, they introduce a resonance with the consciousness of others and peoples' consciousness of the others: "The word itself is both interior and exterior: it is . . . a partial exteriorization of an interior seeking another interior. The primary physical medium of the word—sound—is itself an exteriorization of a physical interior, setting up reverberations in other physical interiors" (Ong, 1967, p. 179). The relationships accomplished through voices singing become even more complex when they also involve the words of another, of a lyricist. Here not only the sound of the voice(s) matter, but also the meaning of the words and the wider system of meaning.

Fourth, music also includes sounds created by musical instruments. These instruments, each reflecting a particular technology, introduce a vast ecosystem of audio components and characteristics, from pitch, timbre, and tonal range to the skill of the musician and the quality of manufacture. The instruments express characteristic sounds, which composers and hearers associate with emotional expression or even ideation. Stringed instruments differ from woodwinds, brass, or tympani, with sounds often associated with symbolic understanding. Beyond the physical characteristics of instruments, composers and performers add auditory characteristics as each instrument allows: volume, tone, pitch, rhythm, beat, vibrato, and so on, together with effects arising from their combination, like harmony and arrangement (Langer, 1957, 129–39). All of these create what Langer refers to as "the emotional tone" or "artistic import" (p. 129).

Fifth, while not essential to its nature, most music as people experience it today depends on writing. Obviously people in oral cultures created and performed music, depending on memory and improvisation. However, writing affected music. Based on his anthropological notes of oral cultures, Carpenter (1972) comments, "Written music became increasingly linear & narrative" (p. 40)—that is, it takes on the characteristics of writing. Liss (2019) sheds light on the process as he traces the history of the development of musical notation, writing that "musical notation began as an ancillary accompaniment to written text" (p 4) and, quoting Wellesz (1962), "Ecphonetic notation seems to have been introduced towards the end of the fourth century.... It appears fully developed in manuscripts of the eighth century and is maintained practically unchanged until the end of the 13th" (p. 35, quoted in Liss, 2019, p. 4). The ecphonetic notation refers to notations for chanting a text: indications of flow and accentuation. The notation helped a cantor in improvisation but did not record a melody. By the ninth century monks had introduced the neume, a notation that combined ecphonetic marks with indications of pitch. By the eleventh century, monks had added the musical staff, with notations that indicated harmony. Liss explains the process:

> In contrast to singular, unison melody organum adds at least one voice to create harmony, usually a perfect fifth or fourth. Variations from parallel and later free organum marked the incipience of true polyphony, utilizing both parallel and oblique motion (upper voice moving while the tenor holds one note) and serves as a precursor to authentic harmony (multiple voices moving in different directions involving variations of pitch and duration). At this spectacular moment in history, the technology of visually capturing musical sounds emerged as necessary.... In the chapter Music in the Twelfth Century from the *New Oxford History of Music*, Dom Anselm Hughes (1962) writes "First of all comes the line, in imagination or in dry-point or in ink, above the top of the text, and from this basis the heights of the notes are computed with more or less accuracy" (290). In other words, a standard is fixed—a conceptual line of which notes can be written above or below and in relative, hierarchically-ordered distances. This transformation can hardly be stressed enough—the lines above and below the standard formed an abstract representation of real sounds. Notes on the page for the first time could be seamlessly translated into notes sung. In other words, sounds could be read for the first time. (p. 7)

Written notations also introduced a "spatial relativity" (p. 8) to the idea of pitch, with its location of high notes and low notes in relation to their positioning on a page. Similarly, written musical notation recorded time, as Liss comments: "The final technological breakthrough in modern music notation derives from creating a standard schema for visually capturing time" (p. 9). In combination, the added technology of writing led to more complex musical compositions. Musicians could visualize the harmonics that they heard and even apply the mathematics of acoustics to add more complexity. They could also record their melodies and transmit them from place to place and time to time. Musical notation interacted with instruments, whose sounds composers could specify; written music allowed the composer to use more instruments and separate sounds than anyone could keep in memory. And the sense of time in music has become something marked out in writing.

A sixth element that helps to shape the ecology of music—and one flowing directly from writing—combines tradition, interpretation, and intention. Like written texts, musical pieces open themselves to interpretation and to an ever-expanding "conversation" about the "text," whether intertextuality, musical performance, or recording. As Ong (2002) points out in reference to literature and literary criticism, "The fact that a text is a text because it can be read means, in short, that a text as text is part of discourse" (p. 497). The discourse takes place between writer and reader, though it may well be deferred over centuries. And every interpretation of a text potentially adds another voice to the discourse. To take on the role of a reader demands that the potential reader must have "an extra-textual code that makes reading possible and applies the code"; without it "the physical inscription remains forever no more than a visible pattern on a surface" (p. 497). To take on the role of, for want of a better term, a critic (or "informed reader"), the reader must also know the tradition: What have those other voices added? What interpretations have emerged over the history of the text? Which other texts interact with these? and so on. Ong draws a parallel to the work of Umberto Eco: "Eco distinguishes two kinds of texts generated by authors, *closed* texts (calculated to elicit a specific response from readers) and *open* texts (designed in a maze-like structure for readers to labor through), although he wisely notes that the 'closed' text is open to more than one interpretation and that the 'open' text is not open to random interpretation" (p. 499, italics in original). All of this applies to musical composition, with composers and conductors "reading" the score, the tradition, and the history to produce something new at every performance. They also have the added "extra-textual code" of instruments and voices and their affordances. For example, contemporary conductors or performers may have access to instruments that the composer did not; they may choose to interpret a piece against a background that did not exist for the tradition (as Britten does in the *War Requiem* with the poetry of Owen). But neither they nor the audience can forget the tradition of meaning and interpretation even as they impose their own intention as a composer or as a performer. One powerful part of the ecosystem of music that affects any theology lies in its sense of history.

A Media Ecology of Theological Music

These characteristics and affordances of music present an enriched opportunity for faith to seek understanding. Both the theological tradition and some ecclesiastical documents agree with Langer that music as a significant form expresses emotion and perhaps more. Such emotion and feeling emerge as a central (and non-reasoned) reflection on faith. Heaney (2012) agrees with the possibility: "If theology is 'faith seeking understanding,' could music not also be theological? Does it not offer us, at the very least, a form of understanding of our faith, and perhaps even an aid in attaining and entering into that faith?" She continues, answering her question in the affirmative, "music offers a form of approach to or comprehension of faith that is different to our linguistic and conceptual understanding of the same, and for that very reason is complementary to it, in theological discourse" (p. 1). Vitz (2005) draws a lesson from Christian history as she discusses how medieval liturgy taught faith and then she observes, "One is reminded of Augustine's account of how he wept as he listened to the liturgical music in Ambrose's church in Milan, and he says that finally his tears of emotion were good (Augustine, 1991, p. 164)" (p. 25). Both Basil the Great and John Chrysostom (fourth century) praised the psychological and emotional impact of music: "according to Ambrose, a psalm softens anger, offers a release from anxiety, and alleviates sorrow" (Anttila, 2013, p. 23). Less positively, reformers like John Calvin and Ulrich Zwingli raised a warning flag about music and its emotional character in churches, feeling that anything other than plain settings of psalms could distract the listener (Bethke, 2015, pp. 48–49). In his history of instrumentation in Catholic liturgical music, Novotny (1962) shows that the Baroque period highlighted an existing stress on emotion: "It was with the coming of the Baroque and its desire for an 'affective representation' (*stile rappresentativo*) in music that instrumental timbre became more expressive and correspondingly less reserved" (p. 101). But this sometimes led to exaggeration:

> According to the philosophy of the Camerata, the text was to be supreme. But, unfortunately, in the field of church music the greatest stress was laid on the affective representation of individual words or phrases of the text, with the composer giving full reign to his personal emotions and the liturgical text being little more than an excuse for the expression of these feelings. The totality of the text, its place in the liturgy, its basically communal spirit were all lost sight of. (p. 101)

Such abuse did not lessen the expressive importance of emotion as a theological experience. In the nineteenth century, Schleiermacher argued that "music is a better way to communicate religious feeling than through words, following Schleiermacher's thought that music cannot be grasped by definite speech, but is an interchange of sounds and feelings. If religion is feeling, then sounds can evoke and interact that feeling" (Lynch, 2018, pp. 5–6). Catholic church legislation, while at times reining in instrumentation, continued to value emotional expressiveness. In a 1928 instruction (*Divini Cultus*), Pope Pius XI connects emotion with liturgical music: "He makes it clear that the Church is not opposing the progress of music in preferring the human voice to any instrument, 'for no instrument can surpass the human voice in expressing emotion'" (Novotny, 1962, p. 108). Later in the twentieth century, in the Lutheran tradition, Blankenburg contrasted the "word—reason—theology" triplet with "voice—emotion—music," to focus on the different effects of reading and singing: "Reading speaks solely to the intellect, but singing takes the emotional side of a person into an encounter with the Word" (Anttila, 2013, p. 11). Anttila continues, showing how this tradition has informed contemporary theology. Referring to Johannes Block, she writes, "To sing the word is not just to understand it, but experience it. To sing a psalm is not to explain it, but to become explained by it. The theology of music is deeply emotional" (p. 11). Liturgical music had other theological purposes as well, as we will see as we examine other affordances of music.

The stress on expressing emotions through the use of voice, musical instruments, and musical styles fits into the wider theological understanding of sacramentality. This tradition, retained more strongly in Catholic theology than in Reformation theology, holds that "material objects and physical actions became means through which humans could encounter divine grace" (Cashner, 2020, p. 45). Its application to music appears as early as Augustine's *De Musica* where he uses Platonic categories to explain how, in hearing music, people experience numbers which take on physical characteristics as the link between body and soul. Music delights because music turns people's minds to God. Anttila (2013) explains:

> Numbers direct our delight toward its right source and force us to inquire about what it is that pleases us in perceivable objects. Augustine's answer is that we can only love beautiful things . . . and that beauty is established in *aequalitas* and *numerositas*. Moreover, God has created everything with numbers, so that even a sinner may be moved by numbers and set numbers into movement. These movements may be less beautiful, but they cannot be entirely without some of the beauty that resides in the numbers. The aim of musical studies is that "with a restored delight in reason's numbers, our whole life is turned to God, giving numbers of health to the body, not taking pleasure from it." This reflects the Augustinian tenet that bodily sensations are the operations of the soul. (pp. 27–28)

The attention paid to the material leading to God continues in different guises to the present. Lynch (2018) traces it in the theological aesthetics of Hans Urs von Balthasar in the later twentieth century and points out how it informs his views of music's theological role, one that focuses more on music's intellectual potential as an analogy: "It is an analogy as there is true likeness between the music and the theological truth. This account of music reflecting the rest of the created world and theological understanding is based on an understanding of creation as united. The analogy is possible because the likeness is already written into creation by God" (p. 23). Lynch also finds the sacramental approach to music in the contemporary work of David Brown, who proposes "a sacramental account of music" (p. 18). Brown "holds that the musical experience is, after all, a bodily experience, but not the less important or sacramental because of that. This highlights the importance for Brown of the embodied nature of musical experience" (p. 15). For Heaney (2012), the sacramental appears as a part of "the theology of the body," dealing with human embodiment and overcoming estrangement in space and time—"our intrinsic difficulty in holding together spirit and matter, which has left us bereft of interiority" (p. 263). Music's existence as sound restores interiority, as Ong argues for all sound, and serves that sacramental means by which through the physical people experience God.

Third, music's relationship with time offers other theological possibilities. Its presentation of time, its presence in Langer's phrase as "audible time," its existence in Begbie's analysis of multiple time measures, its immersive qualities—all take music's hearers beyond themselves. This suggests an experience of the divine: an experience of living in time suspended, a lived eternity. But one must exercise caution here. Begbie (2000) explains:

> Music, so to speak, is "time-out." Sometimes this is taken further: music's most important theological possibility is said to lie in the way it can suggest or approximate to a timeless condition. . . . More specifically, it has been claimed that music can evoke the timelessness of eternity. This in turn is sometimes allied to an appeal to what is perceived to be music's extreme immateriality. Music, we are told, is the most "spiritual" (i.e. non-physical) of the arts. Compared to, say, a painting, it is marked by a high degree of impermanence and insubstantiality, and has very limited referential power; this means it is not nearly so tightly bound to the physical world as many of the other arts. This freedom from physicality, so the argument runs, is one of music's greatest theological virtues. . . . Much of [Begbie's] book is designed to question and challenge this drift of thinking, a drift which derives its momentum from a cluster of overplayed half-truths. I shall argue that many of music's most instructive lessons for theology arise because in and through its "making" it has the capacity for

> an intense and respectful engagement with "given" temporalities integral to the world (human and non-human), and that to take this seriously entails taking with equal seriousness the intrinsic physicality and materiality of musical practices. (p. 34)

Begbie's warning that one ignores the sacramental principle at peril is a good one. Music has theological weight precisely because it connects the physical to the divine. Its affordance for the experience of time opens the possibility of understanding faith in ways other than the written word. At the same time, the distancing from daily time—the "time-out" quality—does provide people with an experience that can offer religious possibilities (Heaney, 2012, p. 157–63.; Lynch, 2018, p. 53–55). Lynch addresses the "time-out" quality as transcendence (p. xix) while Begbie (2000) finds significance in how the multi-temporal aspects of music reveal aspects of theological time.

Fourth, music's creation of spaces also provides room for theological experience. The sounds of music delineate a space (all within earshot) such that it binds its hearers into a reality that opens beyond itself. And because music is sound, the space (even defined by recorded music) is "alive." That space involves several qualities. Composers and performers make an imagined space, a space where anything can take place. In some ways this resembles the work of a filmmaker who creates a virtual world and allows the characters to try out different possibilities within it. Musicians also create a virtual world within the sonic space that can foster theological reflection. But this space, as Ong (1967, pp. 161–69) suggests with other kinds of sound, takes on sacral characteristics: "Acoustic space is not 'pure' space. It is essentially inhabited space" (p. 164). Furthermore, "sound establishes here-and-now personal presence. Abraham knew God's presence when he heard his 'voice'" (p. 113). Vocal sound, especially musical sound, offers a space to encounter the Other. The encounter with a living other provides a theological opening. Lynch (2018) describes several varieties and characteristics of such a space. Musical space allows movement or transcendence. Following Regina Schwartz, she identifies two types; "vertical transcendence, in which the subject goes beyond the immanent world, and horizontal transcendence, which is self-transcendence. . . . [T]ranscendence is a step into the beyond that opens new potential for understanding reality" (p. 77). Such space, Lynch notes, is liminal space (p. 88) that connects the day-to-day world with the transcendent. Similarly, as we have seen, such musical space is affective space (p. 89). Music also creates a social space that allows people to relate in different ways to each other and to God. Mann's (2010) studies of music in the Spanish missions of North America shows how the missionaries created the physical spaces of churches in which the indigenous peoples could experience European music; the native peoples themselves created music in their own, often outdoor, spaces. Both groups used music to create and reinforce social spaces, with performance tied to specific ways of organizing the village life. This also affected gendered relations: "Just as music and ritual performance were agents in the reshaping of social hierarchy in mission communities, they also acted as catalysts in the reshaping of women's roles and social space in the north" (p. 220). The female performer's place in the music production created a new social place. Similarly, music created a place where the community remembered itself, its organization, and eventually its religious identity (p. 202).

The multiple uses of musical space suggest that music serves many functions, often connected with the intentions and motivations of the composer and performer. Liturgical music acts as a form of prayer and praise, as has long been recognized in Christian circles in the phrase "*qui cantat, bis orat*; who sings, prays twice" (Anttila, 2013, p. 11). All liturgical music, from chanted psalms to complex baroque compositions, aim to support prayer and to help the congregation lift their minds and hearts to God. But church music simultaneously functions as "auditory declarations of Christian belief" (Mann, 2010, p. 202), having a pedagogical function. Such pedagogy often takes indirect form, as a kind of background, or as Lynch (2018) terms it, music is "used by theologians as a way of expressing, understanding, or investigating theological truths" (p. 22). Begbie (2000) suggests that theology can come first, with the music serving as an existing reflection on belief when "central doctrinal loci are explored, interpreted, re-conceived and articulated" (p. 5). More explicit pedagogy takes place through hymn singing and song lyrics. Luther "recognized that music touched people deeply and could be used as a powerful tool of evangelization. Luther also knew that popular music with new religious words could be equally effective in teaching Christian doctrine" (Bethke, 2015, p. 48). The seventeenth-century Jesuit scholar Athanasius Kircher argued something similar in his *Musurgia Universalis*: "For Kircher, music added such power to words, that it could move a listener not only to understand the subject of the words, but to physically experience their truth. . . . Kircher says that the experience of Jesuit missionaries around the world provides ample evidence of this miraculous power of music combined with preaching" (Cashner, 2020, pp. 76–77). Both Mann (2010) and Bethke (2015) provide historical examples of how, in Bethke's words, "western choral music was not only used as a tool to distance local people from their inherited religious beliefs, but, more seriously, to subjugate and 'civilize' them" (p 57). Even in non-missionary regions, hymn singing serves to reinforce belief both by setting credal statements to popular music and by repeated singing. Such congregational singing can solidify group identity and religious identification, as shown for example in practices where, until relatively recently, a Lutheran community would not sing a Catholic hymn nor a Catholic one, a Methodist hymn. Anttila (2013), referring to Block's (2002) study, explains the pedagogical power of hymns as connected to "the self-understanding of practical theology. He [Block] aims to define what he calls *hermeneutical hymnology*, in which singing a text requires something more than analyzing and explaining it. The singer is personally involved in the song, leading to an existentialist redefinition of practical theology" (p. 7, italics in original).

The affordances of writing for music additionally open up paths for composers to reflect on their belief. In his overview of the development of musical notation, Liss (2019) comments that the notations for harmony and time allowed medieval monasteries to increase the complexity of their musical performance in order to enhance worship practices and to share their sung religious insights across monasteries. Cashner (2020) explains a much more complex manipulation of composition for theological ends in his discussion of Spanish music of the seventeenth century, in which musicians created "solmization puns." Rather than the familiar (to English speakers) syllables, *do*, *re*, and *mi*, the Spanish system of the time used *ut*, *re*, *mi*, *fa*, *sol*, and *la*. "References to Christ as *sol* (sun) are ubiquitous, and as shown in [an] . . . example by Gutiérrez de Padilla, composers missed no opportunity to put this word on a pitch that could be solmized with that syllable (G, C, or D in the three Guidonian hexachords)" (p. 33). Cashner provides other examples: "At the same time, the syllables themselves could also take on deep symbolic meanings . . . In his 1672 music treatise Andrés Lorente uses the six solmization syllables as an acrostic to help musicians tune 'the spiritual music of the person'—that is, to live with moral virtue. One hexachord leads up to communion with God; the other goes down to perdition" (p. 34). And, presenting a more complex example, he guides the reader through the

> tenor part of a setting by Gutiérrez de Padilla, *Miraba el sol el águila bella*. The part is a virtuoso demonstration of solmization puns. The text of the *estribillo* and *responsión* is made almost entirely of solmization syllables, as in *ella al sol mire y la mire el sol*. Gutiérrez de Padilla sets every syllable to the corresponding pitches so that for much of the piece, singing the lyrics is almost identical to singing the solmization . . .
>
> But the piece is not nonsense—in fact, the poet (perhaps Gutiérrez de Padilla himself) has managed to craft a semantically and theologically coherent text based on an entirely separate conceit relevant to the feast of

the Conception of Mary, that of the Virgin Mary as an eagle. The eagle, Spaniards believed, had the power to look directly at the sun without harming its eyes, and thus the eagle was a fitting symbol for Mary as Immaculate. That Mary was conceived without original sin was enforced as official dogma in Spain long before the rest of the church approved it, and Puebla Cathedral was dedicated to Mary as Immaculate. Gutiérrez de Padilla takes advantage of the hexachordal system, which means that there are usually three possible notes that could be solmized with a particular syllable, to add an additional symbolic layer embodying the eagle conceit through musical technique. To represent the eagle turning to the sun (and therefore Mary seeing the face of God), Gutiérrez de Padilla has the Tenor shift from the soft hexachord, through a ficta alteration, into the natural hexachord . . . He thus quite literally moves *al sol*—both because he moves to a note on *sol* and because he shifts to the hexachord that starts on the *sol* of the previous hexachord. Where Irízar shifted from the soft hexachord down to the natural for moving from heaven to earth, Gutiérrez de Padilla makes the same shift upwards to represent the eagle/Mary looking up to the heavens. (pp. 36–37)

Written musical notation makes this kind of thing easier (if not possible) to compose; in other examples, Cashner shows how composers created theological allusions in the score through the use of black notes and white notes in notating rhythm (pp. 69–70). This dependence of music on writing to create theological emphasis occurs in other places as well. Pelikan (1986) finds similar things in Bach's Passions. In an extended analysis of the *Passion according to Saint Matthew*, he shows how Bach contrasts different experiences of the consciousness of sin with different voices and how the interplay of different choir parts (men's choir, women's choir, and boys' choir) works out an interpretation of Anselm's view of the redemption as satisfaction (pp. 89–101). The ability to compose for different instruments and voices depends more and more on writing as the music becomes more complex.

Another component of the media ecology of the theology in music appears in the interpretive contexts in which musicians and composers worked. This shifted over time, borrowing from the local cultures or placing restrictions on which possibilities musicians could follow, thus channeling their thought in new directions, much as the advent of musical notation did. Early Christianity freely imitated the synagogue's chanting of psalms and hymns as part of its worship, often accompanied by instruments. Novotny (1962) reports that Clement of Alexandria (c. 150–215) allowed the lyre and kithara because biblical passages mention those instruments as used by King David. Within a few centuries, others disapproved of any instrumentation: Novotny quotes

St. Jerome in the fifth century as rejecting these instruments (and the pipes and organ as well) on the basis that they were used in pagan worship (p. 66). By the ninth century, monks again used instruments, like the hurdy-gurdy, to support liturgical singing. Novotny sees a growing environmental influence: "The medieval sacred drama had great influence on the liturgy itself. In these plays, a variety of instruments was used, and the solemn *Te Deum* closing the drama was usually accompanied by the organ and by bells and cymbals" (p. 66). As the surrounding cultures (such as entertainments, royal courts, and village festivals) invented and employed more instruments, these appeared in worship as well through their expansion in Renaissance Europe. But a reaction took place. The sixteenth-century Reformation's theological debates had an impact on music. From within the Catholic tradition, Erasmus criticized the incorporation of the Renaissance musical tradition on several grounds: "The most important was that the words were almost inaudible. Either they were left out completely due to the complexity of the music itself, or they were mispronounced by singers inexperienced in singing Latin. In other words, while the music itself could be beautiful, the main reason for its performance (the contemplation of God) was obscured" (Bethke, 2015, p. 47). Luther objected to complex musical forms and even Latin chants for other reasons, principally that ordinary people could not sing them and thus could not participate in the liturgy: "Thus, he introduced the *chorale*, or congregational hymn, in place of liturgical chants in certain places within the liturgy" (pp. 47–48). Other reformers were not so tolerant. Calvin agreed with Luther on the power of music, but restricted liturgical music to the psalms and biblical canticles, though only unaccompanied ones lest the music distract the congregation from the scriptural words (p. 48). Another of the reformers, Zwingli, felt that any type of art could distract the worshiper and allowed only the spoken word in worship (p. 49). These various positions affected how different reformed churches utilized music. Bethke (2015) traces how these different strands (psalmody, hymnody, and performance) appear in the Anglican Communion's Book of Common Prayer, showing how external theological commitments affected worship and its musical traditions:

> In essence, then, two main theological interpretations of worship became associated with the BCP [Book of Common Prayer] tradition. The first advocated active congregational participation through the singing of metrical psalms. The second preferred an offering of carefully rehearsed choral music sung by a choir while the congregation simply listened and watched. Both interpretations would yield strong musical traditions and thousands of compositions. The "cathedral" theology stimulated

> numerous settings of morning and evening canticles and a vast corpus of anthems. The "parish" theology allowed for the development of psalm and hymn tones, some still sung and loved today. In fact, the English hymn tradition became a hallmark not only of Anglicanism, but dissenting churches too, most particularly the Methodists (Charles Wesley) and Congregationalists (Isaac Watts). (p. 53)

In addition to how churches and congregations performed music, theological commitments determined what music churches performed. Churches in the Reformed traditions focused on biblical materials, such as the Bach *Passions* or Handel's *Messiah*. Those same traditions excluded the Requiem: "As one of their most consistent points of doctrine, Protestants rejected the Christian tradition of intercession for the dead and removed the dead from the world of the living" (Koslofsky, 2000, p. 2). Without a theology of Purgatory or prayers for the dead, there was no need of a requiem Mass or musical settings for the requiem. Theological commitments thus placed boundaries for liturgical music. Where the Catholic Church allowed choir-performed liturgical music to reflect divine beauty (though sometimes urging simpler compositions), the Lutheran church promoted congregational singing; other reformed churches moved music completely out of religious spaces and into concert halls. The existing theological and cultural traditions guide musical expression to favor chants, chorales, hymns, and, more recently, Christian rock.

Handel's *Messiah* stands as an example. With lyrics drawn from both Testaments, it began not as a church work but with its premiere performance in 1742 in the music hall on Fishamble Street in Dublin. Pelikan (1987) continues, "The setting of *Messiah*, which, except for performances in the chapel of the Foundling Hospital, was given in church only once during Handel's lifetime, at Bristol Cathedral on 17 August 1758; and that, moreover, appears to have been the only performance of any of Handel's oratorios in a church" (p. 77). This development of music dealing with religious themes outside of liturgical settings—Lynch (2018) gives the examples of Haydn's *The Creation*, Mozart's *Don Giovanni*, and works of Brahms; and Begbie (2000), of many others—calls to mind Goethal's (1999) contention that theological reflection in art moved out of the Protestant churches into homes, landscapes, and galleries (pp. 149–52).

People reflect on their faith wherever they are and use the media available to them. Heaney (2012) quotes George Steiner to emphasize this point: "Music has long been, and continues to be, the unwritten theology of those who lack or reject any formal creed" (p. 6). This has not gone unnoticed. Beaudoin's (2013) collection highlights the attention that academic theologians now pay to contemporary music, arguing that music, whatever its origins, creates a religious experience and reflects on belief. He categorizes these activities as theology through artistry (p. xix), theology in community (p. xx), and theology through song—that is, as expressed in lyrics (p. xx).

All this does not mean that the more traditional theological methods based in writing cannot apply to understanding music or cannot form the basis for further reflection on music. Commenting on a document by the United States Catholic Conference on music in worship, Caccamo (2007) identifies three judgments ministers should make on music: a musical judgment (quality), a pastoral judgment (appropriateness to the congregation), and a liturgical judgment (suitable to the worship), each principally examining lyrics (p. 47). Following his own interest in moral theology, Caccamo then asks about the ethical influence of music and adds judgments that expand the traditional verbal or writing-based ecology. Calling it "the most readily apparent connection between liturgical music and ethics," he proposes a "symbolic judgment" based on communicating the ideas of the moral life (p. 48)—something solidly within the area of traditional written expression and evaluation. To this he adds an experiential judgment that evaluates the "moral affections." In doing so, he calls attention to experience and environment:

> few question that music can be an extraordinarily powerful means of mediating God's self-communication. . . . Through its consciously emotional power, music opens up a socially acceptable context for affective engagement with God. As it creates sonic, narrative, and temporal environments, liturgical music opens up spaces within the imagination to help worshipers apprehend the presence of God. (p. 49)

Such environments move worshipers from thinking to experience and inform moral judgment. Third, Caccamo suggests a "performative judgment," since, he writes, "I have never been entirely satisfied with the principled and affective approaches to the moral life" shown in the symbolic and experiential judgments (p. 51). Here he suggests that the larger ecology of music in worship comes to bear:

> While often overlooked, the performance of these sorts of musical actions, repeated from week to week over the course of a lifetime, create habits of body and will that are nothing less than properly moral. In part, this is because the formation of Christian moral actors is a matter of forming Christian responders. In the broadest scope, the Christian life is a cycle of call and response. (p. 51).

Both understanding and evaluation of music (from quality to moral impact) involve taking music on its own terms.

Media ecology helps us to notice things about how theology interacts with music: the affordances that shape music and the affordances that allow people (composers, performers, and auditors) to reflect on belief and even to direct that belief in different ways. These complex sets of interactions offer a kind of loose structure to how people "think" theologically in music.

8
ARCHITECTURE

Building Up the Faith

Churches as architecture provide an important public illustration of faith-seeking-understanding, since they combine different media, an ecosystem, and theology in very direct ways. The media ecology approach calls attention both to communication as part of a larger environment and to communication environments in themselves. Church buildings do the same: religion has its own environments, which often have specific functions for religious practice but which also reinforce particular theological perspectives. As with most environments, we take these for granted, so the first step in a media ecology method makes the environment a more direct object of attention.

Religious environments vary, though they have several things in common. Sacred spaces may mark the literal place where some religious or spiritual event occurred: the burning bush that Moses saw, the hill on which Jesus died on the cross, the grotto where a saint had a vision of God, and so on. Other sacred spaces may symbolically connect believers to religious events: the Stations of the Cross in Catholic churches invite people to imagine the places in Jerusalem that Jesus passed along on the way to his death and to call to mind those places whose stories they narrate. A maze indicates one's journey to God, just as an actual pilgrimage symbolizes that journey in another way. Still other sacred spaces become sacred in light of the religious rituals that take place within them: people consecrate church buildings to set them apart for holy actions. Each of these spaces is an environment, and within each of them we find an ecology of communication and of theology.

Each sacred space has a particular theology (or understanding of faith) literally built into it. Marking a place where someone experienced God's presence simultaneously affirms that human beings can experience God's presence (that is, that God does indeed interact with humans) and that humans can recreate such experiences—that those experiences are open to all.

As an introduction to the media ecology of church architecture, this chapter will consider three church buildings that offer three complementary examples of space, building, and belief. Each has its own theology, expressed in its own environment. With these examples in mind, the chapter will analyze the ecology in more detail to think about how people create structures to reflect their belief. As in previous chapters staying within the Christian tradition, the three church buildings represent the Catholic, Presbyterian, and Russian Orthodox understandings of Christian theology.

Within a short walk near Cromwell Road in the Knightsbridge area of west London, three churches represent the three traditions. While many church buildings serve their respective communities, these, by their proximity, provide a good starting place to think about the ecology of built environments, not only the physical buildings but also their histories and their theological foundations.

Catholic

The Oratory church on Brompton Road or, the London Oratory (more properly, the church of the Immaculate Heart of Mary), stands just to the east of the Victoria and Albert Museum and dates to the 1880s, built fifty years after the Catholic Emancipation Act through which Catholics regained legal status in England. The church belongs to the Congregation of the Oratory founded in the sixteenth century in Rome by St. Philip Neri and introduced into England by St. John Henry Newman in 1849. The London foundation, staffed largely by converts to the Catholic Church, set out to build the church in 1874 to mark the silver jubilee of the group in England: "The architectural style and the atmosphere of the church were deliberately Italianate, in order to bring St. Philip's romanità to 19th century London" (Church of the Immaculate Heart of Mary, n.d.). The dedication of the church to the Immaculate Heart of Mary, a style modeled on St. Peter's Basilica in Rome, and the location on a prominent thoroughfare all combine to announce the building as "Catholic," both in theology and style. Contemporary writers noted the ability of the architecture to reflect theology, as reported by Sheppard (1983): "At the opening of the great church in 1884 *The Tablet* commented that it would 'bring home vividly to many that thought can find expression in other forms than words' (26 April 1884, p. 645), and it is easy to feel that the building does indeed assert the ultramontane trend of thought in Victorian Roman Catholicism—especially, perhaps, that of Catholics not born into the Church" (p. 50).

The nave of Brompton Oratory in London, England.
Wikimedia Commons

Modeled on the Renaissance Baroque style of Saint Peter's Basilica in Rome, the church building creates a lofty interior space, with the nave rising several storeys and the cupola reaching a height of two hundred feet. The overall cruciform design creates both worship spaces and individual side chapels, each with a particular theme, and each forming a miniature church space in itself. The sanctuary area stands several steps above the nave floor level and has a large marble altar against the back wall. The altarpiece above that altar represents the Virgin and Child. The rest of the interior of the church features a highly decorated space, with inscriptions drawn from the Gospels around the interior perimeter and baroque statues, including those of the twelve apostles, located throughout the building. Illustrations of the Stations of the Cross line the nave. Ceiling, walls, and sanctuary provide material for meditation, capturing the spectator's attention and designed to aid prayer. This visual environment includes light, color, text, painting, statuary, design, and arrangement of materials, as well as the vestments worn during worship. C. T. G. Formilli, an Italian architect (resident in London) charged with renovations in the 1920s, "declared [his] aim was by his colouring to make the interior 'still more in keeping with the traditions of the Catholic Church'" (Sheppard, 1983, p. 56).

Wooden chairs with a kneeler attached at the back and wooden pews with kneeling benches in the Italian style offer places for worshipers throughout the church; most are oriented to the high altar, though some face the altars of the smaller chapels. Racks of votive candles stand by each altar.

In addition to the visual and architectural environment, the church offers an acoustic one, with a massive pipe organ and senior and junior choirs, both known for their choral performances. During most hours when Mass does not occur, the church remains silent, offering a place of quiet meditation.

The building itself expresses several aspects of theology in general and Roman Catholic theology in particular. The building creates a complex environment for worship, prayer, and reflecting on belief. Architectural features, such as the high nave, evoke a sense of God's grandeur in the visitor and perhaps a concomitant sense of one's own smallness in such a huge space and before God. Statues and other elements of the decor help individuals to visualize events or scenes from both the Old and New Testaments of the Scriptures; textual inscriptions serve a similar purpose: the building appeals to the imagistic and the literate senses. Every surface works to bring the visitor or worshiper to an awareness of God. These same statues reinforce both a cult of the saints (traditional in Catholic theology, which acknowledges the mediation of saints) and an anti-iconoclastic theology of image. The stone altar makes reference to a Catholic Eucharistic theology of sacrifice (that is, that the Eucharist is a sacrifice, united with the sacrificial death of Jesus on the cross). The reservation of the Eucharist at a special altar also symbolizes the real presence of the risen Lord in the Eucharist. Both the dedication of the church and the Marian images reinforce a Marian theology and remind the worshiper of the various Marian beliefs of Catholic theology. Less debated in contemporary Catholic theology, the Italianate style of the church also subtly reinforces the nineteenth-century disputes about ultamontanism, in which theologians and clerics argued for a strong centralizing church government focused on the powers of the papacy. Finally, the building, the decor, the votive candles, the holy water stoups, and other details all express a sacramental theology in which people experience God's action through created things.

Presbyterian

A short walk to the south brings one to St. Columba's church, Knightsbridge, which serves to illustrate the church environment created by the Christian denominations influenced by the Reformation. St. Columba's is affiliated with the Church of Scotland (the Presbyterian tradition).

Though Presbyterians have resided and worshiped in London from the time of King James, the Crown Court Church in Covent Garden (established 1719) provided their first parish. As the congregation grew, it established St. Columba's in the mid-nineteenth century at its present location in 1884 (St. Columba's Church of Scotland, n.d.). Rebuilt after its destruction during the London blitz in 1941, the church presents a high-ceilinged space flooded with light from clear windows. Croot (2004) refers to an "austere design with Georgian and Romanesque references by Sir Edward Maufe, said to derive 'its significance from its very special Scottish circumstances.'" The minimal decor consists of Scottish coats of arms along the sidewalls and one stained-glass window behind the communion table, featuring the cross of St. Andrew, the Holy Spirit as a dove, the nativity, and a scene of St. Columba. A large pulpit stands to the right of the communion table (that is, to the left of the congregation) and a lectern, on the other side. Each pew offers cushioned seating and holders for Bibles and hymnals, but no kneeling benches. A blue carpet runs the length of the nave and into the chancel, with the color scheme reflected in the trim. A large pipe organ dominates the choir loft in the rear. Finally, a small military chapel is situated behind the chancel.

This worship space stands in marked contrast to the Catholic one. Even the casual observer notes the absence of representational art, statues, stained glass, and other decorative elements. The color white dominates. The three elements that fill the chancel (a wooden communion table with chairs for the church elders along the back wall, a lectern for the Scriptures, and a high pulpit with soundboard behind) serve both functional and theological ends.

As in the case of the Brompton Oratory, St. Columba's structure and decor reflect the theology of the congregation. The pulpit, pews, and pew Bibles give witness to an emphasis on the Word of God, that is, on the Reformation commitment to the principle of *sola scriptura*. The wooden communion table signals a de-emphasis on the sacrificial character of the Eucharist. In the reformed tradition, the Eucharist serves as a memorial of the Last Supper—or as a meal that serves as a conduit of grace, but either way, a meal—hence a table rather than an altar of sacrifice. The chairs for the church elders ("presbyters") mark both a rejection of the mediating role of priests and an affirmation of the church governing structures.[1] The downplaying of the role of the priest also stresses the priesthood of all believers. The absence of representations of the saints also marks the rejection of a theology of mediation in which people did not approach God directly but through

---

[1] As appeared in ch. 5, the Reformation translated key terms from the New Testament Greek following theological principles. Hence, "elder" rather than "priest" for the Greek πρεσβύτερος, "presbyteros."

the intercession of saints. The plain decor also extends to the cross. Rather than a crucifix displaying the suffering Jesus, the church features a plain cross. This too comes from the Reformed tradition. An indirect influence on the Presbyterian tradition, the Swiss reformer Ulrich Zwingli "spoke specifically against images of Christ and crucifixes, using the long-standing argument that images could not display the truth of Jesus, who was both human and divine" (Jensen, 2017, p. 185).

As befits a church dedicated to God's Word, the assembly space promotes listening—to the Scriptures, to the sermon, and to the choir—but also study, with Bibles available for reading and consulting during the sermon. The minimal decor of the building also suggests a link to Scotland, to a national identity in which the worship tradition has its roots.

Russian Orthodox

Another short London walk to the north leads to the Russian Orthodox Cathedral of the Dormition. Originally built for the Church of England (in 1846–1849) in a neo-italianate Lombard style and dedicated as All Saints Church, the church passed to the Russian Orthodox in 1956, who rededicated it in honor of the Dormition, the Mother of God. The Russian Orthodox also remodeled the interior while leaving the exterior in the original design. The visitor today enters into a small vestibule, and then into the nave, a space lit by natural light, and sees the iconostasis at the front of the church, with additional icons displayed on the walls as well as on individual stands throughout the open area of the nave. There are no pews or other benches. The interior retains the rectangular structural design of the original church as well as the windows, but the removal of any pews and the placement of the icons clearly marks the church as in the Orthodox tradition. The traditional tripartite division of the church space appears more clearly here than in the other two churches (though it also grounds their designs): the vestibule, clearly present in all three buildings and marking a liminal or transitional space between the outside world and the sacred space of the church; the nave, the space for the assembly; and the chancel or sanctuary ("holy of holies" for the Orthodox), the location of the altar. In the Orthodox tradition, the iconostasis physically separates this space from the rest of the church, a feature lacking in the other churches (but remaining vestigially as an altar railing in some Catholic churches).

The altar stands behind the iconostasis, which also marks the division between the various liturgical actions, representing the division between earth and heaven. The iconostasis itself features several doors used during the liturgy, with the rest of the space covered with icons, each with its own significance:

It always includes the icon of the Incarnation (mother with child) on the left side of the royal [main] door and the second coming of Christ the Pantocrator (Christ in majesty) on the right. The sacrament of the Eucharist, revealed through the doors between the two main icons, is thus the manifestation of Christ in the church during the time between his two comings. Icons of the four Evangelists, the Annunciation, and the Last Supper are set over the royal doors themselves. Representations of the archangels Gabriel and Michael, the 12 Apostles, the feasts of the church, and the prophets of the Old Testament are arranged on the iconostasis. (*Encyclopedia Britannica*, 2007)

Largely situated behind the iconostasis, the altar remains hidden to the nave. From there, during worship priests and deacons celebrate the divine liturgy with chant (punctuated by the responses of the congregation) and incense, adding to the overall media environment of the church. The icons themselves, with their characteristic reversed perspective, serve to draw the viewer into the heavenly reality, to which they provide a window.

Like the other churches, this one also bears the stamp of the theology of its tradition. As indicated above, the royal doors frame the Eucharist as revealing Christ in the community. The icons, like the representational art in the Catholic church, depict saints as well as Mary and Christ. Typically, parishioners bow before them and often kiss them, acknowledging that the material world can reveal the divine. As in the Incarnation the Divine Word took flesh, so that Word makes these physical representations holy. The absence of chairs or kneeling benches indicates standing as the proper posture for prayer, expressing respect for the divine. The congregation kneels only to abase themselves during certain penitential liturgies.

A Media Ecology of Environment

Sacred spaces make use of any number of communication media to evoke religious feeling and to make theological claims. People design religious places in accordance with their own religious beliefs. In some way, too, these religious places, their design, and their construction form a kind of theology—a systematic reflection on belief. A closer analysis of these built environments of faith includes not only decorations but the combination of media (architecture, writing, art, etc.), orientation, scale, place, acoustics, and so on.

Christian churches use particular kinds of decoration to make a theological claim at one level or another. In an early demonstration of this, Ferree (1898) offers an illustrated tour through the great cathedrals of France, commenting on the iconography and teaching the reader how to "read" from the images the biblical stories and the theology that shaped the artwork. Here, the artists adjusted the physical environments created by the buildings themselves with carvings over the doors and throughout the buildings to make the entire building a "Bible in stone" (to use Ferree's phrase). The theology appears not only in the biblical scenes, but also in the choice and juxtaposition of those scenes. For example, at Chartres, as noted in chapter 5, the artists group the figures of Jephthah (Judg 11:30–38), King Louis VIII of France, his daughter Blessed Isabelle, and Zechariah (Luke 1:57–80) by connecting them to Christ's sacrifice. Jephthah, who sacrificed his daughter, prefigures the offering of Christ; King Louis gave his daughter Isabelle to the convent, and she founded convents and churches and achieved holiness. Zechariah's son John the Baptist prepared the way for Christ; at John's birth, Zechariah proclaimed God's praises. The carving, then, reflects a theology of sacrifice and sanctification running from parents to children and invites imitation (Ferree, 1898, p. 163).

That tradition of combining communication elements into more complex meanings goes back at least to the fifth century. Paulinus of Nola (d. 431) in a letter to Severus dated in the year 404, described a newly built basilica and its combination of architectural form, images in mosaic, and poetic verses:

> [The basilica] is venerable not merely through the respect paid to the blessed Felix but also because of the consecrated relics of apostles and martyrs kept under the altar in the tripartite apse. A vault adorned with mosaics provides light for the apse, the floor and walls of which are faced with marble. These are the verses which describe the scene depicted on the vault:
>
> The Trinity shines out in all its mystery. Christ is represented by a lamb, the Father's voice thunders forth from the sky, and the Holy Spirit flows down in the form of a dove. A wreath's gleaming circle surrounds the cross, and around this circle the apostles form a ring, represented by a chorus of doves. The holy unity of the Trinity merges in Christ, but the Trinity has its threefold symbolism. The Father's voice and the Spirit show forth God, the cross, and the lamb proclaim the holy victim. The purple and the palm point to kingship and to triumph. Christ Himself, the Rock, stands on the rock of the Church, and from this rock four plashing fountains flow, the evangelists, the living streams of Christ. (Paulinus, 1967, p. 145)

Paulinus goes on to describe other inscriptions on the plaster where the walls join to the dome of the church and continues, "The whole area outside the apse of the basilica extends with high-paneled ceiling and with twin colonnades running straight through an arch on each side" (p. 146) leading to chapels for private prayer and for the location of funeral monuments. The building served not only to memorialize the martyrs and those buried near the church but also to express the beliefs of the community: in God, the Trinity, eternal life, and the nature of the Christian Church. Paulinus makes this explicit later in his letter: "And if we build our structures, however earthly, with spiritual prayer and study, this becomes a blessed preparation for the heavenly mansions. For even as we erect these buildings in the Lord because we have received the faith, we are ourselves erected by the Lord through the growth of this same faith" (p. 151). The pattern begun so early on in Christianity endured over the centuries, with later church builders imitating what others had done, just as their faith built upon what they had received. Prior reflection of faith in building becomes part of the ecosystem of later construction, as appears in the three London churches, with each encompassing both a theological and an architectural tradition.

Over time other elements of church architecture reflected more subtle aspects of theology. Builders oriented churches with the altar facing east, that is, towards the rising sun, a symbol of the risen Christ, something stressed in the fourth century *Apostolic Constitutions*. Many Catholic churches in the West have a cruciform shape with a transept perpendicular to the nave as a symbol of Christ's cross. The architecture also incorporates other theological understandings: the high roofs of the medieval cathedrals symbolize the heights of the heavens but also evoke in those who enter such buildings a sense of human smallness in comparison to the grandeur of God. In other church buildings, the architecture reinforces understandings or theologies of the role of the worshipers: Do they gather in ways that foster interaction or privacy? Do they stand close to or far from the central sacred places in the building? While Gothic and Renaissance church buildings make clear hierarchical separations between laity and clergy (assigning them places in the nave and chancel or sanctuary), more contemporary church buildings often revert to a Roman style with the people gathered around the altar, stressing a theology of the equality of all people.

Some shrines actually have people pass through a series of buildings, reminding them of their (theological) understanding of the stages we pass through as we approach God. Thus, the ways in which people build worship spaces makes a powerful nonverbal statement. Who stands or sits or kneels where? Does the space lift up our hearts and minds? What about the use of light? The importance of the influence of architecture for theology comes indirectly in a fairly common phrase in theology itself: "lex orandi, lex credendi"—

literally, the law of prayer and worship is the law of belief (Hilgartner, 2009). Theology follows how people pray.

Practice emerges in other ways as well. Gothic churches incorporate a kind of theological geometry in their design, inspired by a commentary of St. Augustine on the book of Wisdom's statement that God "ordered all things by measure, number, weight" (Wis 11:21). And so, "at Chartres, explains Robert Scott, scholars 'believed that geometry was a means for linking human beings to God, that mathematics was a vehicle for revealing to humankind the innermost secrets of heaven. . . . the cosmos was a work of architecture and God was its architect.' These ideas led builders 'to conceive of architecture as applied geometry, geometry as applied theology, and the designer of a Gothic cathedral as an imitator of the divine Master'" (Scott, 2003, p. 125, quoted in Woods, 2005, p. 120). Woods continues, quoting another commentary on Gothic architecture: "The choir at Saint Remi is 'among the most perfect Trinitarian symbols in Gothic architecture,' explains Christopher Wilson, 'for the play on the number three encompasses the triple windows lighting each of the three levels of the main apse and even the number obtained by multiplying the number of bays in the choir elevations—11—by the number of stories, that is 33.' Thirty-three, of course, is the age that Christ reached while on earth" (Wilson, 1990, pp. 65–66, quoted in Woods, p. 121). To add just one more architectural element with a theological purpose: church windows admitted light, and in the Hebrew Bible's wisdom tradition and in the Gospel of John, light refers to both divine illumination and to Christ as "the light of the world." Similar to the basilica described by Paulinas, inscriptions pointed out significance. In the Abbey Church of St. Denis, "An inscription on the doors explained that the light elevated the mind upward from the material world and directed it toward the true light that was Christ" (Woods, 2005, p. 122).

The play and importance of light in churches takes on even more theological significance—and expresses important theological beliefs—as it connects to Christianity's ambivalent attitudes to images. Beyond the particular theology of a given representation, the statues, mosaics, or paintings in Catholic and Orthodox churches affirm an "iconic" theology—one that claims that we humans experience God in a way consistent with our perception. Other Christian traditions ban images, taking an "aniconic" theology—a "non-imaged" approach that holds that we cannot directly experience God and so we should not use images (Goethals, 1990). Goethals, the art historian, shows how two different artistic styles competed within Christianity: one drawn from Judaism and the other from the Greco-Roman world. What, she asks, is the role of the visual arts in religion? Is there a theological purpose to art? While contemporary religion tends to take art and visual images as something given, this was not the case for the early Christians. They were caught between the iconic and aniconic aesthetics. The former made use of representative visual images in worship and in ritual spaces while the latter did not. The split grew directly from the debates over iconoclasm.[2]

Goethals sees the two opposing arguments about images still at work in the context of the construction of medieval cathedrals and in the thinking of two twelfth-century Christian monks: Suger of the Abbey of St. Denis in Paris and Bernard of the Abbey of Clairvaux in northern France. Following Panofsky's (1979) work here, she contrasts two aesthetic impulses. Abbot Suger sought a highly decorated church, affirming the visual arts even as it valued light. Goethals argues that Suger followed the spiritual via *affirmativa*—the view that the created world can lead us to God: "Material objects, whether natural or made by human hands, can inspire devotion, enhance meditation, and lead the soul to the experience of transcendence" (Goethals, 1990, p. 24). For Bernard and the aniconic group, art hindered devotion, providing distraction. For him, the windows of medieval churches take on a theological expression instead of statues or figurative art. The windows admit various colors, patterns, or kinds of light as a theological statement about how the builders understood God's action and God's wisdom. Jesus refers to himself as "the light of the world" (John 8:12; 9:5) and the whole of Johannine theology develops the light-darkness theme.

Goethals demonstrates the connection between aesthetic styles and theological beliefs with these two case studies. Interestingly, she traces how the same conflict continues within Western Christianity through the Protestant Reformation. Here, the reformers, especially Calvin and Zwingli, rejected the Catholic approach to visual images—a theological decision that still influences the decoration of contemporary churches, both Catholic and Protestant, as the designs of the London Oratory and St. Columba's show. The reformers opposed the medieval tradition of highly decorated churches on both theological and pragmatic grounds. Sympathetic to the Old Testament prohibition of images, they also found the "Bible in stone" approach inimical to people reading the biblical text (Goethals, 1990, p. 47–52). Unlike Pope Gregory the Great, they did not want a visual Bible for the unlettered; they wanted everyone to learn to read. Here again, media ecology shows itself with the affordance of cheap printed books making literacy more valuable and reducing the cost of books; religious practice shifts from a focus on images of Bible scenes to the printed

---

[2] See ch. 6 for more detail.

narratives of those scenes. To put it another way, the changing environment of the church buildings marks another shift in media ecology from the Scriptures as performance texts (things to remind one of the memorized narratives) to reading texts. This shift in turn affects what people do in churches and how they participate in religious activities. One change in the environment affects all its parts.

An Ecology of Place

The ecosystem that a church building defines extends beyond the walls of the building in its influence on the reflection on belief. Church buildings mark places. Religious history has long recognized holy places—places where people have encountered God, memorials of those places, or places set aside for sacred activities. The memorial and functional aspects of church buildings also enshrine a theology. In his reflections on ritual, Smith (1987) highlights how the place of worship can affect people's understandings of their belief: "[The place marks] a distinction in the social experience of quality of time that stands at the origin of the absolute spatial dichotomy of sacred and profane, which, in turn generates the other cognitive dualities on which intellection rests" (p. 40). The holy place of a church building creates a sense of holy time and a space in which people experience God's time. That in turn sets the stage for how present and subsequent visitors will reflect on their belief. Both communication and religious scholars have highlighted this. People live in physical places but extend them virtually through communication practices. A church building connects people imaginatively to sacred places through, for example, the images of the Stations of the Cross or the altar standing in for Calvary—to draw two examples from Catholic practices seen in the Brompton Oratory. The Stations of the Cross—fourteen images of places marked out in Jerusalem that Jesus passed through on his way to death on Calvary—bring a distant holy place (that is, recreate that holy place) into the local church. The representational art and the walking from station to station allow the worshipers to exist in two places at once, a physical manifestation of a theological belief, a practice shared by the Orthodox praying before an icon. Soukup (2003) explains:

> Ritual places, as social places, make information available. In a religious sense, this is information about God, about how a worshiping community understands God, about how that community reflects on God. Smith [1987] has pointed out that the ritual actions make the places repositories of social information. But, as we see in Christianity, that information can also reside in the ritual. As the ritual places become rituals, we see a gradual

pattern of substitution for place. At the Reformation an important change occurs when ritual place became more of a symbolic place. (p. 113)

Churches of the Reformation rely less on images than on sermon and books, on more abstract theological expression:

> Communication practices begin to substitute for place: the book for the temple, the liturgical calendar for the way of the cross. [Smith] does note how the symbolic becomes separated from the ritual: the symbolic statement substitutes for the Last Supper. To some extent, this parallels the growing move towards abstraction fostered by communication technology. Written words abstract from face-to-face immediacy; . . . a literate culture values abstraction. (Soukup, 2003, p. 113)

But the abstract can recreate the place. The Hebrew prophet Ezekiel uses a written description of the temple in Jerusalem (chapters 40–48) to make that temple present to the Jewish exiles in Babylon. Similarly, Luther's emphasis on the Word of God was enough to make the Gospels a reality:

> In the Stadtkirch (City Church) of Wittenburg, where Luther often preached, another of Cranach's altarpieces depicts a triptych that displays the Lutheran interpretation of the sacraments (baptism, the Lord's Supper, and confession of sin). In the altarpiece's predella, Cranach depicts Luther himself, preaching in an elevated pulpit and pointing to a crucifix that has materialized before a small gathering of congregants, implying that the words of his sermon successfully conjure the image in the imaginations of his listeners. The scene alludes to a central tenet in Luther's theology—that the preached word has a sacramental dimension. (Jensen, 2017, p. 183)

Place, whether physical or virtual, leads to reflection on belief and influences that reflection. Places affect how people think theologically.

The interior space of a church building also defines an acoustic environment and that, too, influences how people think theologically. All three of the London churches feature music—the chanting of the Russian Orthodox, the choirs of the Presbyterians and Catholics—as well as the spoken word. As Ong (1967, p. 111) frequently pointed out, sound lives ephemerally: it exists only as it passes from existence. Sound both testifies to life—in churches, to the living God—and situates the hearer. People know where they are and their relationships through what they hear. Religious traditions use different instruments to create sounds or a texture of sound—sometimes these embody theological claims. The religious tradition can also adjust aspects of the music itself: instrumental vs. choral, accompanied vs. a capella, single voices vs. polyphony, various tempos, and so on. All of these as well as lyrics can carry particular theological meaning. But the interior of the church building itself adds to the theological significance of the music: to hear Mozart's Requiem or Bach's Passion of St. Matthew performed in a concert hall offers a completely different experience from a performance in a church.

• • •

This consideration of communication and theology points out that each aspect of Christian worship spaces communicates about God and people's relationship with God. The built environments, the places in which people worship manifest a "theology"—a way of thinking about God and the conclusions people draw about God. The key Christian concept of the Incarnation, God's taking on our flesh, grounds Christian understanding of church buildings. Christian worship stresses the physical and its importance; this theological affirmation of the importance of the flesh and of all creation appears in the very fabric of building. It counters those religions that deny the value of the body or try to escape into a purely spiritual world.

Beyond the overall religious heading of "cult" or worship, the media ecology approach examines each of the elements individually and as a complex interacting environment. Media ecology reveals religious places as "communication machines." The variations among churches of different denominations express important theological differences: while all profess a faith in Christ, they show their differences not only in theological books but in the ways that each group designs its worship places. Churches are built in faith to build up faith.

9
RITUAL

Expressing Belief in Action

Standing in the shallows of a river, a minister plunges people dressed in white robes into the waters.[1] Dressed in ornate vestments at the front of a church, a priest pours water over the head of a small child. Seated around a table, a group passes bread and wine among themselves. Hidden behind an iconostasis, the Orthodox priest chants the words of Jesus, "Take and eat . . ." Interpreted and enacted in different ways, all Christian groups or denominations have at least two recognizable rituals—baptism and the Lord's Supper. After all, Jesus himself commanded that his followers do these things ("Go, therefore, and baptize all nations in the name of the Father, and of the Son, and of the Holy Spirit." And, after the Gospels narrate how Jesus took the bread and the cup, he said, "Do this in memory of me").

Rituals span human life, in both religious and nonreligious practice. In religious practice, rituals exhibit the basic characteristics of "public assembly, the repetition of gestures already considered 'ritual tradition' by a community, and the invocation of divine beings" (Bell, 1997, p. 166). Further, in rituals, individuals must "do something in such a way as that the doing itself gives the acts a special or privileged status" (p. 166). Put another way, rituals "denote the performance of more or less invariant sequences of formal acts and utterances not entirely encoded by the performers" (Rappaport, 1999, p. 24). Sets of actions imbued with symbolic meaning, rituals constitute a media ecology of their own: "Media beyond language have served to express matters of sacral belief and practice in every culture. Ceremony, folklore, and myth, as well as drama, come easily to mind as examples" (Sorenson, 2000, p. 118). Rituals combine action with any number of other media: words, often with special language registers; music; special decor; light and darkness; visual images; painting, including body painting; anointing; incense or other odors; particular tools, instruments, or special vessels; furnishings; and so forth. Rituals appeal to the

[1] Portions of this chapter previously appeared in Soukup (2003).

senses in various combinations—what Ong terms the sensorium or the mix of simultaneous impact on sight, hearing, smell, taste, and touch (1967, pp. 1–6). In a ritual, people experience the symbolic meaning, which depends on the ecology: "Symbolic action affirms something: it makes a statement about the conditions of existence in terms of the relations of persons and groups. Ritual, then, is essentially communication, a language in which societies discuss a variety of matters" (Crocker, 1973, p. 49). As focused on matters of existence and ultimate things, rituals enact theology. The mix of the communication elements, the actions, the symbols, the ecology in short, embodies the theology. Following Durkheim, Crocker notes that the context, the environment or ecology, establishes the significance of the ritual (p. 50). Crocker also reports how the anthropologist Victor Turner adduced data from his fieldwork "to show how the symbols used in the rite interact with one another on many levels to create one poetic metaphor after another" (p. 68). A change in ecology, then, changes the meaning. And the theological meaning—the understanding of faith—lies in the ritual.

A ritual specifies each part of the action and each of its accompanying media. As an example, consider the baptismal ceremony for infants in the Catholic Church. The priest, dressed in white vestments greets the parents, godparents, and child at the door of the church and asks two questions: "What name have you given your child?" and "What do you ask of God's church for your child?" When the parents request baptism, the priest then welcomes the child in a ritualized formula and marks the child with the sign of the cross, inviting each of the others to do the same for the child. In the church, gathered around the baptistery, the group reads from the Gospels. After blessing the water, the priest invites the parents and godparents to speak for their child in professing faith and renouncing sin. Only then does he baptize the child, using the specific formula in the Gospels: "I baptize you in the name of the Father, and of the Son, and of the Holy Spirit." From ancient custom, a grammatical or pronunciation error does not invalidate the ritual; however, changing the names (Father, Son, and Holy Spirit) does (Pelikan, 1978, p.31). The ritual continues with the priest anointing the child with scented oil (recalling the anointing of Christ), clothing the child in white, and giving the parents and godparents a lit candle representing the light of Christ. The ritual combines media appealing to each of the senses. And each aspect of the ceremony signifies part of the experience of the ritual. Changing part of it—the holy names, as noted—changes the ritual. This ritual, as any ritual, embodies a theology; here, a theology of incorporation into a group; a theology of enlightenment, of new birth; a theology that sin, present in human life, does not have the last word; a theology of Incarnation, of God's presence in human life.

Media Ecology and Ritual

People need to have a sense of the ritual: "An action is not ritual if the participants are not aware that it is a ritual" (Mead, 1973, p. 91). This does not imply that people immediately understand the ritual. Experience precedes reflection; reflection leads to understanding. In other words, affect comes first, then intellectual understanding. One need not begin with faith to accept or participate in a ritual: "Acceptance is not belief" (Rappaport, 1999, p. 119). Participation in a ritual says nothing about one's interior state. A ritual, however, does interact with belief: "But, paradoxically, it may be, and it surely has been implied by religion's defenders, that the acceptance indicated by liturgical performance, being independent of belief can be more profound than conviction or sense of certainty, for it makes it possible for the performer to transcend his or her own doubt by accepting in defiance of it" (p. 120). The public process of faith-seeking-understanding in ritual offers an invitation to the private: "Acceptance in, or through, liturgical performance may reflect an inward state of conviction; it may also encourage 'the mind,' 'the heart,' and 'the spirit' into agreement with itself" (p. 122). Rappaport argues for interactions among the participant, the community, the community's reflection (or theology), and the individual's process of faith-seeking-understanding:

> But a liturgical order that is not supported by the *conviction* of at least some of the members of the congregations realizing it is in danger of gradually falling into desuetude, of sooner or later becoming a dead letter or, as contemporary usage would have it, "mere ritual." Whereas belief, being volatile, hidden and unpredictable, is not *in itself* sufficiently reliable to serve as the foundation of convention, it is, *in the long run*, indispensable to the perpetuation of the liturgical orders in which conventions are accepted. If liturgical orders are to remain vital they must receive the numinous support of at least some of those who participate in them at least from time to time. (p. 396, italics in original)

Hence the importance of an ecology, which encompasses both the ritual and the people; the ecology provides a framework for understanding. Early Christianity shows this at work in its celebration of the rituals. For example, the Jerusalem church let people experience things first, and then explained them. The fourth century *Catechesis* by St. Cyril of Jerusalem provides an example, explaining their baptism to new adult Christians:

> You were led down to the font of holy baptism just as Christ was taken down from the cross and placed in the tomb which is before your eyes. Each of you was asked, "do you believe in the name of the Father, and of the Son, and of the Holy Spirit?" You made the profession of faith that brings salvation, you were plunged into the water, and three times you rose again. This symbolized the three days Christ spent in the tomb.
>
> As our Savior spent three days and three nights in the depths of the earth, so your first rising from the water represented the first day and your first immersion represented the first night. At night a man cannot see, but in the day he walks in the light. So when you were immersed in the water it was like night for you and you could not see, but when you rose again it was like coming into broad daylight. In the same instant you died and were born again; the saving water was both your tomb and your mother. . . .
>
> This is something amazing and unheard of! It was not we who actually died, were buried, and rose again. We only did these things symbolically, but we have been saved in actual fact. (Cyril of Jerusalem, 435, 3:1–2)

The ritual meaning emerges over time as people hear the explanations and think about what happened. A theology of baptism emerges from that reflection on belief.

Religious rituals differ, of course, from nonreligious rituals like a baseball player's pre-batting movements and gestures or a footballer's celebratory dance after scoring. They differ from civic rituals like voting or observing a memorial day. They differ as well among themselves from other religious rituals. The difference lies in the ecology, the environment, and the meaning of the symbols. The difference lies, too, in the theology attached to the ritual, for each ritual acts as a reflection on faith. For example, above, Cyril explains how each of the elements in the baptism enacts what the person baptized believes. Remaining with this example, to celebrate baptism differently, even subtly, indicates a change in theology. In the sixteenth century, during the Reformation, the Anabaptists rebaptized adults and later practiced only adult baptism, expressing a theology that stressed free will and individual decision (as opposed to a theology of community, in which parents made faith decisions for their children).

How do rituals communicate theology?: "Representations appearing in ritual may evoke emotion and may affect cognition through their aesthetic qualities" (Rappaport, 1999, p. 385). The combination of ritual action and ritual environment (art, music, speech, setting, and place) embody a reflection on belief. Rituals reinforce—they teach, define, and provide a framework. Communication study, as well as anthropology, provide a context to see the ecology of rituals in their theological role.

Rituals reinforce the community, both by teaching and by fostering a sense of identity. Vitz (2005) notes that, during the Middle Ages when only an elite group had the means to become literate (p. 21), religious rituals provided theological education. Such rituals taught by means of a training of the body through the senses, music, sight, vision, and a sense of community (p. 24). The rituals provided a set of actions, motions, and postures, each of which held significance. Religion and religious understanding came through actions, upon which people could reflect. Asking "what did they learn?" Vitz responds that people learned "religion as presence, as affect, and as a calling for response" (p. 25). "Even if one does not understand the words" of the ritual (p. 28), Vitz continues, they learned affect and that emotional tone shaped their behaviors and understanding. By creating an environment, a ritual teaches people how to live in that environment, giving the conditions for an unreflective faith, which later can come to greater articulation. The same thing happens today as people participate in religious rituals. A church wedding, for example, differs from a civil ceremony, even for the nonreligious. The environment creates an affect, which in itself teaches something about the religious meaning of the ceremony. The meaning, the theological understanding, results from the ecology, which itself comes from a reflection on faith gained over many generations.

Carey (1989) sees ritual as also fostering a kind of learning, but a learning of identity occurring in contemporary society in a different way, through communication. To explain his analysis, he draws a distinction between two views of communication: a transmission view and a ritual view. The former, "defined by terms such as 'imparting,' 'sending,' 'transmitting,' or 'giving information to others,' . . . is formed from a metaphor of geography or transportation" (p. 12). This view of communication objectifies communication into packets that move from one person or place to another. Like any object, these can be measured, tested, manipulated, sped up, slowed down, and so on. The spatial metaphor highlights the role of transmitted messages in asserting control at a distance, in assisting with a kind of foreignness as communication comes in from the outside. In contrast to this, Carey offers a ritual view of communication, where communication unites people in a sharing or association, the purpose of which lies in reinforcing the identity of the group, which occurs over time and arises from the group:

> The archetypal case under a ritual view is the sacred ceremony that draws persons together in fellowship and commonality.
> The indebtedness of the ritual view of communication to religion is apparent in the name chosen to label it. Moreover, it derives from a view

of religion that downplays the role of the sermon, the instruction, and admonition, in order to highlight the role of the prayer, the chant, and the ceremony. It sees the original or highest manifestation of communication not in the transmission of intelligent information but in the construction and maintenance of an ordered, meaningful cultural world that can serve as a control and container for human action. . . .

This projection of community ideals and their embodiment in material form—dance, plays, architecture, news stories, strings of speech—creates an artificial though nonetheless real symbolic order that operates to provide not information but confirmation, not to alter attitudes or change minds but to represent an underlying order of things, not to perform functions but to manifest an ongoing and fragile social process. (Carey, 1989, p. 15)

Because Carey draws the metaphor from religion, the application of his ritual view of communication to theology seems straightforward. The theological meaning encoded in the symbolism comes precisely in "the prayer, the chant, and the ceremony." The reflection on faith or belief that defines theology occurs in the repeated actions, "in material form," in the body, and in the community. There remains, of course, room for "the sermon, the instruction, and admonition" but these reflect a different register of theology, a different medium in the ecological mix.

Drawing on sociological and anthropological metaphors, White (1986) suggests a dramaturgical image for the ritual communication of theology. The church, its ministers, and its members play well-defined social roles that encode their understanding of religion and the world. These understandings incorporate theological understandings, often those inherited from the period of the Reformation and the wars of religion that followed. The rise of the mass communication media in the nineteenth century, especially the popular press, offered different roles for the people—different rituals of community, to use Carey's terms. No longer did the religious dramaturgy provide the sole ritual of community identity. The shift in the ecological mix, the addition of a mass medium, affects all roles, and that in turn affects people's self-understanding. The Catholic Church, for example, first adjusted its social self-representation. It "presented itself as a more perfect sub-society upholding traditional order, preserving the timeless wisdom of the past, and maintaining the institutions of family and community. . . . Catholic social teaching provided harmonious and certain answers to all human and social problems, in contrast to endless interest-group debates and revolutionary agitation" (pp. 11–12). Later, with the Second Vatican Council, the Catholic Church again adjusted is social roles to complement and counter the dominant social rituals: "This social dramaturgy is anchored in a type of faith reflection which takes as its starting point not just Catholic tradition but a prayerful analysis of God's redeeming action revealed in the contemporary efforts to build a more human and just order in society" (pp. 12–13). Ritual and ritual identity moved from particular church ceremonies to the ways that religious groups (from small communities to organized churches) interact with other social entities—communication media, governments, business, and so on.

White's analysis suggests, too, how changing one part of the ecology propagates changes to all other parts. This affects not only social performance—that is, the church's performance of social ritual—but also the church's own rituals. A key element of media ecology studies, this conviction holds the intertwined nature of all communication elements and meanings, even if the consequences remain hard to predict. Many have recognized such changes. Ritual, as a more or less self-contained ecology, shows perhaps greater sensitivity to such changes.

Marshall McLuhan (1999b) speculated on this point in a consideration of the consequences of adding the microphone or amplified sound to Catholic rituals such as the Mass. In his analysis, the unamplified Mass counted as a "cool" medium, one that lent itself to prayer and contemplation with all the sensory elements balanced. The Latin uttered by the priest formed a kind of soft aural environment that corresponded to the other ritual elements: light, architecture, odors of incense, movement, and so on. However, the microphone changed the environment and the ecological balance. By overstressing the one sense of hearing, it created a "hot" medium. The amplified voice overwhelmed all the other parts of the environment and focused attention on the speaker, significantly altering the ritual, pulling it into the ambit of other public performances where people experience amplified sound. This had a number of consequences. It eventually helped propel the shift away from Latin to the vernacular languages: "It is not practical to say Latin into a microphone since the mike [sic] sharpens and intensifies the sounds of Latin to a meaningless degree" (p. 112). Second, the amplified sound affects the architecture of the church building, replacing sights with dominant sounds. But the microphone also softens the voice of the speaker, who no longer needs to shout; indirectly it makes preaching softer, both in volume and in content (p. 112). A change in the ecology changes the ritual itself, the participants' experience of the ritual, and the eventual meaning of the ritual. Among the other things that McLuhan notes is a move from meditative prayer to an enforced sense of community rather than the more natural sense of community arising from the ritual itself (p. 114).

More recently Spadaro (2011) took up McLuhan's theme, extending the question about the microphone's impact on ritual to a more generalized question about new communication technologies. As the microphone led to the expansion of sound to the exclusion of other aspects of the ritual, Spadaro argues, new technologies expanded sound still further via radio and Internet so that ritual sound reaches anywhere in the world, both expanding and excluding ritual place. Ironically, this in turn has led to a growing demand for virtual rituals, rituals in electronic spaces like Second Life or Facebook. Churches already exist in these virtual worlds and some do offer virtual rituals. But what status accords to such virtual rituals? "Ritual is concerned with relationships, either between a single individual and the supernatural, or among a group of individuals who share things together" (Mead, 1973, p. 89). Ritual enacts understandings of those elements: the individual, God, and the group. Each of the Christian rituals mentioned at the beginning of this chapter localizes God for the group, perhaps none more so than the Eucharist, in which the community "recreates" the experience of the Incarnation. The relationship with God is focused on the Body and Blood, the person of Jesus. The theology embedded in the ritual stresses physical place when God is everywhere and we are in one place. The virtual world seems to reverse this. Spadaro considers the possibility of "sacraments" in virtual space but concludes that, lacking the physical, they become merely a psychological experience. But this does not lack precedent. He suggests, "There remains open the way for a possible 'digital devotion,' which can somehow be linked to various forms of 'spiritual communion' as the tradition has always known, as evidenced by the Council of Trent" (Spadaro, 2011, p. 111). The digital technologies affect the ecology of ritual, in this instance unbalancing place. Do people, Spadaro eventually asks, really need to occupy the same physical place in order to participate in a ritual?

All of this became an almost universal reality in the responses of the churches to the 2020 Covid-19 pandemic when public health authorities closed churches and other public places of assembly. Most churches quickly moved to different forms of online worship, with Eucharistic services livestreamed, Bible study taking place through video conferences, prayer meetings led by remote ministers, sermons recorded, and so on. For some churches, particularly evangelical churches with a theology of preaching the Word of God both in person and electronically, this presented little change. For most others, the impact of setting up a camera proved much greater. While the structure of the rituals remained the same, their context dramatically changed. Watching a ritual, no matter how familiar that ritual, differs from living in the ritual. A "spiritual communion" is not physical communion (whether receiving the

Body of Christ or joining with others in an experience of community). Spadaro's prediction of "digital devotion" proved correct but these rituals became, in effect and in reality, new rituals, with a different theological outcome. The assembly at prayer moved from a people to a group of individuals. A common place changed to an intention to watch and listen at the same time. Place now encompassed the spaces of home or office and the surroundings of screens. The online rituals literally shrank the church building to the size of a screen; theologically the church became one channel among others, an option rather than an environment.

The technologies, from sound to virtual worlds, move rituals away from a particular location, and in so doing change them and their meaning. As White suggested, these changes occur together with other social changes. When people are everywhere, in cyberspace for example, the place of the ritual becomes less important. Ritual and place form an ecology that matters.

The Physicality of Place

The ritual importance of place shows that place matters for theology. But how? People locate themselves by place, define social relationships (and thus theological ones) by place, and situate themselves before God by place. Joshua Meyrowitz (1985) and Jonathan Z. Smith (1987) explain these functions, from perspectives of communication study and ritual studies, respectively. Both note the connection between physical places (landmarks as well as indoor spaces—the front as opposed to the back of a room, for example) and social spaces. Some spaces remain open to all; other spaces, open to a few, based on rank or occupation. The distinction even appears in linguistic usage in English, as when people say that someone "does not know his or her place" (Meyrowitz, 1985, p. ix; Smith, 1987, p. 45). Place marks social standing, including religious standing. Christian churches feature a tripartite division among vestibule, nave, and chancel or sanctuary: places for the world, the congregation, and the clergy. The distinction carries clear theological meaning about how people approach God.

Meyrowitz, following Goffman, points out that social standing also guides behavior. People take on social roles depending on their place. Actions and behaviors differ dramatically from a wedding and the reception and even more dramatically between a wedding and a beach party. The serving staff at a restaurant behave differently with the customers than with the kitchen staff. This appears in almost every human interaction. Using an analogy to a stage borrowed from Goffman, Meyrowitz highlights how behavior changes with its audience. Soukup (2003) summarizes:

> The public audience (that is, the audience of the public places) calls forth one set of behaviors; the more intimate audience of family and friends, another. Think here of the differing ways that one speaks in a classroom or lecture hall, in a business, in a church, in a public meeting, at home, or relaxing with one's peers (Meyrowitz, 1985, pp. 23–33). In communication terms, physical location provides social information, the things we know about each other and that determine how we relate to one another (p. 37). For media ecology, place provides yet another method of information management. (p. 111)

Such information management includes theological information. People's physical situation affects how they enact religious rituals and thus how they think about God. Meyrowitz points to three key life dimensions where place influences people socially (and, from the perspective of religious ritual, can affect theological thinking): "roles of affiliation or 'being' (group identity), roles of transition or 'becoming' (socialization), and roles of authority (hierarchy)" (p. 52). Religious experience and understanding influences each of the three—group identity, socialization, and authority—and, in turn, is influenced by them. How groups and individuals define each of them reflects the groups' theological orientation. Think, for example, about the Reformation insistence on redefining Catholic ritual away from something performed by a priest (with clear roles of hierarchy) to rituals of the preaching of the Word open to everyone's understanding (with very different understandings of authority). The ritual and people's places within it expressed what they believed.

A change in place can affect all three categories identified by Meyrowitz. And, as Meyrowitz argues extensively, communication media change our sense of place. In his example, television has altered people's sense of place, letting them see things otherwise off-limits—politicians relaxing at home, for example, or the Pope close up. Those views changed how people behave towards those once-unapproachable figures.

Smith (1997) shows the connection of place to religious consciousness, writing that the activity in a place (the sense of place, the social action) makes it holy. People use place to remember, to reenact holy events, and to encounter the Holy (pp. 39–41). Place affects not only religious practice but also one's understanding of the world: "In other words, it is a distinction in the social experience of quality of time that stands at the origin of the absolute spatial dichotomy of sacred and profane, which, in turn, generates the other cognitive dualities on which intellection rests" (p. 40). But "place," as Meyrowitz also indicates, works flexibly. Communication media can become places in themselves. Though Meyrowitz focuses on television—people "go" to a favorite bar or a friend's home, though both of these exist as stage sets on television, as imagined places—the experience of communication media as places extends much farther back in time.

Smith recounts the movement of sacred places from physical locations to mediated or analogous locations. The Hebrew prophet Ezekiel reconstructed the Jerusalem temple for the Jewish exiles in Babylon through vivid descriptions in his writings (chapters 40–48), including not only a physical description but also the social arrangements, with the roles of king, priest, the Jewish people, and the nations specified. Soukup (2003) again summarizes:

> Though Smith does not put it this way, the structure of communication practices begins to substitute for physical places: the book stands in for the temple, the information management of the text for the information management of the ritual. The somewhat restricted access to information in the book to the priest or scribe continued the social restriction of place found in the Temple precincts. The community's worship and prayer mirrors the community's social structures. (p. 112)

Similar things occur in Christianity, with the Book of Revelation substituting the description of the "heavenly Jerusalem" for the Jewish city, expressing the key theological claim that the heavenly place will have no temple, but instead that God will dwell among people. Later Christian practice transposed place to art, with images of the Jewish city of Jerusalem placed around churches to symbolically recreate pilgrimage spaces within the place of the churches:

> As Meyrowitz points out, in communication terms, social place marks out the availability of information. Ritual places, as social places, make information available. In a religious sense, this is information about God, about how a worshiping community understands God, about how that community reflects on God, in short, about theology. Smith has pointed out that the ritual actions make the places repositories of social information. But, as we see in Christianity that information can also reside in the ritual. As the ritual places become rituals, we see a gradual pattern of substitution for place. The Reformation shifted this substitution yet again, replacing or modifying rituals from ritual place as social place to ritual place as social information—"symbolical, historical, or social." . . .
>
> To some extent, this parallels the growing move towards abstraction fostered by communication technology. Written words abstract from face-to-face immediacy. Following Danet, O'Leary (1996) argues that the

> separation of symbolic from ritual correlates with a transfer of performative communication from the spoken text to the written. The analysis and abstraction fostered by the separation of speaker from words—that is, the ability to see our words as separate from ourselves and our speaking, to see our words on a page before us—changes our relationship to language and to practice. It allows people to step outside of ritual and of ritual place; it allows people to focus on social information rather than on physical or social place. In so doing, abstraction reinforces the tendency to create a semiotic system of substitution. (Soukup, 2003, p. 113)

Ritual places facilitate the movement of both social and theological information. The performance in speech and action reinforces what the community believes but also allows the community to transform that belief into other media—art or writing for example. How people think about religious experience shows the mark of the communication tools with which they think (Ong, 1969). And using those communication tools becomes ritualized in its own way.

In the last centuries, people's experience of ritual has dramatically changed, because people's experience of place has changed through dramatic changes in communication. In many ways communication erased place—or distance, at least. For almost two hundred years (since the telegraph) people have no longer needed to be in the same place with another to communicate, though for much of that time, the technology has remained expensive and limited. But at least since the 1970s, things changed for everyone. The anthropologist Edmund S. Carpenter describes the situation in explicitly religious terms:

> Electricity has made angels of us all—not angels in the Sunday school sense of being good or having wings, but spirit freed from flesh, capable of instant transportation anywhere.
>
> The moment we pick up a phone, we're nowhere in space, everywhere in spirit. Nixon on TV is everywhere at once. That is Saint Augustine's definition of God: a Being whose center is everywhere, whose borders are nowhere. (Carpenter, 1972, p. 3)

Electronic communication dissolves place.[2] People can be at home and watch simultaneous events across the world. People can travel the world and simultaneously remain in their offices and homes, linked by smart phones. By the same token, electronic communication shatters social norms. People in their pajamas can view popes, presidents, queens, and movie stars along with their morning coffee, with no need for protocol. People have indiscriminate access

---

[2] The following material to the end of this chapter, with a few changes and additions, previously appeared in Soukup (2003), pp. 114–17.

to social information that formerly defined groups, leading to an uncertainty of who and where they are.

Perhaps it is not so much a loss of place as the substitution of one kind of place for another. Contemporary places are virtual ones and composite ones. People combine physical place with the virtual place of television location, computer simulation, and cell phone conversation. People seldom dwell in one place at a time anymore, but link themselves somewhere else. Part of them remains physically tethered, but another part seeks out the virtual. From their behaviors (and dependence on electronic media), it is clear that people prefer to gather together in places: here and in that virtual somewhere.

Meyrowitz asks what the change in this sense of place has done to us. To help us understand it, he has, as noted earlier, identified three dimensions of change: group identity, socialization, and authority, three things connected with ritual. Because each depends on place, the changing of social place by electronic media has affected each.

Generally, sociologists define groups as individuals bound together by place, people who share the social information that place restricts to their members. While people formed communities of discourse based on written materials (Stock, 1983; Anderson, 1991), electronic media have sped up and expanded the process and provided social information formerly available only face-to-face (Meyrowitz, 1985, p. 135). The wider place introduced by electronic media has led to "the decreasing importance of traditional group ties and the increasing importance of other types of association" (p. 131). Electronic media provide more options for identity formation, exposing people to different social meanings and shared social information across a much larger group:

> To use George Herbert Mead's term, electronic media alter one's "generalized other"—the general sense of how other people think and evaluate one's actions. The "mediated generalized other" includes standards, values, and beliefs from outside traditional group spheres, and it thereby presents people with a new perspective from which to view their actions and identities. (pp. 131–32)

The change in place brought about by electronic media changes groups by increasing both the scope and the rate of information.

Socialization—the ways in which people enter into groups—changes with the shift in their sense of place too. Typically socialization involves the gradual introduction of an individual into a group, through the measured provision of information about the group, its goals, its behaviors, and its practices: "Part of the mystique of any training or socialization process is the belief by the person going through it that when the process is complete, he or she will be 'another person,' a person with special qualities" (Meyrowitz. 1985, p. 155). The Rite of Christian Initiation of Adults provides a good example here, both in its current form and in the form as practiced in the Jerusalem church in the fourth century, quoted above. However, today television and electronic media do not distinguish among groups nor do they aim to keep things secret. This changes both the pace and the practice of entering social groups. The merging of formerly public and private spheres blurs the distinctions among full group membership, stages of socialization into a group, and outsider status. Generally, individuals being socialized into a group learn about the group's ideals first (i.e., public information) and then gain access to more private information as they become more fully socialized. Through electronic media, however, the sequence and amount of information have changed. Individuals learn much about a group's private information and behavior before they become full members of the group. As a result stages of controlled access are bypassed (p. 153). Individuals may well receive information about groups or society in general before they are ready for it; they may lose the sense of becoming a new person through initiation; and they may find themselves partial members of many groups and fully incorporated in none of them. The electronic media's impact on socialization causes an information overload. Such a change in information management also affects the theological role of ritual as a means of socialization and of reflection on faith. New members cannot reflect on their experience in a way controlled by the ritual; both the experience and the theology growing from it have changed.

Finally, Meyrowitz describes a loss of authority stemming from the loss of a sense of place. Authority, he claims, "rests on information control" (1985, p. 160), with people or organizations in authority, by virtue of their places, having more information than others. But electronic media have altered that access, providing information to everyone, sometimes even before political authorities like the President or Congress have it. But the media have chipped away at authority in other ways as well:

> Roles of hierarchy are upset not only by the loss of exclusive control over knowledge directly relevant to role functions (medical data for a doctor, for example), but also by the merging of public and private situations. More than any other type of roles, hierarchal roles depend on performers restricting access to their personal lives. Much human activity is common to all individuals. If high status persons cannot segregate such behavior from their on-stage high status performances, then they appear to be more like everyone else. By providing greater access to, and awareness

of, backstage behavior, electronic media tend to undermine traditional abstractions of status. (p. 167)

Once any authority figure has lost hierarchical place, all authority comes into question. People who have access to once-privileged information in one sector feel that they could also have similar access in others. People who see the more hidden behaviors of some authorities infer it of others. Television changes the workings of authority in ways that many people in authority have not yet understood.

Though Meyrowitz does not discuss it, television and electronic media also affect people's sense of ritual place. Ritual place, according to Smith, directs our attention:

> Ritual is, first and foremost, a mode of paying attention. It is a process for marking interest . . . It is this characteristic, as well, that explains the role of place as a fundamental component of ritual: place directs attention. (Smith, 1987, p. 103)

But the focus of electronic media and television constantly changes and directs our attention from (virtual) place to (virtual) place, making it harder for people to attend to the place they are. At the same time, television and electronic media trivialize place. Because they can be anywhere, people lose their sense of place. The sacred place is just another place. It is not uncommon now for people to make no distinctions in their social behaviors when they enter into churches or other "holy places." The sense of place has changed. And because they have access to virtually anywhere in the world, people hesitate to go to a holy place. What is there that they do not have on television or online? This in some ways describes the problem that Spadaro addresses: many people no longer experience ritual itself as a means to enter into the holy. Television and electronic media have changed social practice to the extent that people experience place differently and therefore experience ritual differently. Research into American church life after the restrictions imposed by health authorities in 2020 identified "the difference between attending and viewing," a "general disconnection between churches and congregants—in terms of both expectations for ministry and how to rightly measure engagement" (Barna Group, 2020).

Just as ritual place changed from public shared spaces to information—the book, the symbol, the image, and the imagination—so now the disembodied information of the electronic media privatize ritual space, a phenomenon exemplified in online religious gatherings. Religious practice depends less on the community in its physical locations and seems more a matter of individualism. "I'm a very spiritual person, but I don't go to church" is a more and more common refrain. The virtual community of virtual places allows people more freedom in choosing their communities of worship.

All three of Meyrowitz's examples touch on religious experience as well as the more general social experience he describes. Group identity, socialization, and authority function within religion, too. Just as television and electronic media changed group definitions by providing access to groups beyond people's physical boundaries, so too have they affected religious groups. Religious groups themselves overlap one another—to the benefit of ecumenism and interfaith dialogue. Religious intercultural dialogue also comes from the breakdown of group definition. On the other hand, religious groups become more porous, with people more likely to switch from church to church. Other groups have lost their mystique, their strangeness, and their cohesion. The shifting group boundaries also affect socialization, since groups can no longer control the flow of information to new members. It is more likely now that people come to join churches on their own terms and come with a great deal of knowledge of both the ideals and the flaws of religious groups.

However, religious authority shows the greatest effect of a change of place and ritual. As with other authority, the loss of a privileged place and the appearance of no longer controlling the flow of information have resulted in a more open questioning of authority, particularly the hierarchical authority that depends on place. The trappings of office—physical separation, special clothing and vestments, and behavioral protocols—are not enough to establish authority. The clergy no longer hold a place of honor and their actions are more likely to be questioned. Church members seek to hold their leaders accountable, despite theological claims that the Church is not a democracy. It is not so much political theory that gives people democratic expectations of the Church, but television's and electronic media's breaking down of the sense of place and opening the flow of information. As Meyrowitz puts it, "electronic media not only weaken authority by allowing those low on the ladder of hierarchy to gain access to much information, but also by allowing increased opportunities for the sharing of information horizontally" (Meyrowitz. 1985, p. 322). As people share more information, the interpretive rules change, lessening authority even more.

As both Smith and Meyrowitz note, the change in place affects the way people think about religious experience—that is, the kinds of theology they engage in. Like all communication structures, people tend to take place for granted, even though it affects how they experience religion and how they think religiously. As place changes, people become more aware of groups, cultures, and their own situatedness. That challenges the ways that people have traditionally thought about the Church. It will also change the ways that people experience God's presence, to invoke a place-based metaphor. On the other hand, if people can change place so easily, then is Carpenter right? Have people become angelic? What does that change do to people's sense of body and embodiedness? To their sense of contingency? The shifting of sense of place not only changes what people think about; the changes in social practice resulting from it will also affect who does the thinking for the Church and how they think. The hierarchical sense of teaching authority and authorized teachers breaks down, since people feel that their perspective is as good as anyone else's. The last twenty-five years have already seen hints of this in the Catholic church, in the adulation that meets Popes on their travels coupled with a willingness to discount what they say or write as chief teacher. The papacy has succeeded in establishing a visual authority but not an interpretive one. The changing of social place means that the Catholic Church will need to develop a new model of authority, one less dependent on position.

In addition to the actions that define them, rituals act as a collective theology, a collective faith-seeking-understanding. Ritual still matters as a source of religious experience but the experience changes with the quality of the ritual. That in turn affects the theology. As the communication culture changes, the very images and powers we attribute to God change—that is, the theology—changes, even if God does not.

10
FILM

Expanding the Sacramental Horizon

Professional theologians, those people who spend their time seeking an understanding of faith, seem to love film, at least judged by the sheer number of books and articles they write about such things. Lindvall's somewhat dated two-part review (2004, 2005) of such writing runs to over one thousand bibliographic items; the years since have seen the publication of perhaps three hundred more such publications. Individuals also find in mass media narratives sources for theological reflection; these levels of engagement suggest some approaches to the media ecology of film as theology. Where earlier periods of Christianity's faith-seeking-understanding drew upon people's immediate experiences, upon biblical material, or upon the works of other Christians (preachers, teachers, saints, or sinners), contemporary Christianity's location in a media-centric world places it in a rich communication and media environment, all aspects of which provide material to its reflection. The same holds true of the communication tools available to those seeking to understand faith. Where past generations of people interested in theology used storytelling, art, painting, sculpture, the written word, the printed word, and almost any other traditional form, today people will just as likely turn to film. The ecology includes both theological writing about film, theological use of film, film critics' attempts to explain the theological in film, and filmmakers' conscious or unconscious wrestling with theology. As the media environment becomes richer and more complex, the theological interaction with that environment simultaneously becomes more complex.

This chapter will use some of the studies of theological engagement with film to show the wider media ecology involved or overlooked in three key approaches. Then it will focus more specifically on how media ecology helps to explain the key theological idea of sacramentality as writers apply it to film.

Theological Engagement with Film

Mitchell (2005) offers a path through the world of theological engagement with film, reporting that over time, theologians have shifted and refined three approaches to film (dialogue, appropriation, and encounter) as they more frequently include film in their studies:

> This has moved through five stages: first, discrimination, which concentrates on the morality of specific portrayals; second, visibility, which focuses on how religious figures or themes are represented; third, dialogue, which promotes theological conversations with particular films; fourth, humanism, which examines how film can promote human progress and flourishing; and, fifth, aesthetics, which ultimately explores how the transcendent may be manifested at the cinema. (p. 738)

Mitchell's overview suggests three general categories to illustrate the movements within the wider ecology of film, theological reflection, and theological expression.

First, as cultural products, films promote a certain exploration of experience through dialogue: "While film has the potential to amuse, to entertain, and to distract, it also has great potential to explore profound theological questions and moral dilemmas" (p. 742). Film content, in other words, can provide data for theology. Many of the theologians who take this approach pull plot devices, characters, and even dialogue from specific films in order to highlight a religious potential. Film content offers a kind of homiletic resource—rather than explicating the meaning of a biblical passage, theologians explicate the meaning of a film. That is, they apply theological tools to different sorts of texts. Mitchell explains, with reference to the writing of Neil Hurley:

> Hurley sets out a "cinematic theology." He famously begins by asserting that "movies are for the masses what theology is for an elite." He attempts, for example, to trace transcendence through a number of contemporary films, suggesting that it is possible to identify signs of grace on the screen. (p. 744)

In terms of an ecology of the filmic experience, the film theologians, of whom there are many in addition to Hurley, appear to approach film as a text, much like any other text. In this, they overlook a number of other qualities of film: the visuality, the multimedia nature of the form, the environment in which people watch films, and so on. They focus on one—important, to be sure—but only one aspect of film in order to find theological themes. In so doing, they reinforce an observation that Marshall McLuhan, one of the great practitioners of media ecology, delighted in repeating: with any medium of communication, people focus on the figure rather than the ground (1999a; 1999c, pp. 100–3). The theologians call attention to what they can reduce to print and thus miss the larger context and power of any visual media.

Second, Mitchell's general category of theological engagement with film (which he refers to as appropriation) describes how film illuminates theology, particularly biblical theology. He describes this approach as one in which theologians use film as a hermeneutic or interpretive lens to see relevance for the Bible today. This category draws closer to a media ecology by examining how films "work" on an audience. Mitchell (2005) describes several pioneering efforts:

> Adele Reinhartz uses *Scripture on the Silver Screen* (2003) to assist in the development of "biblical literacy," while the diverse essays in *Screening Scripture* ([Aichele and Walsh], 2002) demonstrate how "intertextual connections between scripture and film" are possible. . . . Kreitzer [1999] provides a careful reading of different versions of *Bram Stoker's Dracula*, both the novel (1897) and the Coppola film (1992), to illuminate the blood motif in Paul's first letter to the church at Corinth. (p. 744)

A number of theologians who take this approach understand that film does more than convey a meaning. If films act upon viewers, then films share in the sacramental principle, the theological principle that holds that created things become a source of the encounter with God, just as the consecrated elements of the sacrament become the Body and Blood of Christ. Again, Mitchell (2005) explains:

> In *Images of the Passion* (1998) Peter Fraser examines the films which in his opinion best portray Christ's passion, describing them as sacramental films. For Fraser, "the sacramental film allows for the appropriation of spiritual presence sought by the devotional writers, but in a public experience" (p. 5) . . . Fraser suggests that if the *Diary of a Country Priest* (1950) is embraced as the director Bresson intends, then viewers "will be brought into a sacramental experience with the living God" (p. 11). . . . For Fraser, the sacramental film can become an object of "mystical contemplation," and he predicts that in the future films may well become "more prominent in popular practices of Christian piety" (p. 6). (p. 745).

Though these writers and others like them claim a special theological function for film, they seldom explain how films bring about such religious or sacramental experiences.

Because those who claim the sacramental principle also look at what McLuhan termed the figure rather than the background of the media, they limit their analysis to a kind of efficient causality. In other words, they narrow the focus to only one of Aristotle's four causes (efficient cause, material cause, final cause, and formal cause). In an example about a house quoted by Eric McLuhan, the bricks and wood constitute the material cause of the house; the work of the bricklayers and carpenters, the efficient cause; and the goal of a house to live in or to rent, the final cause (McLuhan, E., 2005). Those looking at films as religious often seem to ask, "How does it work?" and limit themselves, as do most communication researchers, to the effects of a given thing on another, whether physical or psychological. In his wider comments on media, Marshall McLuhan urges those who would understand how communication has an effect on people to attend not so much to the efficient causality of physics as to formal causality (McLuhan, 2011). In McLuhan's view, formal cause goes well beyond the oft-cited example of the plan or blueprint, the visual analogy of which misses the point (McLuhan, E., 2005). The formal cause has to do with the nature of the thing, of how it exists in the world, of its defining qualities vis-à-vis other actors. The formal cause of a sermon or talk, Marshall McLuhan holds, is the audience. The formal cause of the radio is made up of "the social and psychic changes that the medium causes in the lives of its users" (McLuhan, 1999c, p. 102). Here, too, in this second general category of the theological impact of film, the theologians do not go far enough to understand the sacramental quality that they have identified in films. The effect may be sacramental, but not as a result of efficient causes. We will return to the "sacramental" efficacy of film below.

Third, Mitchell terms his last general area (encounter) "directorial theology." By this he means that filmmakers can evoke or address theological themes in their work.[1] Mitchell recognizes that theology does find its way into films, though perhaps not completely consciously: "Few directors have studied theology in depth and few consciously attempt to articulate theological themes through their work. Their intention is rarely, if ever, explicitly theological" (p. 746).

Still, this category could encompass a large number of films. For example, two related kinds of film that address theological topics are the Bible film and the Jesus film. The former include all those films that retell Bible stories, from the Exodus to the spread of Christianity; the latter refer to films of the life of Jesus (Baugh, 1997). In many ways these films follow a method that

---

[1] Filmmaking is a collaborative effort, and critics have long debated whether the director has an overall influence akin to the author of a written work. Who bears ultimate responsibility: the director, the writer, the editor, the producer, or some combination? For now, we will refer to "filmmakers" to describe the collaborative effort.

resembles an ancient practice of the rabbinical interpreters of the Scriptures, which attempts to fill in the gaps between the biblical text and the experience of a community: "Observable in numerous literary venues, supplemental exegesis, embellishments, or gap fillers reflect a Second Temple [fourth to first century BCE] author's frequent desire to resolve the incomplete contents of a biblical text" (Bateman, 2010, p. 46). Often filmmakers do the same, adding scenes, creating characters, or otherwise supplementing the Bible. Other times, filmmakers create a theological situation, drawing from the Bible, as Krzsztof Kieślowski does in *The Decalogue* (1988), a series of ten television films with plots based on the Ten Commandments, or from religious studies, as George Lucas does in the *Star Wars* films, with their stark battles between good and evil. A different approach occurs with filmmakers like Ingmar Bergman, whose early films had characters wrestling with issues of faith. While each of these examples of directorial theology places theology at the level of plot or dialogue, other films show an attempt on the part of the filmmakers to do theology through the matter of the film, as Robert Bresson does through editing, camera angle, and acting.

The example of Bresson moves closer to a media ecology of film, because his work makes more conscious use of the full features of the cinematic medium (Schrader, 1972). The claim that film can act sacramentally, or participate in the sacramental principle, needs to find support in the nature of the medium and not just in the reduction of a film to a text. Certainly, narratives matter; dialogue and interpersonal appeal plays its part. But a film is not a film when we abstract its plot or character. A film works, as McLuhan points out in terms of every medium, in ways beyond efficient causality. The same holds for the sacramental principle. The theological tradition holds that sacraments operate not through an efficient causality but through a mystical or transcendent experience of God. A sacrament is efficacious not through the action or authority of a minister, nor through some scientific principle, but rather through God's action. In the theological expression, sacraments bring about what they signify. Any number of theologians have attempted to explain this; Appleyard (1971) does so through an appeal to communication.

The Religious and Sacramental Significance of Film

Several of the theological approaches to film have suggested that film may affect people sacramentally—that is, participate in the sacramental principle. Both theologians and film critics interested in religion try to explain the phenomenon of material things manifesting God's presence as it operates in films.

These approaches draw from multiple disciplines, incorporating communication studies, theology, literary criticism, psychology, sociology, film studies, and so on. As Appleyard (1971) notes, communication offers a set of different starting points for understanding sacraments and, by analogy, the sacramental ecology created by film and theology. Rather than beginning with the theological commentary on film, communication and media ecology ask how film can serve religious expression. This is not just a matter of the content of film (or of music, art, or narrative). Media ecology calls a different approach to mind: Does the form itself have a theological impact? What about genre? What about the ways in which imagination plays a role? What about the ways in which people experience film? From the perspective of communication, film can have religious significance in a number of ways: relationally, ritually, narratively, symbolically or performatively, and imaginatively. Each of these expands on the general idea of a formal cause.

First, the early communication scholars working with Paul Watzlawick (Watzlawick, Beavin, and Jackson, 1967) noted that every interpersonal communication simultaneously expresses a particular content and establishes or reinforces a relationship between the communicators. The same thing applies to mediated communication: watching a film puts us into a relationship with the actors, director, marketing people, audience members, etc. Each of these function as a kind of background against which we experience the film. Each of them works to create the experience of the film, including its theological possibilities. Media ecologists tell us that, beyond these relationships, we also infer meaning from the medium itself and from the context in which we use it. For the theological expression, this means that our entire experience with film and with visual imagery enters in, at least as a kind of background structure of relationships. For each film's content, a web of relationships exists. From a theological view, these relationships image the human relationship with God, much as the Incarnation makes God present in human life; as the Letter to the Colossians puts it, Christ Jesus "is the image of the invisible God" (Col 1:15). Human relationships with one another and with creative expression act as analogy to God's relational nature.

Second, James Carey (1989) proposes a clarification of the workings of communication by drawing a contrast between two approaches in mass media studies. Much of the early U.S.-based research in communication effects followed a metaphor of transportation in which communication media carried a message from one individual or place to another. Such a metaphor, he argues, reinforces a focus on the efficient cause or on one set of effects of communication; in short, it promotes an instrumental view of communication. He draws attention instead to European-based research that tended to place communication in cultural roles. To describe this, he uses the metaphor of ritual, where communicators (whether interpersonally or through some medium) engage in a set of ritual behaviors that lead to mutual influence or coordination of actions. The ritual view broadens an understanding of communication; in fact, Carey highlights the religious aspects of ritual in his explication of the concept. People usually reinforce or gain a sense of self-identity from rituals, take rituals for granted, engage in them for any variety of reasons, define the ritual behavior loosely, and regularly make use of them. For Carey the ritual metaphor for communication calls attention to the larger background in which communication functions and directs attention away from a purely instrumental view.

Without trying to make too much of it, film does have strong ritual aspects both in how people view it (darkened cinemas, with groups of people, often as special events, and so on) and in how people react to it. Film serves to focus people's attention in ways unlike oral or written communication. In some other ways, too, film or cinema has ties to worship. A great deal of research shows how visual images play a role in Christianity (see, for example, Goethals, 1990, 1999; Miles, 1985). Those who wish to study the religious aspects of film should begin there—with images and the ritualistic human experience of images. Goethals (1999) argues that, after the Reformation's removal of art from churches, the development of religious imagery shifted to the arts and entertainment. Art and entertainment themselves start to function as a kind of parallel religious discourse, one freed from the dominance of a religious elite. As the Reformation pushed visual images out of the Protestant churches, these grew separately in the secular realm. Today, people can experience a popular culture that takes on many once-religious forms; they also experience a popular culture that takes on the religious tasks of explaining the world, answering ultimate questions, and so on.

A third way that films take on religious significance comes through narrative. This refers to more than a plotline or summary of film action. Instead, the analysis follows an area called narrative theology, which grows from an appreciation of the storytelling in the oral culture of the Bible. Narrative theology has taken different directions: narrative as religious (auto)biography; "narrative as a formal quality of human experience"; and narrative in the Scriptures (Stroup, 1975, p. 133). The latter two hold greater interest for understanding the media ecology of film and theology.

Crites (1971), drawing from literary criticism and from the history of theology, argues that "the formal quality of experience through time is inherently narrative" (p. 291). As a basic human approach to experience, narrative refers not just to particular stories but to a way of understanding. People organize their experience and understanding in narrative ways. When people come to systematically reflect on their belief (that is, to engage in theology), narrative plays a key role. Crites explains:

> For within the traditional cultures there have been some stories that were told, especially on festal occasions, that had special resonance. Not only told but ritually re-enacted, these stories seem to be allusive expressions of stories that cannot be fully and directly told, because they live, so to speak, in the arms and legs and bellies of the celebrants. These stories lie too deep in the consciousness of a people to be directly told: they form consciousness rather than being among the objects of which it is directly aware. . . .
>
> For these are stories that orient the life of people through time, their life-time, their individual and corporate experience and their sense of style, to the great powers that establish the reality of their world. So I call them sacred stories, which in their secondary, written expressions may carry the authority of scripture for the people who understand their own stories in relation to them. (p. 295)

Though Crites does not advert to it, this description of narrative fits well with the practices of oral cultures (Ong, 1982). The long human history before writing led to structures of memory and consciousness that honed narrative as a way to remember. But narrative is not just a story. Rather the entire structure of understanding (religious) experience takes on the form of narrative. This falls, like any communication, into the realm of formal cause.

Crites turns to St. Augustine's *Confessions* to find confirmation of this approach. The *Confessions*, probably the first instance of a spiritual autobiography, examines the inner form of experience. Augustine finds in memory the key means of organizing experience (Crites, 1971, pp. 298–99); that organization has the design of a narrative constructed of images. Here Augustine draws on an understanding of memory based on classical memory techniques (Yates, 1966), where images have places, mark places, and serve to store associated memories. In many of the instructions on memory, the rhetor (for these places developed out of rhetoric and played a constitutive role in the basic educational system for which Augustine had been an instructor) learned to walk figuratively through the places in memory, looking upon the images stored there; these in turn provided links to the ideas remembered. The speaker then needed only to draw the narrative together. For Augustine, according to Crites, "all the sophisticated activities of consciousness literally re-collect the images lodged in memory into new configurations, reordering past experience. But that would be impossible were it not for the much more naïve functioning of memory itself, preserving the images drawn from experience" (p. 299). In the *Confessions* Augustine finds God in these places of memory, even when he had not stored the divine image there. Crites, following Augustine, discovers that the structure of experience is narrative, a narrative drawn on the images of memory, and the structure itself has theological implications. One wonders that Crites and other proponents of narrative theology did not think immediately of film, a medium that structures itself on image and narrative.

Some have criticized Crites for an unproven theory of the role of the image, for the potentially unreliable nature of narrative, and for the unsuitability of narrative for theological concepts (Hartt, 1984). While the epistemological critique holds merit, particularly as to the correspondence of narrative and concept, it fails to note the radical disjunction in human thought brought about by the kinds of theoretical conceptualization introduced by writing. Writing leads to different ways of handling concepts and, according to Ong, of different kinds of conceptual thought. So Hartt, for example, is absolutely correct that narratives do not offer the same kinds of concepts that philosophical analysis does. However, Hartt does not investigate the status of the kinds of concepts that appear in oral discourse, nor how much people still make use of those kinds of concepts or of narrative patterns in thought. If the contemporary communication situation has changed, becoming more oral (or embracing, in Ong's term, "secondary orality," 1978a), then the older patterns of understanding and thinking will reassert themselves. Humans never lost the ability to think in narratives; they added more kinds of thought with writing. The residual narrative patterns still offer a consistent approach to think through a problem, as film studies clearly shows.

Other approaches to narrative begin with the Gospels and move from there to the possibilities of narrative for theological expression. Navone (1984) roots his approach to narrative theology in an analysis of human thinking and how it interacts with God's action or "God's story." He presumes that the structure of God's revelation correlates with the structure of human thinking. Characterizing narrative theology as a kind of "Christian anthropology," he connects this kind of theology to the Incarnation: "If the Word of God incarnate is the life story of God, the narrative theologian will critically reflect on that story for learning to know God" (p. 11). Like Crites, Navone finds the basis of narrative theology in the patterns of human consciousness and the role of images in human memory. To establish this point, he turns to the work of theologians who follow the transcendental method, investigating with them the conditions for the possibility of knowing in general and of knowing God in particular:

> Our life stories and their narrative expressions reflect the transcendental-categorical structure of human consciousness. Our transcendental awareness, the world of our interiority, seeks objectification in external interaction with other persons and with our environment, with the tendency to manifest itself in all the dimensions of our life story. . . .
>
> Even our most spiritual knowledge involves the work of imagination. (p. 13)

For Navone, narrative theology consists of examining how people "react to and appropriate the story of Jesus" (p. 15). After demonstrating the method by a reading of key Gospel texts, he offers a series of "theses for a theology of story" (pp. 143–53). These include:

> 2.6 The human action that defines a story is a declaration of a basic faith. . . .
>
> 2.6.11 Since the communication and expression of faith transcends all conceptual knowledge, both its expression and communication lie in the symbolic mode of consciousness, symbol being defined as the best possible expression of an unknown content. . . .
>
> 2.62 Images, and the stories that contain them, provide models and motives for the decisions and action that shape our lives. (pp. 145–46)

Writing some years after Crites, Navone addresses in more detail the epistemological problem of narrative and, by grounding his work in the narrative form of the Gospels, he maintains a parallel between narrative in theology and narrative in oral cultures.

Another theologian who urges a narrative methodology, John Shea (1980) sees stories as a means to connect individuals with a tradition, one often taken for granted (p. 77) but that helps people make sense of their lives through a kind of dialogue that compares one story to another (p. 79). The tradition (or the existing narratives) provides a context: "A concern of contemporary living searches the tradition for perspectives and values which resonate with it" (p. 82); in turn, the tradition "widens the scope of the concern and so makes possible a new approach to it" (p. 83). Presuming the kind of hermeneutic described by Gadamer as fusion of horizons (1975, pp. 337–41, 358), Shea argues that people make meaning, particularly religious meaning, through a matching of stories. Everyone has a story (p. 87) and the stories have a religious dimension—they go beyond any one individual because they affirm ultimate meaning (p. 88). People do not tell stories unless they have a hope that the stories resonate with others or with the tradition: "Narrative is an inherent quality of experience and so a primal form of human discourse. Therefore, if theistic faith is to be rooted in experience, it seems it will have a preference for expressing itself in story" (p. 88).

Stories can take on many forms and many topics. While Shea focuses on the religious story, what he writes about "stories of faith" applies to all narratives, since in his view all narratives—even nonreligious ones—affirm an implicit faith. He lists seven elements of such stories:

> (1) People relate stories of coming to faith. These are tales in which the initiative of God is stressed. (2) Within these stories the reality of God is acknowledged and God language enters into the conversation. (3) A felt-perception of how the reality of God relates to us is expressed and conveyed in images. (4) The images generate further stories which explore the relationship. (5) These stories yield insights and values. (6) The insights and values have implications. They push toward strategy and action. (7) The faith-motivated behavior yields another set of stories, the stories of enacted faith. (p. 90)

The process is a recursive one and could apply to any narrative. Over time, these narratives will lead to a more explicit faith.

Narrative theology offers a way to understand how film can have a sacramental impact. The very process of story and image evokes a response to something beyond a given narrative. Navone, Shea, and Crites all suggest this. For Navone, "human stories are implicit answers to the fundamental questions that arise concerning life and death" (p. 146). People, as Crites (1971) argues, think of themselves and order their memories in narrative terms:

> From the sublime to the ridiculous, all a people's mundane stories are implicit in its sacred story, and every mundane story takes soundings in the sacred story. But some mundane stories sound out greater depths than others. Even the myths and epics, even the scriptures, are mundane stories. But in these, as well as in some works of literary art, and perhaps even in some merry little tales that seem quite content to play on the surface, the sacred stories resonate. (p. 296)

Not only does such a view of narrative connect to self-understanding; it also suggests how people outside of the religious elite express their understanding of faith, that is, their theology, when other options remain closed to them. Each of these unofficial narrative theologians also includes images as fundamental to the narrative process, another point of contact for film. Film, then, in narrative content and style, in image, and in form touches its audience in a way consistent with the sacramental principle.

Fourth, as noted already, Appleyard (1971) turned to communication to help explain that principle. To get there, he begins with symbols, since sacraments (like narratives) involve the "symbolic mode of consciousness." He then couples the understanding of symbols with the idea of performative utterances. Following Langer, Appleyard notes two kinds of symbols: discursive and expressive or presentational (p. 186). The former result from a logical reasoning, but the latter operate differently: "So long as it functions as 'a vehicle for the conception of object,' the symbol is inextricably bound up with the concept of the object which it 'symbolizes'" (p. 186). To explain this, he cites Coleridge on symbol: "It always partakes of the reality which it renders intelligible; and while it enunciates the whole, abides itself as a living part in that unity of which it is the representative" (Coleridge, 1858, pp. 437–38, quoted in Appleyard, 1971, p. 187). Appleyard finds a further explanation in the philosophical theology of Karl Rahner:

> The basic principle of his [Rahner's] ontology of the symbol is that "all beings are by their nature symbolic, because they necessarily 'express' themselves in order to attain their own nature." "A being comes to itself by means of 'expression,' in so far as it comes to itself at all. The expression, that is, the symbol . . . is the way of knowledge of the self possession of self, in general" (Rahner, 1961, p. 230). So he defines symbol as "the self-realization of a being in the other, which is constitutive of its essence" (p. 234). (p. 187)

The symbol, then, presents something to human consciousness by representing it as an expression, related to itself but different. It does so directly, as a "presentation," and not as a process of reasoning. The symbol moves something, to return to communication terms, from one medium to another—from an object to language, from an experience to an image, and so on. The symbol plays an essential role in people's coming to know.

Appleyard next connects the symbolic mode to action, to the action of structuring the social world. The symbols (first language, but other kinds of symbols as well) have an effect on people because of the way that people use language, not just to describe or denote but to persuade, command, promise, obligate, connect—all of the social relations possible. In sketching this out, in terms of sacramental signification, Appleyard follows J. L. Austin's more communicative, or speech-act, theory of language (pp. 188–91). Such a theory seems well suited to oral cultures, since those cultures do not separate words from experience, as writing allows. For Appleyard, these two understandings, of the cognitive role of symbol and of the social action of symbol, help to illuminate how the sacramental principle works in human consciousness. While Appleyard is, of course, interested in the theological and religious use and actions of that sacramental principle, his analysis applies to some extent to the impact of film in general as well as to film's potential role in theological expression. As a medium of images and of multiple media of communication, film relies on presentational symbols. As a social medium, film also partakes in the performative register of language. Once again, an examination of the ecology of the film suggests ways that a film might function theologically.

Fifth, Blake (2000), a film critic, offers yet another way to regard films as participating in the sacramental principle and, in so doing, brings together a number of the threads that have emerged from the different communication and theological theorists presented here. Blake presumes the validity of auteur criticism, that is, the approach that regards a film as the result of a director's vision and ideas. He also accepts as fact that film images function symbolically and that these can have the force of archetypes (pp. 2–3). Because many directors of films that theologians have identified as religious deny any religious intent, Blake chooses to examine the films themselves rather than any authorial intention. He does this by reference to "imagination" (pp. 5–6), the human faculty that stores up, draws on, and shapes images of the kind described by Crites and Augustine. Blake explains further:

> Through the imagination artists remember and forget, recall, repress, and reconstruct their world. The artist, perhaps more perceptively than the rest of us, sees some elements of the story as important and worth sharing with a larger public and struggles, at times intuitively, to find the images and words to re-create that world. In bringing these experiences to the screen, filmmakers interpret and articulate them in a way that is consistent with their own imagination, shaped as it is by a particular web of previous experiences and beliefs. (p. 6)

Along with ideological critics, Blake argues that a host of cultural, familial, educational, psychological, national, religious, gender-related—and the list goes on—elements influence the imagination, shaping it to unconsciously take for granted ways of seeing the world, of imaging the world. Blake wishes to tease out the religious influences, since he seeks to find them in the films of individual directors, even when those directors do not make or seek to make a theological film.

Is there a religious imagination? Sociological evidence offers an affirmative response. Using national survey data, Andrew Greeley conducted an analysis of differences in approaches to the world among adherents to different religious traditions. Seeing religion as "encoded in the personality by symbols" (1990, p. 39), Greeley connects the imagining of the world—the symbolic thinking that emerges more clearly with images—to religion. For Greeley "religion operates in the same area of the personality where artistic expression and scientific insight flourish" (p. 36). Further, "religion is a system of symbols which acts to establish powerful, pervasive, and long-lasting moods and motivations in men by formulating conceptions of a general order of existence" (p. 37). Greeley's data analysis (detailed in his book) supports his hypothesis that a group's religious background does indeed influence the images through which they view the world.

To describe the differences in the religious imagination, Greeley turned to the theological work of David Tracy, who drew a contrast between analogical and dialectical approaches to God in the Catholic and Protestant traditions (Tracey, 1981). Studying the history of theology and the work of key thinkers, Tracey notes, "Two major conceptual languages have served as the principal candidates for this task in theology [to reflect on the original religious language]: analogical and dialectical languages" (1981, p. 408). The former articulates "similarity-in-difference" (p. 408) while the latter, "dissimilarity in similarity" (p. 409). Greeley correlated this insight into theological method with his sociological data on how U.S. Catholics and Protestants view the world, concluding that the Catholic imagination leans towards analogical thinking and the Protestant towards dialectical. He explains:

> My central argument will be that Catholics differ from other Americans in that their imaginations tend to be more "sacramental" (or to use David Tracy's word, "analogical"). By that I mean that Catholics are more likely to imagine God as present in the world and the world as revelatory instead of bleak. Much that is thought to be distinctively Catholic results from this distinctive style of imagining—the importance of community, institution, and hierarchy; the emphasis on ritual and ceremonial; the interest in the fine and lively arts; devotion to saints, angels, holy souls, and especially the Mother of Jesus; reverence for status and images; the use of blessings, medals, and prayer beads. (p. 4)

In other words, "Catholic [theological] 'classics' assume a God who is present in the world, disclosing Himself in and through creation. The world and all its events, objects, and people tend to be somewhat like God. . . . Protestant classics, on the other hand, assume a God who is radically absent from the world . . . The world and all its events, objects, and people tend to be radically different from God" (p. 45). Ever the careful sociologist, Greeley stresses that these are tendencies and not a zero-sum division. Supported by other sociological investigations from Durkheim and Weber, Greeley suggests that the narratives (writ large—the whole way of explaining the world) of the two groups lead to dramatically different ways of seeing the world and interacting with it. Blake expands on this idea:

> For Catholics, God is present in the world. Logically, then, salvation comes through the human community with God at its center. For Protestants, God is absent. Salvation, then, must be achieved by the person who breaks away from the sinful world and approaches God as an individual. (p. 9)

Such attitudes overflow into ways of decorating churches, obligations to others in the community, dependence on others, and a host of other things, including film.

Using this model, Blake examines films of six key American directors who grew up in the Catholic tradition, looking for signs of a Catholic or analogical imagination. The key theological markers for Blake are sacramentality (finding God in the material creation), mediation, and community. To give just one example, here is Blake's brief discussion of sacramentality:

> In keeping with the ... notion of the Catholic present-God, as opposed to a Protestant absent-God, a Catholic imagination will tend to "see God in all things," and therefore the material universe, like the objects in front of the camera, have a sacred or sacramental character to them. These objects will signify a supernatural value and meaning beyond their immediate material surface. For a Catholic film maker, "things" will have a spiritual meaning, revealing the world as the arena of God's presence. By contrast, the critic, screenwriter, and director Paul Schrader, a former Calvinist divinity student, maintains that the spiritual can be reached more effectively in films of "sparse means," when all the decoration and distraction have been removed. For one with a formal Protestant education, like Schrader, the material universe is antithetical to the spiritual. To reach spiritual realities, his dialectical Protestant imagination insists that materiality be removed from the scene. (p. 13).

Blake thus provides a fifth approach to understand how a film might participate in the sacramental principle: through the imagination. The media ecology of film vis-à-vis theology invites a closer look at images and their roles in both forming and expressing the imagination.

Rather than examining only the "content" (or "figure," to use McLuhan's term) of films for a possible theological role, the media ecology approach encourages a look at the ground, particularly at relationships established by films (with the audience, with actors, and with cultural entities), at the ritual role played by films, at narrative as itself a theological enterprise (especially given its long role in oral cultures), at the symbolic and performative nature of filmic expression, and at the imagination as a producer of film. Though not explicitly discussed, each of these elements interacts with other elements of the ecology of film: the history of art and image, the modalities of watching films, the tradition of script writing, the economic structure of the industry, and so on. Overall, the impact of the film does not come only from the plot, story, or special effects, but from the way of seeing and experiencing. In this, the theology (the understanding of faith experience) plays one role; a second comes from the capacity of film to create a religious or faith experience.

• • •

All of this suggests that theology does not remain solely under the control of the professional theologians or even of the Christian churches. The larger discussion here moves the consideration of theology out into popular or secular culture. Religious impulses do not disappear from people's lives when they walk out the door of a church. There is a "popular" theology embedded in contemporary culture, a (perhaps not entirely consistent) way of interpreting the world and asking those ultimate—and ultimately "religious"—questions that Navone and Greeley identify. This popular theology may not use the concepts of Christianity, or it may borrow some and reject others. What makes it a theology is that there is a more or less systematic approach—in this instance expressed in a film—to answering religious questions. The format is narrative and the medium follows the aesthetic rules of expression of images. Almost any narrative-driven, successful film in one way or another offers something that takes the audience beyond themselves and beyond the film. Often good and evil (or a battle between good and evil) characterize such stories. But these can take on many faces of evil: these are not only the obvious external evils of destruction or violence, but also the interior evils of jealousy, loneliness, broken relationships, power, betrayal, and deception.

The media ecology of film and theology offers a dual lesson on how film participates in the sacramental principle and how film has become a locus for popular theology, done in a form quite distinct from the tradition of a written theology.

11
SOCIAL MEDIA

Opening Up the Theological Ecosystem

In the first decade of the twenty-first century, a loose Christian community formed around the websites and blogs of several Evangelicals dedicated to a further understanding of the "End Times," particularly as described in the book of Revelation. The group created a kind of "virtual ekklesia" or church (Howard, 2011). The individual members for the most part had never met offline but found encouragement, support, and teaching in their fellowship independent of any congregation or denomination. Made insular by their central belief in the End Times, they nevertheless celebrated their version of Christianity in frequent communication. More than this, the teachings of the most frequent writers created a theological body of texts central to the group's identity.

From early on in the history of the Internet, scholars have distinguished "religion online" from "online religion" (Helland, 2000). The former term refers to the ways that established churches or congregations make, create, or use online resources—posting information about religion (doctrine, belief, organizational structure, and services), responding to questions, and creating a virtual presence to support their physical presence wherever that may be. The latter, a phenomenon loosely akin to radio or television evangelists' conducting preaching and worship through the media, refers to people's use of the Internet and its affordances to worship together without being physically together, to create religious communities or groups of all kinds, and to participate in religious activities.

The rise of online religion suggests another site for a media ecology of theology. The rise of the Internet in the latter part of the twentieth century illustrates how the communication ecosystem changed and how it changed theology. The Internet began in a fairly well-established communication environment, one marked by both individual (or interpersonal) communication media and practices as well as a variety of mass media and their associated practices. Each medium and its attendant practices not only fostered communication but also functioned as a kind of information management—the shaping of ideas, the storage of thought and information, the access to and sharing (or restriction) of that information, and so on. For example, printed materials fostered fairly concise expression, thoughts presented in ways structured for reading rather than hearing, indexed material, and resources available openly to those who could purchase or borrow the publications. Breaking this down further, each print medium had its own organizational pattern: newspapers with key articles on the first pages, highlighted by headlines whose size indicated the value of the article; magazines with longer articles arranged by topics; academic journals with essays prepared in more or less rigid formats to facilitate the location of information. Similarly, television content followed a set of generic conventions, with different kinds of programming signaling different kinds of thought—commentary, comedy, drama, or news. Even the programming schedule marked importance and hierarchy by time of day or by interruption for vital news. In short, the communication world managed relationships, ideas, knowledge, social structures, interaction, business, and even religious reflections.

In that pre-Internet world, personal and interpersonal communication rested on face-to-face interactions, telephony, letter writing, and the postal system. Larger-scale interactions—those characteristic of a community, church, city, or state—made use of group or mass media. The cultural, religious, or legal systems interacted with these communication systems to protect, limit, or promote discourse. In the United States, where the chief media systems took shape over the hundred years previous to the rise of the Internet, newspapers and magazines first came to economic independence and gained the Constitutional protection of free speech, defined in parallel to the interpersonal rights of speech in free assembly. Both appear in the First Amendment together with a guarantee of freedom of religion, the practice of which at that time included both assembly and the use of printed materials like the Bible. The Courts later extended the Constitutional protection of speech, the press, and assembly in various degrees to film, radio, and television. As older media, print also had developed business models that in some ways influenced those of the other mass media. As even older phenomena, religious practices, preaching, and theology existed alongside the media and made use of them, usually to support belief or to spread ideas. These formed part of the public sphere, of the communication world, alongside political, economic, cultural, educational, and other types of expression. In turn, the interpersonal and mass media interacted with these spheres. While not determinative of a given social reality or expressive style, the communication media allowed particular patterns of thought and expression and, once people adopted them, reinforced those choices.

This communication world, with its rhetorical, legal, and economic structures, had its problems, limitations, and characteristic styles of communication. Although the Constitution guaranteed the right of free expression to all citizens, the press critic A. J. Liebling had trenchantly remarked that in the United States "freedom of the press is guaranteed only to those who own one" (1960, p. 109). Similarly, the other mass media had erected barriers to entry, many based on cost but some on scarcity of bandwidth (i.e., radio and television), others on an editorial gatekeeping process that filtered publication through expert judgment, and others on educational level. In religious discourse or theology, education and ordination placed limits on expression. In this communication environment, the right to communicate and the practice of communication more often meant the right to receive (approved) information from established sources. As many critical communication scholars have pointed out, this particular ecology of communication limited thought as much as it promoted it. Educated formally or informally within the system, people literally could not imagine things outside the system.

Theology itself developed a set of practices within this communication environment that in some ways mirrored what had happened with the media. While older methods of theological reflection, like preaching, art, and music, remained in the churches, these lost credibility as "theology." Churches, universities, and seminaries usually restricted that title to official or doctrinal statements and to work carried on in approved academic fashion—the presentation of papers at conferences and the publication of reviewed articles and books. By the mid-twentieth century, theology as a subject matter and as a work of the Christian churches had both expanded and constricted. It had expanded in terms of the specialized topics addressed: biblical theology, systematic theology, pastoral theology, historical theology, feminist theology, liberation theology, the theology of culture, ecumenical theology, and so on—each with particular methodologies for study. But theology had also constricted to the discourse of a highly trained elite who policed themselves and in various ways submitted to the authority of a religious or denominational body. Theology had become an academic discipline as well as a specialized discourse of the Christian churches. The ordinary reflection on belief—Anselm's faith-seeking-understanding—no longer seemed like theology.

An Ecology of the Internet

An analysis based on the media ecology model asks what changes when something new enters into a communication system. In this instance, the Internet came into the communication ecosystem as briefly describe above. Envisioned as an incremental improvement, the Internet linked computers to facilitate sharing data, something in the manner of the telephone system networks it initially used. However, the Internet offered other affordances (Ling, 2004, pp. 23–27) by allowing a variety of uses with its flexible design. Individuals and institutions did not need to use these options but could; they could also adapt, adjust, or invent other uses for the Internet structure. In these ways, the Internet was not deterministic but open. One key flexible factor resulted from how the Internet organized information. Data traveled digitally and computer operators quickly realized that binary storage could represent any kind of information: numeric, textual, visual, acoustic, and so on. Computer networks, then, provided not only communication links but also data storage and data processing. When reduced to binary representation for storage, all information appeared alike. With the development of the graphical interfaces of the World Wide Web, nonspecialists could easily access complex data. Further, cataloguing and indexing services made information easier to locate. Improvements in processing and transmission made the Internet more convenient. Software developments allowed anyone to prepare and publish online material. Portable devices for accessing the Internet soon made it ubiquitous.

Interestingly, almost every aspect of the Internet existed in some form before the rise of the Internet and the World Wide Web. That is, people did not invent the Internet or its uses from scratch, but they followed where its openness led. As a network communication system, the Internet differs slightly (but significantly) from telegraph and telephone systems: it does not require a dedicated connection but breaks information into packets which reach their destinations through divergent paths, allowing more efficient use of the system. As information storage, the online system resembles the symbolic storage of books and libraries, but with greater capacity and with immediate access. Its indexing and cataloguing found initial models in books and libraries, but included vastly more references, shifted to database management, and later added powerful algorithms to evaluate and rank information. Access via portable devices grew with the improvement of cellular technologies and with the recognition that, from the perspective of network transmission, voice and data do not differ at all. One could account for much of the Internet's growth in this way. The key development resides not so much in the physical infrastructure but in a new understanding of information—physically, the Internet is an information management system that offers different views of and uses for the information linked to its network structure. As such, it affects and reshapes the entire communication environment.

Just as the Internet itself resembles earlier communication technologies, the impact of the Internet resembles that of earlier developments in communication. Like the printing press (Eisenstein, 1979), the Internet has increased the volume of material available to the public, the speed at which it circulates, and the variety of its content. By removing barriers to material reproduction (as the printing press did by substituting mechanical copying for manual labor) and consequently increasing information storage (as the printing press did in the form of new books), the Internet effectively removes the need to choose which information to publish and store. Its networked storage has room for everything. Like the printing press, which created new forms for the display of information, whether words typographically arranged on a page (Eisenstein, 1983, pp. 63–66; Ong, 1982, pp. 120–23.) or words fashioned into new genres like the essay or academic article and consequent memory systems (Eisenstein, 1979, p. 84; 1983, p. 57; Yates, 1966, p. 131), the Internet's neutrality toward information—typographic, verbal, graphic, aural, or visual—has created new forms for presenting information. Like the telegraph, which increased the speed of communication, erased the factor of distance, and transformed communication into digital information (Standage, 1998), the Internet has extended digital information around the globe. Like the radio, which further removed communication from physical connection through its use of the wireless electromagnetic spectrum, the Internet reaches practically everywhere that a radio signal can go. The Internet (and the social media it supports) also manifest what economists call "network effects." That is, it provides an "explicit benefit" to users who "align [their] behavior with the behavior of others" (Easley and Kleinberg, 2010, p. 509)—the more people who use the network the more valuable it becomes, connecting more people and devices. Ultimately, the impact of the Internet depends not so much on any one particular factor but on the combination of things that leads to a dramatic reinterpretation of information management. Conceptually as well, then, the Internet is an information management system.

In one way or another, all communication manages information. Simple conversation exchanges information between people. Storytelling in groups helps to shape information, store it, and pass it along from one generation to another (Ong, 1982; Assmann, 2006). Writing fixes information in symbolic forms and thus more efficiently and more securely stores it. Learning systems like those of classical rhetoric teach as much ways to organize thought and information as ways to present it intelligently and pleasingly. Indeed a significant part of rhetoric (and other educational systems) addresses the need to remember or store information in ways that facilitate recall. Each development in communication technology has led to a new way of storing and accessing knowledge. For example, the index in a book (something not really practical until the advent of printing with its identical pages; Ong, 1982, pp. 123–24) presents information as objects, subject to readily located places on a page. Ong argues that such things result in a new "noetic economy" or way of thinking, citing the postprint growth of science, mathematical logic, dictionaries, and intertextuality, all made easier through newly developed information storage (1982, pp. 130–32). Seeing words on a page makes people think differently of words, of communication itself. These become objects rather than activities and, as objects, open to manipulation. Similarly, later developments like film and television extend the information effects of drama and storytelling, making it possible to simulate and manipulate more and more complex situations.

Because it combines so many communication forms into one overarching view of data, the Internet continues the communication processing of information, but in ways not fully apparent yet, given its relative youth. However, research into network effects suggests that distributing information management and storage across a wide system lowers the effective cost of managing that information, increases the amount of information available to each member of the network, and increases the perceived value of that information. Another network effect favors standards, fostering uniformity for data storage and consequently easing the wider use of that data (Easley and Kleinberg, 2010, pp. 509–10). Increasing the availability of data and fostering the ways people think with and about them, this network effect indirectly reshapes how people learn, think, and work. For example, online sites combine text, graphics, animation, images, sound, and video in approaches that move people away from text-only definitions of knowing. YouTube serves as an example of the visualization of thinking with its abundance of display, not unlike *Pilgrim's Progress*' Vanity Fair (Laytham, 2012, p. 51), but now equipped with algorithms to decide what people want, teaching yet another kind of information management even as it remains somewhat hidden from users (Detweiler, 2013, p. 420). These approaches to thinking even affect physics and mathematical education resources, which combine equations with graphical and photographic representations of the phenomena they describe, linking the abstract with the concrete. Here and in other disciplines, the whole movement to the purely symbolic representation of knowledge has slowed. Similarly, a subject like ethics now involves case studies, enacted in dramatic portrayals.

Though they could have developed in many different ways, some features of the Internet and the social networking sites available online also lead to specific noetic consequences. The search algorithms of Google, for example, make information retrieval rapid and seemingly comprehensive. Much like the news industry, as Bernard Cohen (1963) observed, this organized presentation of information "does not tell people what to think, but what to think about"; in addition, Google's search results may have an even more powerful effect by telling people what information to think with, and teaching them that thought consists of doing things with that information. Google's algorithms, like data standards, have both positive and negative consequences—not all information exists online nor does all information lend itself to the kinds of storage Google excels at searching. Not all information fits into standard categories. Further, and perhaps more important, not all thought consists of data manipulation. Similarly, Wikipedia and other online encyclopedias provide crowdsourced information, drawing on the expertise of large groups and depending on the self-correcting processes of massive peer review. Such online resources both promote and limit thought, shape and constrain thinking. Another Internet feature that helps to shape the contemporary noetic economy appears in blogs and social network posts—personal commentary and narratives, some of which are interactive. Virtually available to anyone with Internet access, blog and social media commentary widens the scope of any discussion, giving a public voice around the world to people seldom heard. Creating a blog or social media post requires neither credentials nor licensing, but only access to the Internet and the knowledge to use simple software. On the other hand, the form of a blog or post seldom fosters sustained argument. Here the communication environment offers wider participation at the risk of less in-depth participation. A less-reflected-upon feature of this noetic economy of abundant information takes advantage of the unconscious rhetorical bias towards repeated information. Anything met often enough and reinforced through many sources carries the presumption of believability. This results in a kind of contradiction of Cohen's claim that communication media do not tell people what to think but what to think about. Sadly, unsupported claims, if repeated often enough, do tell people what to think. Finally, and a bit ironically, the social networking structure of the Internet requires no preexisting community to support communication interaction; instead, it creates an online community (whether permanent or fleeting) from virtual passersby. As Howard (2011) found in his case studies of the virtual ekklesia of End Times believers, this feature of the Internet gave place for theological discussions not occurring in established churches but also sheltered people from criticism as they moved in and out of these communities.

Other characteristics of the initial noetic economy of the Internet, as noted already, include an expansion of thought beyond verbal argument to include visual images, graphics, video, and drama, together with their characteristic ways of presenting information—both a photograph and a play organize information and have done so for generations. However, the Internet makes more visual and audio information available to more people than any previous communication tool. The Internet gives human beings more information to think about, more tools to think with, more approaches to that information, and more ways to organize and recall that information.

Foley (2006) likens the level of participation, the kinds of participation, and the embedding of thought through participation in the online world to oral cultures that simultaneously store, share, and shape information in the active processes of storytelling:

> Thus, oral tradition and the Internet share some core characteristics. Neither medium is a static retrieval mechanism for data; each is ever-evolving and brought into being by the performer and computer user. Both are demonstrably kinetic, emergent, creative activities, and both are linked to actual performance (as opposed to being predetermined and fossilized within the covers of a book). Finally, and because of these shared features, oral tradition and the Internet are phenomenologically distinct from our default, prosthetic (because text-modeled) concept of memory. To put it aphoristically, oral tradition and the Internet mimic the way we think. (p. 96)

From a media ecology perspective, the process Foley describes may work in a more circular fashion. Oral tradition and the Internet may mimic the way we think initially—all those borrowings from earlier communication structures mentioned earlier—but they also shape and reinvent the way we think. They redefine information management and the noetic economy in which we live. And they can define the world for us.

Though not specifically concerned with noetic processes, Laytham (2012), in a theologically informed critique of the technologies underpinning the social media world, offers a different set of metaphors (drawn from entertainment) to describe its theological information management: pleasure, play, attention, leisure, and audience (p. 11). Each acts as a heading for a theological perspective based on how people use the media and thus how they think. Each of them correlates with ways that people have used older media and how those media indirectly influence their thinking. Laytham refers to these as "a kind of cultural competency, or linguistic fluency, or normative practice" (p. 9). These represent a shift in the theological paradigm, which Lindbeck (1984) had proposed as falling into three types: one "emphasizing the cognitive aspects of religion and stresses the ways in which church doctrines function as informative propositions"; a second "focuses on . . . the 'experiential-expressive' dimension of religion, and it interprets doctrines as noninformative and non-discursive symbols of inner feelings, attitudes, or existential orientations"; the third "attempts to combine these two emphases" in a kind of two-dimensional matrix (p. 16). A focus on the media ecology illustrates more clearly how the media environment affords the tools by which people move from cognitive to experiential to expressive in various combinations.

Media Ecology and (Online) Theology

The communication environment, with its information management created by the Internet and networking technologies, provides the context for theology today, whether it occurs on- or offline. As part of this larger social world, theology cannot claim immunity to these forces. The changing ecology has several consequences: these touch upon the noetic economy of theology, the participants and authority of those doing theology, the topics addressed by theology, the approaches to doing theology, and the way that theology might understand its own environment.

Changes resulting from a developing communication environment have happened before to theology, but perhaps not as dramatically. Religion and theology literally organized the Western world's calendar until the civil, business, and online calendars took over (Detweiler, 2013, p. 12). Theology tended to keep to its own world, though other things influenced it. Over fifty years ago, Ong (1969) asked how theology and theologians used communication media. Among other things, he argued that they used them to think and to share information, but more significantly from a noetic perspective, to shape acceptable arguments and to widen their circle of peers. That is, improved communication—and in 1969 Ong had in mind the post, the telephone, television, travel, and book distribution—led to more contact among theologians and to a greater diversity of cultures and ideas entering into theological dialogue. Today, of course, no longer is one culture, methodology, or understanding seen as defining theology; every local theology (a concept not explicitly reflected upon those fifty years ago) must take into account other local theologies. Contemporary theology has heard previously unrepresented voices, voices sometimes suppressed by the ecosystems in which theology previously existed—such as women's voices, non-Western voices, and indigenous voices. The world of theology has become richer and more complex due to the increased ease of communication. Theology takes account of global concerns more now than even twenty years ago. People experience the world differently and must reflect theologically in a different fashion in this Internet age.

People also express themselves differently: the essay, which emerged after years of familiarity with printing technologies, represents only one form for theology today. Ong (1969) argued that the essay freed theology from the polemic and dogmatism of an earlier age in theology; now, the possibilities of the Internet offer new freedom for expression. While academic theology will not disappear, it increasingly shares the stage with narrative theologies, visual theologies, musical theologies, multimedia theologies, and every other kind of faith-seeking-understanding available online. This noetic shift, a result of the information management fostered by online resources described above, leads to a broader consciousness of method, perhaps more fragmented and data-driven thinking, and less long-form argumentation. Commentary—a form present in patristic homilies, oral tradition, and rhetorical culture (Assmann, 2006, p. 74)—has returned to theology in the online world.

Second, because anyone with access to the Internet can enter into online discussions or publish materials, the community of those doing theological reflection (if not the academic theology community) has become much more open. Anyone who wishes to may post on theological topics. In one of the few empirical studies of the people and content of religious blogging, for example, Campbell (2010a), sampled three hundred and sixty-seven Christian bloggers and found that, of those who stated a profession, 34 percent were pastors and another 28 percent either mission workers, teachers, or students of theology (p. 259). Put another way, 38 percent came from outside the established theological communities. Given the nature of the study, Campbell does not review "official" theological sites—the doctrinal webpages of churches; the pages of theological journals, professional associations, or schools; nor the webpages with formats other than blogs. While many official theological sources exist that somehow authorize their participants (i.e., through academic credentials or ordination or through some other approval process), many other voices also appear online. Some of these offer an ongoing process of faith-seeking-understanding, returning theology to its roots, while others, like those Howard (2011) studied, argue for a particular reading of the Scriptures. One key difference that emerges in the online world is that these are (from the perspective of religious bodies or schools) unofficial, unlicensed, or unapproved sites; even if they may work as religious professionals offline, the bloggers and site managers have by and large not sought any church approbation for their online work. The Internet requires none and, as a communication medium appealing to a younger audience, opens theology to groups different from the usual creators and readers of theology.

Campbell (2010a) did find a fairly consistent conservatism in the blogs that she reviewed. Developing ideas from an earlier study (Campbell, 2007), she divides the idea of "religious authority" into four types of authority: "religious hierarchy, religious structures, religious ideology, and religious texts" (Campbell, 2010a, p. 257). The content analysis of the blogs showed that "bloggers were 12 times more likely to affirm a category of religious authority in their blogs than they were to challenge or speak critically about them" (p. 260). Where bloggers did challenge theological ideas or enter into debates, they tended to take the side of traditional church teachings and oppose newer approaches to theology, such as feminist theology. This study, which Campbell identifies as consistent with other recent studies (p. 269) indicates that, while the Internet has broadened the participation in theology, it has also served to empower traditional religious authorities and traditional theological teachings. Campbell suggests that some of this may result from the demographics of the blogging population: overwhelmingly male, largely affiliated with the churches, and traditional in their beliefs (pp. 270–71). She also notes that Cheong, Halavais, and Kwon (2008) argue that the blogs tend to take an educational approach, but—more significantly here—also "build alternative frameworks for religious interpretation and that religious bloggers operate outside the realms of the conventional nuclear church" (Campbell, 2010a, p. 272). Revisiting the online religious world, Campbell (2021) tracked how the concept of authority has developed online. Scholars describe traditional religious authority as role based, as exercising power or control over religious discourse, and as relational (pp. 22–29). However, different approaches emerge online and help to illustrate how the online ecology has influenced theology. The authority of what Campbell terms "religious digital creatives" comes from "algorithmic" sources, or a trust in automated systems that rank postings and ideas (p. 29–31). That model leads to several categories of people exercising religious authority online: media influencers, thought leaders, and digital leaders (pp. 33–34). From this initial evidence, the alternative noetic system fostered by the Internet has only begun to create different approaches to doing theology in the realm of online work, including blogs, websites, and content curation. The Internet has also allowed these online theologians to operate outside of church supervision and to help create an atmosphere of public opinion in the church.

But traditional sources of theological teaching—usually denominational groups—have not ignored this growth. They themselves create online materials, often imitating the forms popularized by blogs and social media posts. Some use the affordances of the internet to reinforce tradition and traditional theology. For example, the Catholic Church uses the Pope's Twitter and other social media accounts as well as online papal activities to highlight both the ministry and teaching office of the papacy. Sometimes this leads to a kind of theological clash between old and new theological attitudes baked into the technologies, as appears in the Vatican websites: "Just as the real-world Church is centered on the papal office and the Vatican hierarchy, the Church's virtual presence reflects a similar pattern. However, . . . this pattern is challenged by the post-Conciliar ethos of the Church which supports the precepts of the Second Vatican Council (1962–1965), and which includes an emphasis on evangelization through social communications, a commitment to the role of the laity, closer relations with other religions, and the pursuit of religious freedom" (Lynch, 2015, p. 97). Other efforts, especially the Pope's Twitter account, as noted by Narbona (2016), both build on existing authority and manifest digital authority by drawing on the "rules imposed by new technology": appropriateness, timeliness, technical specialization, and relationship (p. 94). Here, Narbona concludes, the Pope has effectively achieved a "transforming or transcendental leadership," one that depends on the demands of the technology: number of followers and retweets (p. 106).

The restrictions on church attendance imposed by the pandemic of 2020 led to a more active social media presence of official denominational sites, often from the bottom up, with local parishes or churches joining to conduct services, lead prayer, answer questions, and organize groups. Others have created online religious experiences through spiritual resources (see, for example, pathwaystogod.org) or even virtual pilgrimages (Golan and Martini, 2018). What the different denominational groups do in the online world typically reflects both their own theological tradition and their view of communication media. Campbell (2010b) presents evidence that "the choices made by religious internet users are often strongly informed by the religious communities to which they belong. These choices related to internet use and innovation are also often guided by previously established views about religious authority, community, and even older mediums such as printed text" (pp. 21–22).

Third, the online world has just begun to affect the topics of theology. Where academic theologians might address specialized topics and provide a wealth of materials, the Christian bloggers and social media users take a more limited approach. In the specific area of theology, which Campbell codes as "religious ideology," she found that the bloggers most frequently address topics such as theological debates, the nature of God, Christian practices, salvation, sacraments, and the nature of the Church (2010b, pp. 262–63). Detweiler's (2013) examination of the impact of digital technologies leads him to see a "shift from the study of God driven by reason to the *experience* of God rooted in *revelation*" (p. 11). Howard's (2011) study of the End Times online community found a more single-minded focus on the Bible, particularly the Book of Revelation. He noted that this group almost exclusively appealed to the authority of the Bible (as Campbell also found for many of the bloggers) or to a personal revelation. In choosing topics for theological discussion, Howard's group depended more on issues raised by the group and less on a catechism or a set of church doctrines. Topics emerge in almost random orders and not arranged by any syllabus—the FAQ (frequently asked questions) has replaced the *Summa* as the guide to theology, something consistent with the information management tools afforded by the Internet.

Fourth, the characteristics of the information management of the online world have affected the approaches people take to theology. In addition to the noetic effects leading to the practices of commentary already mentioned, online theology exhibits network effects, with more popular sites becoming even more popular, thanks to the ranking algorithms of Google or the cross-posting with other online publishers. Social networking sites like Facebook and microblogging technologies like Twitter encourage people to follow particular online personalities, who become—in the language of older communication research—opinion leaders and gatekeepers, setting the agenda for subsequent discussions. Popular blogging software and Web 2.0 designs encourage responses to online material, with the post and response formats creating a kind of written conversation. These create new theological methods where the reflection on faith takes place in fits and starts, among many people, moving from one concern to another, often responding to current events. Clergy may or may not play a part in people's online religious search or in any religious quest; online theology may provide people with knowledge and support apart from any organized religious group or, depending on the approach, may lead people to an organized church. Finally, indexed by search engines, online posts and commentaries appear without context and must make sense apart from any particular tradition.

Fifth, the online world and its information management create a pull on traditional theology to better understand its new environment. The characteristics already mentioned should move churches and academics to sustained reflection on several topics, not the least of which is ecclesiology. What does a church or an assembly mean in a world in which location or distance fades into the background, where people join with others based on a virtual connection? For example, does Howard's virtual ekklesia really describe a church? The traditional understanding of a church rests on proximity, shared memory, shared texts, shared beliefs, shared worship, and shared actions—on a particular way of managing the information that defines the group. What happens when people no longer use those information management technologies?

Sixth, the flourishing world of online religion challenges traditional understandings of religious authority, whether doctrinal or ministerial. The question investigates the qualities or characteristics of church authority: its creed, its exercise of authority, its understanding of ministry, and the person of the minister who has traditionally exercised authority in both the local church and the larger denominational Church. Do bloggers and influencers take the place of a teaching office? Similarly, the information management techniques growing from the new communication patterns lead to questions about doctrine, belief, and the definition of each. What role does the increased public sphere or public opinion in the church play? Does the noetic economy of the Internet reduce belief to a set of facts? Every summary of faith runs this risk (something which has long tempted the church) but the online world actually promotes this kind of thinking. Current events, particularly the sex abuse scandals involving the Catholic Church but also other denominations (another part of the religious ecosystem) reinforce the challenge to ministerial authority appearing online. In fact, a parallel existential authority arises with the voices of victims, many of them organized in online groups. Voices, previously suppressed by Church or academic theology, now appear with their own authority and, based on that, have also begun to find a place in academia. This contemporary media ecology phenomenon shows parallels to the change in church and theology afforded by the printing press.

Each of these questions addresses a particular area of theology. A much larger question begins with our understanding of human nature. Every anthropological theology begins with human experience and often takes approaches to thinking and epistemology as givens. The Internet and its ubiquity offer an opportunity to ask how much information management defines human thinking and human being. While the question begins in epistemology, it ends in a theology.

• • •

This brief look at the media ecology of the Internet, as applied to the theological work of the Church, argues that the information management techniques and practices afforded by the Internet's communication tools have already begun to reshape the practices of theology and have the possibility to do so more radically. Professional theologians and churches have only recently shown an awareness of these changes as they see some traditional approaches to religious reflection decrease and others become obsolete. The deeper theological need—faith-seeking-understanding—has not disappeared, but only taken on new forms and new tools, inviting new groups of people to publicly "do theology."

12
CONCLUSION

Faith-Seeking-Understanding in Popular Culture

In an age of lists and online information systems, a popular faith-seeking-understanding is easy to find, as three examples will demonstrate.

The Criterion Collection, a film distributor which dedicates itself "to publishing important classic and contemporary films from around the world" (2020b) has created a list, "faith on film," which it describes as "films [that] underline both our need to ask eternal questions and the paradoxical power of a visual medium to capture the intangible" (2020a). This list includes titles (arranged alphabetically) from *Andrei Rublev* (1966), *Androcles and the Lion* (1952), *Au Hasard Balthazar* (1966), *Babette's Feast* (1987), *Breaking the Waves* (1996), to *Wings of Desire* (1987), *Winter Light* (1963), and *Wise Blood* (1979); chronologically they span the years from 1922 to 2007. Even without the editorial guidance of distributors, academic theologians long ago discovered film as a new theological source (for a sampling, see Deacy and Ortiz, 2008; Deacy, 2012; Hurley, 1970; Marsh, 2004; Stone, 2000; Johnston, Detweiler, and Callaway, 2019; Pope, 2007).

Despite the quip that "the devil has all the best tunes," popular music also generates its lists of theologically-themed songs; highlighted in the music press, they represent almost every genre from country-western to Gospel to rap to rock (Donnelly, 2018; Eliezer, 2020; Savage, 2018). Here, too, academic theologians have followed, exploring the songs that evoke the sacred or express belief (for a sample, see Beaudoin, 2013; Compier, 2013; Cone, 2001).

Television, too, has its lists, which include films for television and serialized dramas (Kirsch, 2014; Gander, 2020). The theological community has noticed these as well (Callaway, 2016; Frederick, 2016; Rosenthal, 2002; Taylor, 2008; Wetmore, 2012). Finally, some specialized websites bring these discussions online. One, *Pop Theology*, "examines the intersections of pop culture and theology, religion, and spirituality.... It's our hope that the articles here inspire readers to think beyond the screen or the page and to, as Clive Marsh notes in his book *Cinema and Sentiment* [2004], 'push the "more" dimension of popular culture"' (Parker, 2019).

Faith-seeking-understanding can appear anywhere, including in today's (and yesterday's) popular culture. In his exploration of theology and popular culture, Lynch (2005) offers this guide in defining popular culture, drawn from a number of sources: "[W]e can think about popular culture as the shared environment, practices, and resources of everyday life"; popular culture refers to "culture more as a 'way of life' for particular people in particular contexts, rather than simply as a collection of texts and other cultural products" (p. 15). This concluding chapter juxtaposes the faith-seeking-understanding in popular culture to the faith-seeking-understanding in academic theology. As this book has argued, all theology emerged from the media ecology or shared environments and practices of Christian believers—and it still does. What differs in these faith-seeking-understandings lies in the ways that they manage information, in the affordances of their media ecologies.

The artistic expressions in contemporary media follow a pattern that Goethals (1999) first identified with the visual arts after the Reformation: the movement of artistic expression out of churches and into other spaces, such as homes, galleries, or public spaces. For most reformers, their theological reasoning did not reject artistic expression per se, but only its place (or the appropriateness of certain communication styles) in the reformed churches. That people would continue reflecting on their belief independently of church support or church location should not come as a surprise, because people usually try to make sense of their encounter with God, to reflect both on experience and on the faith that grounds it. Faith-seeking-understanding characterizes many lives and, as this book illustrates, so do the media ecosystems that touch everyone. Faith-seeking-understanding forms part of an ecology—a motivation and a tradition for different kinds of expression for some, a template for others. The media ecosystem provides means of thought and expression and a reservoir of content. As theology, faith-seeking-understanding guides different kinds of communication. As theology, it takes many forms of expression, though today people more likely regard "theology" as closely reasoned technical written documents. Clearly, such documents (academic papers, church declarations, letters from church leaders, sermons, etc.) have an important place in the religious universe, but to privilege these to the exclusion of all else impoverishes the great tradition of Christian theology. The fact that the "professional" (academic and ecclesiastical) members of the ecosystem have begun to pay attention to faith understood in different popular communication media marks an important change. The works listed above illustrate an ecosystem of artists and intellectual interpreters, together with their chosen communication media and technology. They also hearken back to the popular arts that shaped the history of theology—the work of the people, including artists, musicians, architects, performers, and so on. As such, the rediscovering of popular culture by theology illustrates the evolution of a media ecology as it comes to terms with theology and of a theology as it comes to terms with its media.

A media ecology approach to theology helps to illuminate the fact that, as theology takes on almost all forms of communication or expression, it also changes or develops them. This happens in at least three ways. First, historically, Christian theology has clothed itself in oral expression, written texts, artistic works, musical composition, architecture, printed books, films, digital works—and more than can come to mind—as well as in a multitude of languages. One change to the media occurs in translation. Some of these forms translate more easily into others: writing, for example, can fairly readily move from language to language; oral expression can shift to written texts. These typically semiotic approaches map meaning systems from one register to another. With different media, some have attempted an intersemiotic approach to explain or to guide the move from one medium to another (Hodgson and Soukup, 1997; Soukup and Hodgson, 1999), with the focus often on cognitive meaning. Such methods show at least the possibility of identifying the different kinds of theology and describing them in written form, thus offering a vantage point for evaluation. They also reveal evidence of Christianity's willingness to support different modes for its faith-seeking-understanding and indeed to act as patron for different expressions, ranging from academic theology (supported in schools and seminaries) to art and architecture (supported in church building) to music (supported in liturgical settings).

Second, the recent media ecology of theology has expanded its participants—or better: its acknowledged participants. By providing easier access to communication in online forums like websites, blogs, video sharing, and so on, the media ecology invites more voices into recognized theology—a similar phenomenon to what happened in the sixteenth century as the printing press offered the affordance of access to uncensored voices. The current environment also more readily acknowledges the theological voices of previously excluded groups—women and members of different ethnic groups, for example—and the contributions of artists, musicians, architects, and others. Though individuals from all these groups have long helped the Christian churches reflect on belief, their work often did not fit the dominant paradigms of theology or into the dominant groups that controlled academic theology.

Third, a closer look at the present ecology of theology and media expression shows an added dimension of content. What we call professional or churchly theology (Pelikan, 1971, p. 4) (that is, theology historically created by bishops, preachers, or academics) takes place as reflection on belief by "commenting" on the privileged expressions of others—scriptural texts, liturgical formulae or practices, conciliar decrees, and theological statements created by other churchly groups—often by systematizing them or by clarifying them and resolving conflicts among them. This still occurs today in academic theology, but academic theology as well as some theology expressed by bishops and preachers has gone beyond these sources to acknowledge that popular culture also offers content for reflection and comment. While the ecology of theology always incorporated a degree of intertextuality, the contemporary ecology has expanded that to include vastly more "texts" (well beyond written examples). It has also recognized a "popular theology"—that is, theological reflection appearing in popular culture.

This last change to the media ecology of theology deserves more discussion. Theological gatekeepers—largely the academic theologians rather than ecclesiastical authorities—have come to see popular culture as a theological field. In 2005, Lynch argued for the importance of popular culture to theology—something that has achieved success—and highlighted, as we saw in the introduction to this book, four approaches people have taken as they bridge popular culture and theology:

> 1. the study of religion in relation to the environment, resources and practices of everyday life (in particular, asking about how popular culture shapes religious belief and activities or is appropriated by religious groups, how religion is represented in popular culture, and how religious groups interact with popular culture);
>
> 2. the study of the ways in which popular culture may serve religious functions in contemporary society;
>
> 3. a missiological response to popular culture;
>
> 4. the use of popular cultural texts and practices as a medium for theological reflection. (p. 21)

The first three of these approaches have more interest for religious studies and for the sociology of religion, but the fourth shows how academic theologians have turned their attention to popular theology. Lynch specifies some of the ways in which they do so. First comes the long tradition of theological scholars commenting on film, claiming with Miles (1996) that "film is an important focus for theological reflection precisely because films are an important cultural medium through which contemporary issues and concerns are explored" (Lynch, 2005, p. 37). Second, we meet "writers who *explore popular culture in relation to biblical texts*" (p. 38, italics in original). In many ways this group extends the tradition of commenting on texts beyond the privileged texts of theology (the Bible, for example) to contemporary expressions of faith-seeking-understanding. Third, another approach "involves *exploring popular culture in relation to particular theological questions and concepts*" (p. 39, italics in original). These academic theologians examine the faith-seeking-understanding of contemporaries who wrestle with typically traditional theological problems like the nature of salvation, the work of the redeemer, the person of Christ, or the possibility of forgiveness. Finally, Lynch identifies those who "*explore popular culture as a source of methods for doing theology*" (p. 40, italics in original). This latter approach has traditional academic theology recognizing that other media (especially the media most common in popular culture like film and music) have their own existing methods for both expressing ideas and for understanding those ideas. In all of these, the media ecology tradition helps to clarify what has occurred: the traditional gatekeepers of theology encounter somewhat familiar material (people's reflection on their belief) outside of the ecosystem that they know best. In a kind of merger of ecosystems, they have widened their worlds to encompass what turns out to be the older, larger ecosystem of faith-seeking-understanding in many media, each with its own affordances and settled means of interpretation. The tradition of theology flowing from the information management systems of writing has rediscovered other valid information management systems for faith-seeking-understanding. From the methodological perspective of academic theology, "the relationship between theology and popular culture can be clarified further if we think of popular culture as a particular context within which theological reflection takes place" (Lynch, 2005, p. 97). "Context" here describes the media ecology.

Writing cultures foster more critical analysis of expression and so it comes as no surprise that academic and churchly theology, like any highly developed information management system, sees itself as normative, that is, as able to interpret its traditions and evaluate the adequacy of people's faith-seeking-understanding. Where ecclesiastical groups hold the power to exclude or anathematize contrary views, academic groups aim to critique. Lynch (2005) describes a two-fold process: first, the reflection on belief and second, a questioning: "[A]s a normative discipline, theology will involve asking critical questions about how true, good, or constructive these particular values, beliefs, practices, and experiences are" (p. 98).

Of the many ways in which people engage this questioning, one seems especially suited to the meeting of the two media ecosystems of written texts and popular culture's other modes of expression. Inspired by the work of Paul Tillich, theologians have tried to correlate theological questions with the concerns emerging in culture—what Tillich terms a "correlational approach" to theology (Browning, 1991). This approach asks how the questions and answers in contemporary expression (popular culture or the historical media systems) interact with the questions and answers in the theological or credal traditions. In other words, the correlational approach in contemporary theology tries to make the media ecologies, often taken for granted, more explicit, so that the theological world can fit them into its own analytical framework. Within the media ecology tradition, this describes part of McLuhan's (1962, 1964) project to call attention to the role of the form of communication in addition to its content, to move it from "implicit" to "explicit." This approach proves fruitful only when it allows the one ecosystem to interpret or understand rather than to judge or appropriate another. That is, correlating with popular culture does not mean that Christian churches should "baptize" popular culture and lay claim to it, as can happen in the writings of some theologians commenting on film. Instead, the process should recognize that popular culture has its own ways to manage information—to manage its faith-seeking-understanding—and bring those to awareness.

Media ecology in the service of theology attempts to identify those affordances of the various media in which people express their faith-seeking-understanding. Among all the possible aspects of music, for example, which best suit the exploration or expression of an understanding of faith? Among all the possible aesthetic, narrative, temporal, and figurative aspects of film, which suit the exploration of faith? Just as theology can shape the ecosystem of media through its traditions of orthodoxy, orthopraxis, and interpretation, so too do the media environments shape theological expression, as we have seen most powerfully with writing. But the same holds true for art, music, architecture, and the rest of popular culture, whether that popular culture emerged in the first century, the twelfth century, the sixteenth century, the twentieth century, or the current century. As theology takes on different media forms, the media change theology. This book has explored some of those affordances and some of the changes over the centuries of Christianity. Many of them have become so familiar that people seldom think of them. And one of them—writing and printing—has become so powerful for theology that people seldom recognize the others, leaving them to silently influence how faith seeks understanding.

While much remains for further exploration, three things stand out. First, the process does not end. A new generation of theological thinkers has begun to examine a wider range of popular culture with collections devoted to Rene Girard (Duns and Witherington, 2021); the Marvel universe (Stevenson, 2021); Prince (Harwell and Jenkins, 2021); horror (Grafius and Morehead, 2021); sports (Tucker and Halstead, 2020); and *Westworld* (Gittinger and Sheinfeld, 2020); and books focused on popular digital culture platforms like YouTube (Laytham, 2012); Facebook, Instagram, Twitter (Detweiler, 2013); or practices like selfies (Detweiler, 2018). Many of these authors, falling under Lynch's fourth category, apply a theological critique while asking how people should live with or how they might know themselves in these media. Contemporary theology has also turned its attention to the technology itself, a process begun long ago by Jacques Ellul (Bennett, 2008), and insightfully examined in depth by Gay (2018). The correlations between theological themes and the popular imagination have begun to include the ecologies of technology, storytelling, music, images, and even time.

Second, as McLuhan pointed out in his wonderful image, "the 'content' of a medium is like the juicy piece of meat carried by the burglar to distract the watchdog of the mind" (1964, p. 18), media content blinds us to the media ecology in which we exist. That danger affects not just what we understand but how the systems of reflection work. Every media ecology as it reaches a kind of stasis becomes invisible—something that this book has tried to show by examining many communication systems in which theology has operated. But we can easily overlook the fact that every media ecology also excludes as well as includes. McLuhan and McLuhan (1988) proposed in their "laws of the media" that every new medium enhances some things, makes others obsolete, retrieves some practices, and reverses still others. The process of media ecology affects our perceptions of how communication works and in some ways erases our historical memory. Relatively little research exists on those voices or forms excluded from the inheritance of faith-seeking-understanding; what tends to survive in Christian theology survives in the telling of the "victors," those whose theological interpretations met with wide approval. We typically know of unacceptable reflections on belief only through their condemnations. The affordances of the various communication media have allowed dominant voices, especially official and churchly theology, to find tools to exclude. For example, Augustine's mastery of rhetoric diminished the force of Pelagius' arguments. We've seen another example in the discussion of the ecology of the King James or "authorized" Bible translation (see ch. 5), undertaken to support the Anglican Communion's (and the king's) views over and against that of the Puritans. Other examples exist, perhaps not in the written records, but in the traces of popular theology of dissident or marginalized groups. An important task for a media ecology of theology remains to search out these voices to better understand how communication tools enabled (or disabled) their reflection on belief. In other words, a further media ecology should ask, "who's left out?" and "why?"

Third, the emergence of academic authority over theology shows how a given group can use its mastery over aspects of a communication system (in this case, educational practices, writing systems, and information management) to claim power within a discourse or communication domain. Media ecology study can shed light on the artificiality of that power, since people often take both power and its artificial nature for granted. As a grounding for a theological critique of technology, Gay (2018) points this out as he sketches the roles that economics, monopoly capitalism, the scientific method, nationalism, and some versions of Protestantism play in the rise to dominance of Western technology. But theology itself depends on a different set of affordances in the communication ecology for its own legitimacy as a source of critique. Herein lies yet another area requiring more research. How have the affordances of media ecology led to the human, intellectual, and communication alignments that characterize current practices?

BIBLIOGRAPHY

Achtemeier, P. J. (1990). "*Omne verbum sonat*: The New Testament and the Oral Environment of Late Western Antiquity." *Journal of Biblical Literature* 109: 3–27.
Aichele, G., and R. Walsh, eds. (2002). *Screening Scripture: Intertextual Connections between Scripture and Film*. Harrisburg, Pa.: Trinity Press International.
Anderson, B. R. (1991). *Imagined Communities: Reflections on the Origin and Spread of Nationalism*. Rev. and extended ed. London: Verso.
Anttila, M. E. (2013). *Luther's Theology of Music: Spiritual Beauty and Pleasure*. Berlin: de Gruyter.
Appleyard, J. (1971). "How Does a Sacrament 'Cause by Signifying'?" *Science et Esprit* 23: 167–200.
Assmann, J. (2006). "Form as a Mnemonic Device: Cultural Texts and Cultural Memory." In *Performing the Gospel: Orality, Memory, and Mark. Essays Dedicated to Werner Kelber*, ed. R. A. Horsley, J. A. Draper, and J. M. Foley, 67–82. Minneapolis: Fortress.
Augustine. (1991). *Confessions*. Trans. H. Chadwick. Oxford: Oxford University Press.
Bailey, K. E. (1991). "Informal Controlled Oral Tradition and the Synoptic Gospels." *Asia Journal of Theology*, 5: 34–54.
Bandura, A. (1977). *Social Learning Theory*. Englewood Cliffs, N.J.: Prentice Hall.
———. (1986). *Social Foundations of Thought and Action: A Social Cognitive Theory*. Englewood Cliffs, N.J.: Prentice Hall.
Barna Group. (2020). "What Churches Might Miss When Measuring Digital Attendance." https://www.barna.com/research/watching-online-church/.
Bateman, IV, H. W. (2010). "Second Temple Exegetical Practices: Extra-biblical Examples of Exegesis Compared with Those in the Book of Hebrews." *Southwestern Journal of Theology* 53, no. 1: 26–54.
Baugh, L. (1997). *Imaging the Divine: Jesus and Christ-figures in Film*. Kansas City, Mo.: Sheed & Ward.
Beaudoin, T., ed. (2013). *Secular Music and Sacred Theology*. Collegeville, Minn.: Liturgical Press.
Begbie, J. S. (2000). *Theology, Music, and Time*. Cambridge: Cambridge University Press.
Bell, C. (1997). *Ritual: Perspectives and Dimensions*. New York: Oxford University Press.
Bennett, S. (2008). "The City's Curse, the Church's Plight: Technology, Communication, and the Sacred: An Ellulian Perspective." *Proceedings of the Media*

Ecology Association 9: 1–14. https://www.media-ecology.org/resources/Documents/Proceedings/v9/v9-01-Bennett.pdf.

Bethke, A.-J. (2015). "The Theology behind Music and Its Performance in Anglican Worship: An Historical Exploration of Anglican Theological Attitudes to Music, Starting with the 1549 *Book of Common Prayer* and Finishing with an Anglican Prayer Book 1989." *Journal of Theology for Southern Africa* 153: 46–61.

Blake, R. A. (2000). *Afterimage: The Indelible Catholic Imagination of Six American Filmmakers*. Chicago: Loyola Press.

Block, J. (2002). *Verstehen durch Musik: Das Gesungene Wort in der Theologie*. Tübingen: A. Francke.

Bobb, L. (2019). "Music and Spirituality: The Resurgence of Faith in Popular Music." *No Basic Girls Allowed*, November 18, 2019. https://nobasicgirlsallowed.com/music-and-spirituality-the-resurgence-of-faith-in-popular-music/.

Bobrick, B. (2001). *Wide as the Waters: The Story of the English Bible and the Revolution It Inspired*. New York: Simon & Schuster.

Bonnot, B. R. (2001). "Communication Theology: Some Basics." *Catholic International* 12: 25–27.

Boyle, M. O. (1999). "Evangelism and Erasmus." In *The Cambridge History of Literary Criticism*, vol. 3, *The Renaissance*, ed. G. P. Norton, 44–52. Cambridge: Cambridge University Press.

Browning, D. (1991). *A Fundamental Practical Theology*. Minneapolis: Fortress.

Bruce, F. F. (1978). *History of the Bible in English: From the Earliest Versions*. 3rd ed. New York: Oxford University Press.

Bryant, J., and D. Zillmann, eds. (2002). *Media Effects: Advances in Theory and Research*. 2nd ed. Mahwah, N.J.: Lawrence Erlbaum Associates.

Burke, D. G. (2007). "The First Versions: The Septuagint, the Targums, and the Latin." In *A History of Bible Translation*, ed. P. A. Noss, 59–89. Rome: Edizioni di Storia e Letteratura.

Caccamo, J. F. (2007). "Been There, Sung That: How the Music of Worship Shapes People of God." *Liturgy* 22, no. 1: 47–54.

Callaway, K. (2016). *Watching TV Religiously: Television and Theology in Dialogue*. Grand Rapids: Baker Academic.

Campbell, G. (2011). *Bible: The Story of the King James Version, 1611–2011*. Oxford: Oxford University Press.

Campbell, H. A. (2007). "Who's Got the Power? Religious Authority and the Internet." *Journal of Computer-Mediated Communication* 12: 1043–62. http://jcmc.indiana.edu/vol12/issue3/campbell.html.

———. (2010a). "Religious Authority and the Blogosphere." *Journal of Computer-Mediated Communication* 15: 251–76.

———. (2010b). *When Religion Meets New Media*. London: Routledge.

———. (2021). *Digital Creatives and the Rethinking of Religious Authority*. London: Routledge.

Carey, J. W. (1989). "A Cultural Approach to Communication." In *Communication as Culture: Essays on Media and Society*, 13–23. Boston: Unwin Hyman.
Carpenter, E. (1972). *Oh, What a Blow That Phantom Gave Me!* Richmond, BC: Holt, Rinehart & Winston.
Cashner, A. A. (2020). *Hearing Faith: Music as Theology in the Spanish Empire*. Boston: Brill.
Catholic Church. (1983). *Code of Canon Law*. (Trans., Canon Law Society of America). Vatican City: Libreria Editrice Vaticana. http://www.vatican.va/archive/ENG1104/_INDEX.HTM.
———. (1993). *Catechism of the Catholic Church*. Vatican City: Libreria Editrice Vaticana. http://www.vatican.va/archive/ENG0015/_INDEX.HTM.
Chandler, D. (2013). "Technological or Media Determinism" (web publication). http://www.aber.ac.uk/media/Documents/tecdet/tecdet.html.
Cheong, P., Halavais, A., and Kwon, K. (2008). "Chronicles of Me: Understanding Blogging as a Religious Practice." *Journal of Media and Religion* 7: 101–31.
Church of the Immaculate Heart of Mary (Brompton Oratory). "History of the Church." The London Oratory. Retrieved October 15, 2020 from https://www.bromptonoratory.co.uk/history-of-the-church.
Clark, L. S. (1998). "Building Bridges between Theology and Media Studies." Plenary presentation to the 53rd annual meeting of the Catholic Theological Society of America, Ottawa, Ontario, June 12, 1998.
———. (2005). *From Angels to Aliens: Teenagers, the Media, and the Supernatural*. New York: Oxford University Press.
Clark, L. S., and S. M. Hoover. (1997). "At the Intersection of Media, Culture, and Religion." In *Rethinking Media, Religion and Culture*, ed. S. M. Hoover and K. Lundby, 15–36. Thousand Oaks, Calif.: Sage Publications.
Cohen, B. C. (1963). *The Press and Foreign Policy*. Princeton: Princeton University Press.
Coleridge, S. T. (1858). "The Statesman's Manual." In *The Complete Works of Samuel Taylor Coleridge*, ed. W. G. T. Shedd, 1: 437–38. New York: Harper and Bros.
Compier, D. H. (2013). *Listening to Popular Music*. Minneapolis: Fortress Press.
Comstock, G. L. (1987). "Two Types of Narrative Theology." *Journal of the American Academy of Religion* 55, no. 4: 687–17. http://www.jstor.org/stable/1464681
Cone, J. H. (2001). "Everybody Talkin' 'Bout Heaven Ain't Goin' There': Black Spirituals as Theology." In *Religion in a Secular City: Essays in Honor of Harvey Cox*, ed. A. Sharma, 129–41. Harrisburg, Pa.: Trinity Press International.
Criterion Collection. (2020a). "Faith on Film." https://www.criterion.com/shop/collection/99-faith-on-film/list.
———. (2020b). "Our Mission." https://www.criterion.com/about.
Crites, S. (1971). "The Narrative Quality of Experience." *Journal of the American Academy of Religion* 39, no. 3: 291–311.

Crocker, C. (1973). "Ritual and the Development of Social Structures: Liminality and Inversion." In *The Roots of Ritual*, ed. J. D. Shaughnessy, 47–86. Grand Rapids: Eerdmans.

Croot, P. E. C., ed. (2004). "Religious History: Foreign Churches." In *A History of the County of Middlesex*, vol. 12, 272–74. London: Middlesex County. Woodbridge: Boydell & Brewer.

Crystal, D. (2010). *Begat: The King James Bible and the English language*. Oxford: Oxford University Press.

Csikszentmihalyi, M. (1991). *Flow: The Psychology of Optimal Experience*. New York: Harper & Row.

Cyril of Jerusalem (435?). *Catechesis, Mystagogia*. PG 33: 1087–91.

Dalli Regoli, G. (1983). "The Relationship between Text and Image in Some Groups of Central Italian Illuminated Manuscripts of the 12th Century." *Text and Image, ACTA* 10: 63–76.

Deacy, C. (2012). *Screening the Afterlife: Theology, Eschatology and Film*. London: Routledge.

Deacy, C., and G. W. Ortiz. (2008). *Theology and Film: Challenging the Sacred/Secular Divide*. Malden, Mass.: Blackwell.

Detweiler, C. (2013). *iGods: How Technology Shapes Our Spiritual and Social Lives*. Grand Rapids: Brazos.

———. (2018). *Selfies: Searching for the Image of God in a Digital Age*. Grand Rapids: Brazos.

Donnelly, M. S. (2018). "25 Songs about God + faith." *Pop Crush*, March 30, 2018. https://popcrush.com/pop-songs-about-god-and-faith-justin-bieber/.

Dulles, A. (1971). *The Church Is Communication*. Volume 1 of *Multimedia International*. Multimedia International.

———. (1989). "Vatican II and Communications." In *Vatican II: Assessment and Perspectives, Twenty-Five Years After (1962–1987)*, ed. R. Latourelle, 3: 528–47. New York: Paulist Press.

Dunn, J. D. G. (2001). "Jesus in Oral Memory: The Initial Stages of the Jesus Tradition." In *Jesus: A Colloquium in the Holy Land*, ed. D. Donnelly, 84–145. New York: Continuum.

Duns, R. G., and T. D. Witherington, eds. (2021). *René Girard, Theology, and Pop Culture*. Lanham, Md.: Lexington Books.

Easley, D., and J. Kleinberg. (2010). *Networks, Crowds, and Markets: Reasoning about a Highly Connected World*. Cambridge: Cambridge University Press.

Ebel, J. G. (1969). "Translation and Cultural Nationalism in the Reign of Elizabeth." *Journal of the History of Ideas* 30, no. 4: 593–602.

Edwards, M. U., Jr. (1994). *Printing, Propaganda, and Martin Luther*. Berkeley: University of California Press.

Eisenstein, E. L. (1979). *The Printing Press as an Agent of Change: Communications and Cultural Transformations in Early-Modern Europe*. Cambridge: Cambridge University Press.

———. (1983). *The Printing Revolution in Early Modern Europe*. Cambridge: Cambridge, University Press.

Eliezer, C. (2020). "15 Rock Classics that You May Not Have Thought Were about Religion." *Tone Deaf*. Last modified September 20, 2021. https://tonedeaf.thebrag.com/15-songs-about-religion/.

Ellingworth, P. (2007). "From Martin Luther to the Revised English Version." In *A History of Bible Translation*, ed. P. A. Noss, 105–9. Rome: Edizioni di Storia e Letteratura.

Encyclopedia Britannica (2007). "Iconostasis." Retrieved October 6, 2021 from https://www.britannica.com/technology/iconostasis.

Evans, P. (1997). Review of *Britten: "War Requiem,"* by Mervyn Cooke. *Music & Letters* 78, no. 3: 466–68.

Ferree, B. (1898). "Bibles in Stone." *New England Magazine* 24, no. 3: 162–77. https://babel.hathitrust.org/cgi/pt?id=uiug.30112004280647&view=1up&seq=174.

Foley, J. M. (1990). *Traditional Oral Epic: The Odyssey, Beowulf, and the Serbo-Croatian Return Song*. Berkeley: University of California Press.

———. (2006). "Memory in Oral Tradition." In *Performing the Gospel: Orality, Memory, and Mark*, ed. R. A. Horsley, J. A. Draper, and J. M. Foley, 83–96. Minneapolis: Fortress.

Fraser, P. (1998). *Images of the Passion: The Sacramental Mode in Film*. Westport, Conn.: Praeger.

Frederick, M. F. (2016). *Colored Television: American Religion Gone Global*. Stanford, Calif.: Stanford University Press.

Funk, R. W., and R. W. Hoover. (1994). Introduction to *The Five Gospels: What Did Jesus Really Say?* 1–38. San Francisco: Harper.

Gadamer, H.-G. (1975). *Truth and Method*. New York: Seabury.

Gander, M. (2020). "The Best TV Shows with Religious Themes." *Ranker*. Last modified September 22, 2021. https://www.ranker.com/list/best-shows-with-religious-themes-v1/molly-gander.

Gay, C. M. (2018). *Modern Technology and the Human Future: A Christian Appraisal*. Downers Grove, Ill.: IVP.

Gerbner, G. (1970). "Cultural Indicators: The Case of Violence in Television Drama." *The Annals of the American Academy of Political and Social Science* 388: 69–81.

Gerbner, G., L. Gross, M. Morgan, and N. Signorielli. (1980). "The Mainstreaming of America: Violence Profile No. 11." *Journal of Communication* 30, no. 3: 10–29.

Gibson, J. J. (1979). *The Ecological Approach to Visual Perception*. London: Houghton Mifflin.

Gittinger, J., and S. Sheinfeld, eds. (2020). *Theology and Westworld*. Lanham, Md.: Fortress Academic.

Goethals, G. T. (1990). *The Electronic Golden Calf: Images, Religion, and the Making of Meaning*. Cambridge, Mass.: Cowley Publications.

———. (1999). "The Imaged Word: Aesthetics, Fidelity, and New Media Translation." In *Fidelity and Translation: Communicating the Bible in New Media*, ed. P. A. Soukup and R. Hodgson, 133–72. Franklin, Wis.: Sheed & Ward.

Golan, O., and M. Martini. (2018). "Digital Pilgrimage: Exploring Catholic Monastic Webcasts." *The Communication Review* 21, no. 1: 24–45.

Goody, J. R., and I. Watt. (1968). "The Consequences of Literacy." In *Literacy in Traditional Societies*, ed. J. Goody, 27–84. Cambridge: Cambridge University Press.

Grafius, B. R., and J. W. Morehead, eds. (2021). *Theology and Horror: Explorations of the Dark Religious Imagination*. Lanham, Md.: Fortress Academic.

Graham, W. A. (1987). *Beyond the Written Word: Oral Aspects of Scripture in the History of Religion*. Cambridge: Cambridge University Press.

Greeley, A. M. (1990). *The Catholic Myth: The Behavior and Beliefs of American Catholics*. New York: Scribner.

Grint, K. and S. Woolgar. (1997). *The Machine at Work*. Cambridge: Polity.

Hadas, M. (1954). *Ancilla to Classical Reading*. New York: Columbia University Press.

Hamlin, H., J. Maltby, and H. Moore. (2011). "The 1611 King James Bible and Its Cultural Politics." In *Manifold Greatness: The Making of the King James Bible*, ed. H. Moore and J. Reid, 117–37. Oxford: Bodleian Library.

Hartt, J. (1984). "Theological Investments in Story: Some Comments on Recent Developments and Some Proposals." *Journal of the American Academy of Religion* 52, no. 1: 117–30.

Harwell, J. H., and K. E. Jenkins. (2021). *Theology and Prince*. Lanham, Md.: Fortress Academic.

Havelock, E. A. (1963). *Preface to Plato*. Cambridge, Mass.: Belknap Press of Harvard University Press.

———. (1978). *The Greek Concept of Justice: From Its Shadow in Homer to Its Substance in Plato*. Cambridge, Mass.: Harvard University Press.

Heaney, M. L. (2012). *Music as Theology: What Music Says about the Word*. Eugene, Ore.: Pickwick.

Hearon, H. E. (2004). "The Implications of 'Orality' for Studies of the Biblical Text." *Oral Tradition* 19, no. 1: 96–107. DOI: https://doi.org/10.1353/ort.2004.0092.

Helland, C. (2000). "Online-Religion/Religion-Online: Virtual Communities." In *Religion on the Internet: Research Prospects and Promises*, ed. J. K. Hadden and D. E. Cowan, 205–33. Amsterdam: JAI.

Hilgartner, R. (2009). "*Lex Orandi, Lex Credendi*: The Word of God in the Celebration of the Sacraments." *Catechetical Sunday*, September 20, 2009. Washington, D.C.: United States Conference of Catholic Bishops. https://www.usccb.org/beliefs-and-teachings/how-we-teach/catechesis/catechetical-sunday/word-of-god/upload/lex-orandi-lex-credendi.pdf.

Hitchcock, J. (1971). "More and Tyndale's Controversy over Revelation: A Test of the McLuhan Hypothesis." *Journal of the American Academy of Religion* 39, no. 4: 448–66.

Hodgson, R., and P. A. Soukup, eds. (1997). *From One Medium to Another: Basic Issues for Communicating the Scriptures in New Media*. Kansas City, Mo.: Sheed & Ward.

Hoffmann, G. (1999). "Renaissance Printing and the Book Trade." In *The Cambridge History of Literary Criticism*, vol. 3, *The Renaissance*, ed. G. P. Norton, 384–91. Cambridge: Cambridge University Press.

Hoover, S. M. (1995). "Media and Moral Order in Postpositivist Media Studies." *Journal of Communication* 45, no. 1: 136–45.

Horsfield, P., and P. Teusner. (2007). "A Mediated Religion: Historical Perspectives on Christianity and the Internet." *Studies in World Christianity* 13, no. 3: 278–95.

Horton, D., and R. Wohl. (1956). "Mass Communication and Para-social Interaction: Observations on Intimacy at a Distance." *Psychiatry* 19, no. 3: 215–29.

Hosseini, S. H. (2008). "Religion and Media, Religious Media, or Media Religion: Theoretical Studies." *Journal of Media & Religion* 7, nos. 1–2: 56–69.

Howard, R. G. (2011). *Digital Jesus: The Making of a New Christian Fundamentalist Community on the Internet*. New York: New York University Press.

Hughes, D. A. (1962). "The Birth of Polyphony." In *The New Oxford History of Music II: Early Medieval Music up to 1300*, ed. D. A. Hughes, 270–85. London: Oxford University Press.

Hurley, N. P. (1970). *Theology through film*. New York: Harper & Row.

———. (1978). *The Reel Revolution: A Film Primer on Liberation*. Maryknoll, N.Y.: Orbis.

———. (1993). *Soul in Suspense: Hitchcock's Fright and Delight*. Metuchen, N.J.: Scarecrow.

Hutchby, I. (2001). "Technologies, Texts and Affordances." *Sociology* 35, no. 2: 441–56.

Innis, H. A. (1951). *The Bias of Communication*. Toronto: University of Toronto Press.

Jensen, R. M. (2017). *The Cross: History, Art, and Controversy*. Cambridge, Mass.: Harvard University Press.

———. (2000). *Understanding Early Christian Art*. London: Routledge.

Jinbachian, M. (2007). "History: The Septuagint to the Vernaculars: Introduction." In *A History of Bible Translation*, ed. P. A. Noss, 29–57. Rome: Edizioni di Storia e Letteratura.

Johnson, M. F. (2005). "Aquinas's *Summa Theologiae* as Pedagogy." In *Medieval Education*, ed. R. B. Begley and J. W. Koterski, 133–42. New York: Fordham University Press.

Johnston, R. K., C. Detweiler, and K. Callaway. (2019). *Deep Focus: Film and Theology in Dialogue*. Grand Rapids: Baker Academic.

Kaster, R. A. (1988). *Guardians of Language: The Grammarian and Society in Late Antiquity*. Berkeley: University of California Press.

Keen, S. (1970). *To a Dancing God*. New York: Harper & Row.

Kelber, W. H. (1994). "Modalities of Communication, Cognition, and Physiology of Perception: Orality, Rhetoric, Scribality." *Semeia* 65: 193–216.

———. (2013a). "Interpretation of Narrative and Narrative as Interpretation: Hermeneutical Reflections on the Gospels (1987)." In *Imprints, Voiceprints, and Footprints of Memory: Collected Essays of Werner H. Kelber*, 33–54. Atlanta: Society of Biblical Literature.

———. (2013b). "Narrative and Disclosure: Mechanisms of Concealing, Revealing, and Reveiling (1988)." In *Imprints, Voiceprints, and Footprints of Memory: Collected Essays of Werner H. Kelber*, 55–74. Atlanta: Society of Biblical Literature.

———. (2013c). "On the History of the Quest, or: The Reduction of Polyvalency to Single Sense (2004)." In *Imprints, Voiceprints, and Footprints of Memory: Collected Essays of Werner H. Kelber*, 237–64. Atlanta: Society of Biblical Literature.

———. (2013d). "Orality and Biblical Scholarship: Seven Case Studies (2007)." In *Imprints, Voiceprints, and Footprints of Memory: Collected Essays of Werner H. Kelber*, 297–331. Atlanta: Society of Biblical Literature.

———. (2013e). "The History of the Closure of Biblical Texts (2010)." In *Imprints, Voiceprints, and Footprints of Memory: Collected Essays of Werner H. Kelber*, 413–40. Atlanta: Society of Biblical Literature.

———. (2013f). "The Work of Walter J. Ong and Biblical Scholarship (2011)." In *Imprints, Voiceprints, and Footprints of Memory: Collected Essays of Werner H. Kelber*, 441–64. Atlanta: Society of Biblical Literature.

———. (2013g). "The Works of Memory: Christian Origins as Mnemohistory (2005)." In *Imprints, Voiceprints, and Footprints of Memory: Collected Essays of Werner H. Kelber*, 265–96. Atlanta: Society of Biblical Literature.

Kennedy, D. (1912). "St. Thomas Aquinas." In *The Catholic Encyclopedia*. New York: Robert Appleton Company. http://www.newadvent.org/cathen/14663b.htm.

———. (1999). *Classical Rhetoric and Its Christian and Secular Tradition from Ancient to Modern Times*. Rev. and extended ed. Chapel Hill: University of North Carolina Press.

Kenyon, F. G. (1971). *Books and Readers in Ancient Greece and Rome*. 2nd ed. Folcroft, Pa.: Folcroft Library Editions.

King, N. (1991). "The Mind's Eye and the Forms of Thought: Classical Rhetoric and the Composition of Augustine's *Confessions*." PhD diss., New York University.

Kirsch, A. (2014). "Finally, a TV Show that Truly Takes Religion Seriously." *The New Republic*, August 5, 2014. https://newrepublic.com/article/118977/leftovers-turns-religion-entertainment.

Knapp, M., and H. Knapp. (1978). *One Potato, Two Potato: The Folklore of American Children*. New York: Norton.

Koslofsky, C. M. (2000). *The Reformation of the Dead: Death and Ritual in Early Modern Germany, 1450–1700*. London: Palgrave.

Kreitzer, L. J. (1999). *Pauline Images in Fiction and Film*. Sheffield: Sheffield Academic.

Langer, S. K. (1953). *Feeling and Form: A Theory of Art Developed from Philosophy in a New Key*. New York: Scribner's Sons.

———. (1957). *Problems of Art: Ten Philosophical Lectures*. New York: Scribner's Sons.

Laytham, D. B. (2012). *iPod, YouTube, Wii Play: Theological Engagements with Entertainment*. Eugene, Ore.: Cascade Books.

Lazarsfeld, P. F., B. Berelson, and H. Gaudet. (1944). *The People's Choice: How the Voter Makes Up His Mind in a Presidential Campaign*. New York: Columbia University Press.

Liebling, A. J. (1960). "The Wayward Press: Do You Belong in Journalism?" *The New Yorker*, May 14, 105–12.

Lindbeck, G. (1984). *The Nature of Doctrine: Religion and Theology in a Postliberal Age*. Philadelphia: Westminster.

Lindvall, T. (2004). "Religion and Film: Part I: History and Criticism." *Communication Research Trends* 23, no. 4: 3–44.

———. (2005). "Religion and Film: Part II: Theology and Pedagogy." *Communication Research Trends* 24, no. 1: 1–37.

Ling, R. (2004). *The Mobile Connection: The Cell Phone's Impact on Society*. Amsterdam: Elsevier.

Liss, B. (2019). *A Media Ecological Approach to the History of Music Notation: The Neume, Staff and Mensural Rhythm*. Paper presented at the 105th annual convention of the National Communication Association, Baltimore, Maryland, November 14–17.

Lord, A. B. (1960). *The Singer of Tales*. Cambridge, Mass.: Harvard University Press.

Lynch, A. P. (2015). "Digital Catholicism: Internet, the Church, and the Vatican Website." In *Annual Review of the Sociology of Religion*, vol. 6: "Religion and Internet," ed. L. Borzano, G. Giordan, and E. Pace, 97–113.

Lynch, D. A. (2018). *God in Sound and Silence: Music as Theology*. Eugene, Ore.: Pickwick.

Lynch, G. (2005). *Understanding Theology and Popular Culture*. Malden, Mass.: Blackwell.

Maltby, J., and H. Moore. (2011). "Origins of the Project." In *Manifold Greatness: The Making of the King James Bible*, ed. H. Moore and J. Reid, 41–59. Oxford: Bodleian Library.

Mann, K. D. (2010). *The Power of Song: Music and Dance in the Mission Communities of Northern New Spain, 1590–1810*. Stanford, Calif.: Stanford University Press.

Marcuse, H. (1979). *The Aesthetic Dimension: Toward a Critique of Marxist Aesthetics*. London: Macmillan.

Marrou, H. I. (1956). *A History of Education in Antiquity.* Trans. G. Lamb. New York: Sheed & Ward.

Marsh, C. (2004). *Cinema and Sentiment: Film's Challenge to Theology.* Milton Keynes: Paternoster.

Martini, C. M. (1994). *Communicating Christ to the World: The Pastoral Letters.* Trans. T. M. Lucas. Kansas City, Mo.: Sheed & Ward.

McBrien, R. (1981). "Faith, Theology, Belief." In *Catholicism,* study ed., 23–30. San Francisco: Harper & Row.

McCarthy, M. C. (2007). "'We Are Your Books': Augustine, the Bible, and the Practice of Authority." *Journal of the American Academy of Religion* 75, no. 2: 324–52.

McCombs, M. (2014). *Setting the Agenda: The News Media and Public Opinion.* 2nd ed. Cambridge: Polity.

McCombs, M. E., and D. L. Shaw. (1972). "The Agenda-Setting Function of Mass Media." *The Public Opinion Quarterly* 36, no. 2: 176–87.

McGrath, A. E. (2011). *Christian Theology: An Introduction.* 5th ed. Malden, Mass.: Wiley-Blackwell.

McInerny, R. and J. O'Callaghan. (2010). "Saint Thomas Aquinas." In *Stanford Encyclopedia of Philosophy,* ed. E. N. Zalta. http://plato.stanford.edu/archives/win2010/entries/aquinas/.

McLuhan, E. (2005). "On Formal Cause." *EME: Explorations in Media Ecology* 4, nos. 3–4: 181–209.

McLuhan, M. (1962). *The Gutenberg Galaxy: The Making of Typographic Man.* Toronto: University of Toronto Press.

———. (1964). *Understanding Media: The Extensions of Man.* New York: McGraw-Hill.

———. (1999a). "International Motley and Religious Costume." In *The Medium and the Light: Reflections on Religion,* ed. E. McLuhan and J. Szklarek, 75–78. Toronto: Stoddart.

———. (1999b). "Liturgy and the Microphone." In *The Medium and the Light: Reflections on Religion,* ed. E. McLuhan and J. Szklarek, 107–16. Toronto: Stoddart.

———. (1999c). "Religion and Youth: Second Conversation with Pierre Babin." In *The Medium and the Light: Reflections on Religion,* ed. E. McLuhan and J. Szklarek, 94–104. Toronto: Stoddart.

———. (2011). "Formal Causality in Chesterton." In *Media and Formal Cause,* ed. M. McLuhan and E. McLuhan, 73–82. Houston, Tex.: NeoPoiesis.

McLuhan, M., and E. McLuhan. (1988). *Laws of Media: The New Science.* Toronto: University of Toronto Press.

Mead, M. (1973). "Ritual and Social Crisis." In *The Roots of Ritual,* ed. J. D. Shaughnessy, 87–101. Grand Rapids: Eerdmans.

Meier, J. P. (2001). *A Marginal Jew: Rethinking the Historical Jesus.* Vol. 3: *Companions and Competitors.* New Haven, Conn.: Yale University Press.

Metzger, B. M. (2001). *The Bible in Translation: Ancient and English Versions.* Grand Rapids: Baker Academic.

Meyrowitz, J. (1985). *No Sense of Place: The Impact of Electronic Media on Social Behavior.* Oxford: Oxford University Press.

Milburn, R. (1988). *Early Christian Art and Architecture.* Berkeley: University of California Press.

Miles, M. R. (1985). *Image as Insight: Visual Understanding in Western Christianity and Secular Culture.* Boston, Mass.: Beacon Press.

———. (1996). *Seeing and Believing: Religion and Values in the Movies.* Boston: Beacon.

Miller, G. R., and M. Burgoon. (1978). "Persuasion Research: Review and Commentary." *Annals of the International Communication Association* 2, no. 1: 29–47.

Mitchell, J. (2005). "Theology and Film." In *The Modern Theologians: An Introduction to Christian Theology Since 1918*, 3rd ed., ed. D. F. Ford and R. Muers, 736–59. Malden, Mass.: Blackwell.

Morris, C. (1972). *The Discovery of the Individual: 1050–1200.* New York: Harper & Row.

Narbona, J. (2016). "Digital Leadership, Twitter and Pope Francis." *Church, Communication and Culture* 1, no. 1: 90–109.

Navone, J. J. (1984). *Gospel Love: A Narrative Theology.* Wilmington, Del.: Michael Glazier.

Navone, J. J., and T. Cooper. (1981). *Tellers of the Word.* New York: Le Jacq.

Nayar, S. J. (2014). *Dante's Sacred Poem: Flesh and the Centrality of the Eucharist to the Divine Comedy.* London: Bloomsbury.

Neustadt, R. E., and E. R. May. (1986). *Thinking in Time: The Uses of History for Decision Makers.* New York: Free Press.

Nichols, A. (1988). "What Theology Is." *New Blackfriars* 69, no. 819: 383–92. Revised 2009. http://www.christendom-awake.org/pages/anichols/theology.htm.

Nordenfalk, C. (1995). *Book Illumination: Early Middle Ages.* Geneva: Skira.

Norton, D. (2000). *A History of the English Bible as Literature.* Cambridge: Cambridge University Press.

Novotny, R. J. (1962). "Instrumental Music and the Liturgy." *The American Ecclesiastical Review* 146, no. 2: 94–112. https://www.catholicculture.org/culture/library/view.cfm?recnum=2980.

Nuovo, A. (2010). "The Book Trade in the Italian Renaissance: Structure and Regulation." 46th Annual Erasmus Lecture given at the University of Toronto, October 21, 2010. http://www.medievalists.net/2010/11/14/the-book-trade-in-the-italian-renaissance-structure-and-regulation/.

O'Donnell, J. J. (n.d.a). "Augustine: Elements of Christianity." James J. O'Donnell. Faculty website hosted by Georgetown University. Last Modified November 10, 1994. Retrieved April 25, 2011 from http://www9.georgetown.edu/faculty/jod/twayne/aug2.html.

———. (n.d.b). "Augustine: Texts and Translations." James J. O'Donnell. Faculty website hosted by Georgetown University. Last Modified November 10, 1994. Retrieved April 24, 2011 from http://www9.georgetown.edu/faculty/jod/augustine/textstrans.html.

Ong, W. J. (1958). *Ramus: Method, and the Decay of Dialogue: From the Art of Discourse to the Art of Reason.* Cambridge, Mass.: Harvard University Press.

———. (1967). *The Presence of the Word: Some Prolegomena for Cultural and Religious History.* New Haven, Conn.: Yale University Press.

———. (1969). "Communications Media and the State of Theology." *CrossCurrents* 19, no. 4: 462–80.

———. (1975). "The Writer's Audience Is Always a Fiction." *PMLA* 90, no. 1: 9–21.

———. (1978a). "Literacy and Orality in our Times" *ADE Bulletin*, Serial No. 58: 1–7.

———. (1978b). "Technology Outside Us and Inside Us." *Communion: International Catholic Review* 5, no. 2: 100–121.

———. (1982). *Orality and Literacy: The Technologizing of the Word.* New York: Methuen.

———. (1992). "Maranatha: Death and Life in the Text of the Book." In *Faith and Contexts*, vol. 2, ed. T. J. Farrell and P. A. Soukup, 128–61. Atlanta: Scholars' Press.

———. (2002). "Technological Development and Writer-Subject-Reader Immediacies." In *An Ong Reader: Challenges for Rurther Inquiry*, ed. T. J. Farrell and P. A. Soukup, 497–504. Cresskill, N.J.: Hampton Press.

Ong, W. J., and W. Altree. (2002). "Why Talk? A Conversation about Language with Walter J. Ong Conducted by Wayne Altree." In *An Ong Reader: Challenges for Rurther Inquiry*, ed. T. J. Farrell and P. A. Soukup, 363–403. Cresskill, N.J.: Hampton Press.

Oster, J. (1999). "'God Loves Stories,' Jews Love Questions: I. B. Singer Questions God." *Journal of the Short Story in English* 32. https://journals.openedition.org/jsse/164.

Panofsky, E. (1979). *Abbot Suger on the Abbey Church of St. Denis and Its Art Treasures.* Princeton: Princeton University Press.

Parker, R. (2019). "About Pop Theology." *Pop Theology*. from https://poptheology.com/about-pop-theology/.

Parry, A. (1971). Introduction to *The Making of Homeric Verse: The Collected Papers of Milman Parry*, by M. Parry, ed. A. Parry. Oxford: Clarendon.

Paulinus of Nola. (1967). *Letters of St. Paulinus of Nola*. Vol. 2: *Letters 23–51*. Trans. P. G. Walsh. Westminster, Md.: Newman.

Pelikan J. (1971). *The Emergence of the Catholic Tradition (100–400)*. The Christian Tradition: A History of the Development of Doctrine, vol. 1. Chicago: University of Chicago Press.

———. (1974). *The Spirit of Eastern Christendom (600–1700)*. The Christian Tradition: A History of the Development of Doctrine, vol. 2. Chicago: University of Chicago Press.

———. (1978). *The Growth of Medieval Theology (600–1300)*. The Christian Tradition: A History of the Development of Doctrine, vol. 3. Chicago: University of Chicago Press.

———. (1986). *Bach among the Theologians*. Philadelphia: Fortress.

Plude, F. F. (1995). "How Communication Studies Can Help Us to Bridge the Gap in our Theology Metaphors." *New Theology Review* 8, no. 4. https://www.religion-online.org/article/how-communication-studies-can-help-us-to-bridge-the-gap-in-our-theology-megaphors/.

Pope Francis. (2018). "Judas and the Good Shepherd." *Angelus*, March 16, 12–13. https://angelusnews.com/faith/judas-and-the-good-shepherd/.

Pope Pius XI. (1928). "*Divini Cultus* on Divine Worship." *Adoremus*. https://adoremus.org/1928/12/on-divine-worship/.

Pope, R. (2007). *Salvation in Celluloid: Theology, Imagination, and Film*. London: T&T Clark.

Postman, N. (1970). "The Reformed English Curriculum." In *High School 1980: The Shape of the Future in American Secondary Education*, ed. A. C. Eurich, 160–68. New York: Pitman.

Postman, N., and C. Weingartner. (1971). *The Soft Revolution: A Student Handbook for Turning Schools Around*. New York: Delacorte.

Pym, A. (2007). "On the Historical Epistemologies of Bible Translating." In *A History of Bible Translation*, ed. P. A. Noss, 196–215. Rome: Edizioni di Storia e Letteratura.

Quintilian. (1856). *Institutes of Oratory*. Ed. L. Honeycutt. Trans. J. S. Watson. https://penelope.uchicago.edu/thayer/e/roman/texts/quintilian/institutio_oratoria/home.html.

Rahner, K. (1961). "The Theology of the Symbol." In *Theological Investigations*, vol. 4. Trans. K. Smyth. London: Darton, Longman, & Todd.

Rappaport, R. A. (1999). *Ritual and Religion in the Making of Humanity*. Cambridge: Cambridge University Press.

Reid, R. S. (1994). "When Words Were a Power Loosed: Audience Expectation and Finished Narrative Technique in the Gospel of Mark." *Quarterly Journal of Speech* 80, no. 4: 427–47.

Reinhartz, A. (2003). *Scripture on the Silver Screen*. Louisville, Ky.: Westminster John Knox Press.

Reisinger, M., B. Scalia, and E. Hicks. (n.d.) "St. Mary's Seminary & University Guide to Academic Writing." St. Mary's Seminary & University. Retrieved November 9, 2020 from http://www.stmarys.edu/wp-content/uploads/2017/09/SMSU-Guide-to-Academic-Writing_Rev-2017.pdf.

Rosenthal, M. (2002). "'Turn It Off!': TV Criticism in the *Christian Century* Magazine, 1946–1960." In *Practicing Religion in the Age of the Media: Explorations* in *Media, Religion, and Culture*, ed. S. M. Hoover and L. S. Clark, 138–58. New York: Columbia University Press.

Safire, W. (2007). "On Language: Suspension of Disbelief." *New York Times Magazine*, October 7. https://www.nytimes.com/2007/10/07/magazine/07wwln-safire-t.html.

Savage, M. (2018). "5 Pop Songs You (Probably) Didn't Know Were about God." *BBC News*, March 28. https://www.bbc.com/news/entertainment-arts-43547436.

Schillebeeckx, E. (1979). *Jesus: An Experiment in Christology*. Trans. H. Hoskins. New York: Seabury.

Scholes, R., and R. Kellogg. (1966). *The Nature of Narrative*. New York: Oxford University Press.

Schrader, P. (1972). *Transcendental Style in Film: Ozu, Bresson, Dreyer*. Berkeley: University of California Press.

Scott, R. A. (2003). *The Gothic Enterprise: A Guide to Understanding the Gothic Cathedral*. Berkeley: University of California Press.

Shea, J. (1978). *Stories of God: An Unauthorized Biography*. Chicago: Thomas More Press.

———. (1980). *Stories of Faith*. Chicago: Thomas More.

Shelton, D. E. (2008). "The 'CSI Effect': Does It Really Exist?" *National Institute of Justice Journal* 259. https://nij.ojp.gov/topics/articles/csi-effect-does-it-really-exist.

Sheppard, F. H. W., ed. (1983). "The London Oratory." In *Survey of London*. Vol. 41: *Brompton*, 50–57. British History Online. http://www.british-history.ac.uk/survey-london/vol41/pp50-57.

Silver, C. (2010). "Dura-Europos: Crossroad of Cultures." *Archeology*, August 11. http://www.archaeology.org/online/features/dura_europos/.

Silverstone, R. (1994). *Television and Everyday Life*. London: Routledge.

Smith, J. Z. (1987). *To Take Place: Toward Theory in Ritual*. Chicago: University of Chicago Press.

Society of Jesus. (1970). *The Jesuit Ratio Studiorum of 1599*. Trans. A. P. Farrell. Washington, D.C.: Conference of Major Superiors of Jesuits.

Sorenson, J. L. (2000). "Ritual as Theology and as Communication." *Dialogue: A Journal of Modern Thought* 33, no. 2: 117–28.

Soukup, P. A. (1983). *Communication and Theology: Introduction and Review of the Literature*. London: World Association for Christian Communication.

———. (2003). "The Structure of Communication as a Challenge for Theology." *Teologia y Vida* 44: 102–22.

———. (2006). "Recent Work in Communication and Theology." In *Cross Connections: Interdisciplinary Communication Studies at the Gregorian University: Saggi Celebrativi per il XXV Anniversario del CICS*, ed. J. Srampickal, G. Mazza, and L. Baugh, 121–46. Rome: Editrice Pontificia Universita Gregoriana.

———. (2011). "Recent Writing on Communication and Theology." *Media Development* 58, no. 3: 3–8.

———. (2012). "Orality, Literacy, Education, and Theology." Paper presented to the 13th annual convention of the Media Ecology Association, New York, June 7–10.

———. (2013). "A Media Ecology of the King James Version." *Translation* 3: 150–72.

Soukup, P. A., and R. Hodgson, eds. (1999). *Fidelity and Translation: Communicating the Bible in New Media*. Franklin, Wis.: Sheed & Ward.

Spadaro, A. (2011). "Liturgy and Technology." *La Civiltà Cattolica* 3860: 107–20.

St. Columba's Church of Scotland (n.d.). "Our History." St. Columba's. Retrieved October 18, 2020 from https://www.stcolumbas.org.uk/our-history.

Standage, T. (1998). *The Victorian Internet: The Remarkable Story of the Telegraph and the 19th Century's On-Line Pioneers*. New York: Walker.

Stern, D. (1992). Introduction to *The Book of Legends: Sefer Ha-Aggadah: Legends from the Talmud and Midrash*. ed. H. N. Bialik and Y. H. Rivnitzky, trans. W G. Braude. New York: Schocken.

Stevenson, G., ed. (2021). *Theology and the Marvel Universe*. Lanham, Md.: Fortress Academic.

Stock, B. (1983). *The Implications of Literacy: Written Language and Models of Interpretation in the Eleventh and Twelfth Centuries*. Princeton, N.J.: Princeton University Press.

Stone, B. P. (2000). *Faith and Film: Theological Themes at the Cinema*. St. Louis, Mo.: Chalice.

Strate, L. (2004). "A Media Ecology Review." *Communication Research Trends* 23, no. 2: 2–38.

Stroup, G. W., III. (1975). "A Bibliographic Critique." *Theology Today* 32, no. 2: 133–43.

Switzer, J. (2010). "What Is Theology?" *U.S. Catholic*. https://uscatholic.org/articles/201004/what-is-theology/.

Taylor, B. (2008). *Entertainment Theology: New-Edge Spirituality in a Digital Democracy*. Grand Rapids: Baker Academic.

Taylor, S. L. (2005). "Reason, Rhetoric, and Redemption: The Teaching of Law and the *Planctus Mariae* in the Late Middle Ages." In *Medieval Education*, ed. R. B. Begley and J. W. Koterski, 68–80. New York: Fordham University Press.

Tilley, T. W. (1985). *Story Theology*. Wilmington, Del.: M. Glazier.

Tilley, T. W., and A. A. Zukowski. (2001). "Narrative and Communication Theology in a Postliterate Culture." *Catholic International* 12, no. 4: 5–11.

Tracy, D. (1981). *The Analogical Imagination: Christian Theology and the Culture of Pluralism*. New York: Crossroad.

Tucker, J., and P. Halstead, eds. (2020). *Sports and Play in Christian Theology*. Lanham, Md.: Fortress Academic.

Turner, W. (1910). "Logic." In *The Catholic Encyclopedia*. New York: Robert Appleton. http://www.newadvent.org/cathen/09324a.htm.

Uberoi, J. P. S. (1978). *Science and Culture*. Delhi: Oxford University Press.
Van den Broek, R. (1995). "The Christian 'School' of Alexandria in the Second and Third Centuries." In *Centres of Learning: Learning and Location in Pre-Modern Europe and the Near East*, ed. J. W. Drijvers and A. A. MacDonald, 39–47. Leiden: Brill.
Van 't Spijker, I. (1995). "Learning by Experience: Twelfth-Century Monastic Ideas." In *Centres of Learning: Learning and Location in Pre-Modern Europe and the Near East*, ed. J. W. Drijvers and A. A. MacDonald, 197–206. Leiden: Brill.
Van Zwieten, J. W. M. (1995). "Scientific and Spiritual Culture in Hugh of St. Victor." In *Centres of Learning: Learning and Location in Pre-Modern Europe and the Near East*, ed. J. W. Drijvers and A. A. MacDonald, 177–86. Leiden: Brill.
Vitz, E. B. (2005). "Liturgy as Education in the Middle Ages." In *Medieval Education*, ed. R. B. Begley and J. W. Koterski, 20–34. New York: Fordham University Press.
Ward, R. F., and D. J. Trobisch. (2013). *Bringing the Word to Life: Engaging the New Testament through Performing It*. Grand Rapids: Eerdmans.
Watzlawick, P., J. H. Beavin, and D. D. Jackson. (1967). *Pragmatics of Human Communication: A Study of Interactional Patterns, Pathologies, and Paradoxes*. New York: Norton.
Weitzmann, K. (1947). *Illustrations in Roll and Codex: A Study of the Origin and Method of Text Illustration*. Princeton, N.J.: Princeton University Press.
Wellesz, E. (1962). "Music of the Eastern Churches." In *The New Oxford History of Music*. Vol. 2: *Early Medieval Music up to 1300*. Ed. D. A. Hughes, 14–50. London: Oxford University Press.
Wetmore Jr., K. J. (2012). *The Theology of Battlestar Galactica: American Christianity in the 2004–2009 Television Series*. Jefferson, N.C.: McFarland.
White, R. A. (1986). "The New Communications Emerging in the Church." *The Way*, supplement 57: 4–25. from https://www.theway.org.uk/article.asp.
Williams, R. (1961). *The Long Revolution*. London: Chatto & Windus.
Wilson, C. (1990). *The Gothic Cathedral: The Architecture of the Great Church, 1130–1530*. London: Thames & Hudson.
Wilson, E. J., and D. L. Sherrell. (1993). "Source Effects in Communication and Persuasion Research: A Meta-Analysis of Effect Size." *Journal of the Academy of Marketing Science* 21, no. 2: 101–12.
Wolf, M. (2007). *Proust and the Squid: The Story and Science of the Reading Brain*. New York: HarperCollins.
Woods, T. E. (2005). *How the Catholic Church Built Western Civilization*. Washington, D.C.: Regnery.
Woodward, I. (2007). *Understanding Material Culture*. Los Angeles: Sage Publications.
Wright, B. J. (2017). *Communal Reading in the Time of Jesus: A Window into Early Christian Reading Practices*. Minneapolis: Fortress.
Yates, F. A. (1966). *The Art of Memory*. Chicago: University of Chicago Press.

INDEX

Abbey of Clairvaux, 148–49
Abbey of St. Denis, 148–49
Abelard, 66
acoustics: performance, 121; space, 123, 124, 125, 130, 142, 145, 151, 190
aesthetics, 121, 149, 156, 186; film, 172, 208; theological beliefs, 149
affordances, 7, 8–9, 37, 124, 130, 205; definition, 9; of the Internet, 187, 190, 198; of music, 120–21, 124, 126, 128, 130; of narrative, 46–47; of oral cultures, 34; of printed books, 69–71, 78, 149; of writing, 67–68, 132
agenda setting, 5
Aggadah, 43
agonistic behavior, 25
Albert Magnus, 41, 56, 58–59, 101, 102
alliteration, 23, 26, 37, 68, 89, 93
Ambrose, 53–54, 127
analogical imagination, 185
analogical sense: of Scripture, 105; of theology, 184
analogy: in music, 129; in theology, 54
Anglican Communion, 85, 86, 91, 120, 134, 210
Anselm, 3, 14, 17, 49, 133, 189
Aquinas, Thomas, 41, 50, 56–59, 61, 62, 102
architecture, 56, 102, 139–45, 147, 148, 158, 159; Gothic, 147–48
Aristotle, 6, 26, 56, 57, 174
art, 8, 14, 36, 41, 50, 72, 75, 95–104, 107, 110–17, 121, 123, 134, 135, 145, 148–50, 163, 164, 177, 205; functions, 96
artifact, 8, 9, 78
Athanasius, 41
audience, 54, 56, 92, 100, 111; as part of ecosystem, 96; for art, 100, 111; for film, 173, 174, 176, 186; for music, 121, 123, 126; for ritual, 162; for social media, 194, 197; role of audience in oral world, 21, 28–31; writer's audience, 68–69
Augustine, 2, 4, 29–31, 50–56, 59, 65, 127, 148, 164, 178, 183; on commentary as theological method, 56; *Confessions*, 178–79; *De Doctrina Christiana*, 55; *De Musica*, 128; media forms, 53; on literacy, 55; on word, 54
aural communication, 21, 35, 159, 191
authority, 53, 54, 66, 71, 74, 107, 108, 162, 165–69, 175, 178, 189, 197–200, 210; art, 105; online, 197; printing, 75; shifting authority, 66, 71, 74

Bach, J. S., 133, 135
Bandura, Albert, 5
baptistery at Dura-Europos, 97–98
baroque: architecture, 141; music, 127, 131
Basil the Great, 127
basilica, 140, 141, 146, 148; architectural form, 146

beauty, as theological category, 96, 113, 128, 135
belief, 1–4, 7, 10, 13–15, 203–7, 209, 210; architecture, 140–51; art, 94–110; film, 178; music, 131–37; oral forms, 17–20; ritual, 153–65; social media, 187–200; stories, 33, 34, 39–46; writing, 66, 75
Bernard of Clairvaux, 113, 149
Bible, 114, 207, 210; ecology of, 71–74; impact of printing, 74; impact of writing, 71; in art, 101, 111; in church design, 143, 144, 149; in film, 173–75, 177; in narrative, 34, 39; in preaching, 31; interpretation, 74, 115; teaching about, 55, 58; translation, 77–93
Biblia pauperum, 116
Boethius, 89
Book of Common Prayer, 134
Book of Kells, 106–7, 116
booksellers, 62, 73
Britten, Benjamin, 119–20, 126
Brompton Oratory, 140–43, 150
Broughton, Hugh, 92–93

Calvin, John, 63, 85, 86, 114, 149; on images, 114; on music, 127, 134; theological influence, 185
Caravaggio, 115
Carey, James, 157–58, 176–77
catacomb art, 95
catechesis, 96, 102, 155; in art, 102; of St. Cyril of Jerusalem, 155
cathedral, 101, 133, 145, 147–49; as memory palaces, 102; Bristol Cathedral, 135; Cathedral of Chartres, 101, 148; Cathedral of the Dormition, 144, 145; Coventry Cathedral, 119; Puebla Cathedral, 133; theology in Anglican Communion, 134
chant, 119, 125, 133, 134, 145, 158
church buildings: acoustic environment, 151; architecture, 102, 139–45; Cathedral of the Dormition, 144–45; London Oratory, 140–42; San Apollinare Nuovo, 100; St. Columba, Knightsbridge, 142–44; St. Mary Madeleine Vézelay, 102
Cicero, 53, 59, 89
cinematic theology, 172
Cistercian renewal, 113, 114
Clairvaux: see Abbey of Clairvaux
Clement of Alexandria, 96, 133
commentary, 31, 60, 72, 99, 148; as information management, 199; as theology, 27, 30, 50, 53, 56, 72, 196; in art, 99, 104, 106; in film, 176; oral practice, 66
cross, 96, 100–103, 110–13, 143, 144, 146, 147, 154, 156; in Book of Kells, 106–7; stations of, 41, 42, 139, 141, 150, 151
crucifix, 103–7, 144
cultivation theory, 5
curriculum, classical, 51
Cyril of Jerusalem, 31, 155, 156

dance, 14, 26, 123
Dante, 13, 41
dialogue: between film and theology, 172, 175, 180; in oral culture, 45
dictionaries, 70, 71, 80, 82, 192
digital culture, 205, 209; devotions, 160; ecology of the Internet, 190–99
Divine Comedy, 41; as theological narrative, 41
doctrine, 1–2, 46, 60, 72, 78, 99, 110, 187, 195, 199, 200; in art, 115–16; in music, 131, 135
Douay translation of Bible, 84, 86, 88
dramaturgy, ritual communication, 158, 159
Dungalus, 110
Dura-Europos, 97, 98; *see also* baptistery at Dura-Europos

ecclesiology, 11, 86, 200
ecphonetic notation, 125
education, 49–63, 82; Albert the

Great, 56; Aristotelian, 57; classical, 18, 51–56; dialectic, 57; grammar/rhetoric, 52; Hugh of St. Victor, 58; in early print cultures, 60–63; in oral cultures, 38; in print culture, 66, 72, 82; Jesuit system, 61; medieval, 56–60; Ramist system, 60; Richard of St. Victor, 58; through art, 111; through ritual, 157
Eisenstein, Elizabeth, 60, 62, 67, 70–74, 79, 81, 83, 91, 191
End Times, church of, 187, 193
English language development, 87
entertainment: as teaching tool, 25, 34, 36; through art, 101; through music, 134; through film, 177
Erasmus, 82, 83, 134
Eucharist, 41, 65, 97, 99, 108, 109, 111, 114, 115, 142, 143, 145, 160; theology, 65, 113–14, 142
Eusebius, 29
exegesis, 59, 75, 175; visual, 99

faith, 1–3, 33–47, 49, 66, 71, 73–75, 78, 97–100, 104, 120, 127, 130, 145, 147, 152, 166, 171, 175, 180, 186, 199, 200; expressed in art, 107–16; expressed in film, 171; expressed in popular culture, 203–5; expressed in ritual, 154–59; faith seeking understanding, 1–16, 39, 66, 73, 75, 78, 102, 116, 119, 126, 139, 189, 196, 204, 207–9; stories of, 28, 30, 33–47, 181
film, 14, 38, 45, 171–86, 203, 207, 208; as exegesis, 175; as narrative, 37–38, 45, 177; Bible, 173; cinematic theology, 172; formal cause, 174; ritual, 177
formulaic thought, 23, 24, 26, 73

Gerbner, George, 5
gestures, 26, 46, 153, 156
Goethals, Gregor, 95, 97, 98, 100, 102, 105–7, 111, 113, 114, 116, 148, 149, 177, 204

gospel, 7, 17–31, 34, 40, 91, 97, 119, 148, 151, 179, 180, 203; as information management, 20
Gottschalk of Orbais, 65, 66
Greeley, Andrew, 183–86
Gregory of Nyssa, 31, 52
Gutenberg, Johannes, 79–80

Handel, 135
harmony, 121, 124, 125, 132
Havelock, Eric, 20, 21, 26
hermeneutics, 180; filmic, 173; hymnology, 132
hierarchy, religious, 52, 86, 131, 162, 166, 168, 184, 197, 198
Hincmar of Reims, 65
homiletics, 32, 99, 172
Hugh of St. Victor, 58
humanism, 60, 61, 80, 83, 172
hymn, 131–35; hymnody, 115, 134

icon, 98, 107, 109, 116, 144, 145, 150; theology, 148–49
iconoclasm, 61, 107, 109, 112, 114, 149
iconoclasm debate, 109, 142, 149
iconography, 99, 100, 102, 145
iconostasis, 144, 145, 153
illumination, manuscript, 7, 96, 105, 106, 116, 148
image: education, 57–59; memory, 22; story, 45; religious images, 95–117; theology, 96, 113
Incarnation, the, 11, 96, 102, 107, 109, 110, 114, 145, 152, 155, 160, 176, 179
information management, 7, 14, 20, 22, 188, 191–93, 194, 196, 199, 200; in Aquinas, 59; in educational systems, 49, 50, 52, 57–59, 69; in electronic media, 188, 195–96; in medieval education, 57; in memory systems, 22, 58; in narrative, 33; in oral discourse, 20, 25, 26, 30, 34; in print, 60–67, 70, 75; in Ramus, 60–61; in rhetoric, 57; in ritual, 162–63; in social media, 188, 191–93, 198–200; in storage medium, 73; in story, 38; writing, 49, 65–66, 68

230 | Index

interiority, 35, 42, 44, 45, 73, 124, 129, 180
interpretation, 31, 36, 44, 51–55, 58, 71–72, 74, 92, 98–107, 115–17, 126, 133, 151, 197, 207, 208; impact of print on, 71–74; in art, 98–107, 110, 115; incorporated in architecture, 150–51; systems of, 51–55, 58

Jensen, Robin, 41, 96, 98–103, 110–12, 114–16, 144, 151
Jerome, 52, 53, 84, 89, 134

King James Bible, 77–94
Kircher, Athanasius, 131

Langer, Susanne, 120, 121, 123, 124, 127, 182
language, 184; educational systems, 51; film, 181–83; Latin, 72, 159; oral culture, 24, 34; print, 70; ritual, 164; translation, 78, 80–94
Latin, 72, 78–80, 82–89
lex orandi, lex credendi, 147–48
literacy, 26, 50, 173; consequences of, 36, 60, 112, 149; in ancient world, 18, 50, 52, 55
liturgical, 206
liturgy, 41, 98, 102, 108, 135, 205; art, 96, 98–100, 113, 115; Bible, 66; medieval, 127; music, 119, 120, 127, 128, 131, 134–36; theology, 110, 128, 206
Lomard, Peter, 57, 58
Luther, Martin, 62, 72, 80, 115, 131, 134, 151
Lynch, Gordon, 13, 128–131, 135, 198, 204, 206, 207, 209
lyrics, 131, 132, 135, 136, 152

manuscript, 69, 71, 73, 79, 82, 90, 113; Bible, 66, 84; manuscript illumination, 96, 104, 105, 116
Manutius, Aldus, 80, 82
McLuhan, H. Marshall, 33, 38, 159, 160, 172–75, 185, 208, 209

Mead, Margaret, 155, 160
media ecology, definition, 6
media ecology characteristics: emotion, 128; environment, 145; film, 176; hearing, 121; interiority, 124; interpretation, 126; musical pitch, 125; online, 187; ritual, 153; sound, 124; space, 123; time, 121, 122; tradition, 126; voice, 124; writing, 124
media ecology contexts: ancient Christianity, 96; book trade, 80, 81; iconoclasm, 107; iconography, 99; illumination, 105–7; internet, 190; language, 87, 88; libraries, 84, 85; manuscript illumination, 104; media, 90, 91; music, 120; narrative, 35; politics, 85, 86; printing, 79, 80; reception, 92–94; rhetoric, 88–90; ritual, 155; scholarship, 82, 83; symbols, 97; theology, 91, 92; translation, 83, 84; worship, 108
media effects, 5
memory, 22, 24, 25, 37, 179, 194, 200
memory systems, 22, 23, 34, 38, 41, 49, 53, 58, 59, 60–62, 191; art, 101; buildings, 101–2; film 178, 179; Ramus, 63; writing, 68, 73; oral memory, 19–22, 26–30, 33
Meyrowitz, Joshua, 123, 161–63, 165–68
Mitchell, Jolyon, 172–74
monastery, 57, 58, 73, 101, 113
montaigne, 88
montanus, 84
multimedia, 41, 46
music, 119–37, 207–9; Bach, 133; characteristics, 121; elements, 121; in oral cultures, 26, 29; popular music, 203–5; relation to space, 131; relation to time, 129; temporality, 122; theological role, 41, 129; time in, 121
music, attitudes toward: Anglican Communion, 134; Calvin, 134; Catholic Church, 136; Erasmus, 134; Jerome, 134; Luther, 134

musical notation, 124, 125
Musurgia Universalis, 131

narrative, 20–24, 33–47, 49, 96, 105, 136, 196; in art, 41, 105; in film, 176–81; in music, 136; in oral cultures, 23–26; rabbinic, 42, 43; stations of the cross, 41; theological form, 21, 31, 40–44; written, 40
narrative theology, 30, 44–47, 180, 181, 196
neume, 125
noetic economy, 24, 30, 32–34, 45, 192–97, 199, 194, 200

Ong, Walter, 8, 21–26, 33–38, 45, 50, 57, 58, 60, 61, 67–70, 72–74, 122–24, 126, 129, 130, 151, 154, 164, 178, 179, 191, 192, 195, 196
online religion, 187
oral culture, 17–38, 49, 50, 58, 67–69, 124, 177–80, 182, 186, 194
oral performance, 21, 29, 30, 37, 52, 62
oral tradition, 19, 28, 31, 194
Origen, 51, 52

Pantocrator, 101, 145
Parry, Milman, 21
Paulinus of Nola, 111, 146, 147; on church architecture, 146
Pelikan, Jaroslav, 1–3, 60, 65, 78, 107–11, 133, 135, 154, 206
performance text, 28, 66, 150
polemics, 2, 72, 196
popular culture, 12, 13, 111, 177, 203–9; theology, 204
preaching, 30–32
printing, 60–63, 65–67, 70–71, 72–75, 79–80; affordances, 70; consequences, 71; in Reformation, 72; theological mindset, 72–75
Processus Sathane, 49

Quintilian, 52

Radbertus of Corbie, 65
radio, 174, 187–89

Rainolds, John, 85, 86
Ramus, Peter, 58, 60, 61, 73
Ratramnus of Corbie, 65
Reformation, 71, 74, 83, 91, 110, 112, 113, 128, 142, 143, 149, 151, 156, 158, 162, 163, 177, 204; attitudes to images, 112, 149; attitudes to music, 131, 134; preached word, 151; printing, 72, 80
religious imagination, 183–85; Catholic imagination, 185
Renaissance, 22, 61, 80, 83, 113, 115, 119, 134, 141, 147
rhetoric, 22, 30, 31, 51, 52, 78, 88–90, 178, 192; Augustine, 55–57
ritual, 33, 37, 41, 98, 102, 114, 116, 131, 149–51, 153–69, 177, 184, 186; communication, 157; definition, 153; digital environments, 160; dramaturgy, 158; environment, 159; identity, 157; place, 161, 162; sense of place, 164

sacrament, 108, 114–16, 128, 151, 160, 173–76, 181–83, 185
sacramental imagination, 95, 108, 116
sacramental principle, 110, 114, 116, 130, 142, 173, 175, 181–83, 185; definition, 108; in film, 173–76, 181, 184; in music, 129; Reformation, 115, 151
Scripture, 29, 30, 53, 55, 63, 66, 74, 77–84, 92, 99, 111, 115, 116, 142, 175, 178
sensorium, 67, 154
sermon, 72, 144, 151, 158, 174
significant form, 120, 127
Singer, Isaac Bashevis, 44
social learning theory, 5
solmization, 132
sound, 28, 35, 54, 68, 98, 122–24, 127, 130, 151, 159, 160; musical, 121, 124, 125, 129, 130
St. Columba's church, 142–44
Stations of the Cross, 41, 42, 150
story, 19–21, 25, 27, 28, 33–47, 97, 116, 178–81, 183, 186; storyteller, 34, 36,

37, 40, 41, 44, 47; storytelling, 19, 34, 36, 40, 42, 45, 177, 191, 192, 194
Suger of St. Denis, 149
symbol, 7, 58, 96–99, 102, 107, 111, 116, 120, 124, 133, 146, 147, 148, 151, 154, 156, 158, 167, 180, 182, 184, 195; discursive, 195; Eucharist, 114, 142; presentational, 182, 183

television, 36–38, 44–46, 79, 162–68, 187–89, 192, 195
theology, 1–3; art, 95–104, 107–16; as commentary, 27, 30, 50, 56, 99, 104, 106, 196; as faith seeking understanding, 1–3; as written texts, 71–75, 207; Bach, 133; communication, 8, 10–13; definition, 1–3; directorial, 174–75; dramaturgy, 158; Eucharistic, 41, 65, 108–12, 114–15, 142; film, 172–86; images/icons, 108–15, 142, 148; in architecture, 147; in light, 148–49; in preaching, 30, 31, 160; in ritual, 50, 150, 154, 156–57; popular culture, 13, 205–8; online, 187–89, 195–200; visual, 98–100
translation, 77–94, 205; Boethius, 89; formal equivalence vs. dynamic equivalence, 89, 90; Jerome, 52, 89; Nida, Eugene, 90
two-step flow of information, 5
Tyndale, William, 84, 87, 88

Ussher, Ambrose, 92, 93
Utrecht Psalter, 105

vernacular language, 62, 72, 77, 80–81, 83, 159
vestments, 108, 141, 153, 154, 168
video, 6, 160, 192, 194, 205
visual: *see* art; image
Vulgate Bible, 71, 83, 89

War Requiem, 119
web, 187–99
worship, 97, 102, 187, 200;

architecture, 141–45, 147–50, 152; art, 108–10, 112–15; film, 177; music, 120, 132–34, 136; ritual, 163, 168
writing, 65–71; affordances, 68–69; effects of, 67–69; impacts, 69; in culture, 18, 24, 31, 32; media ecology, 66, 71–75; thought, 50, 67; theological impact, 62, 71

Yates, Frances, 22, 24, 41, 57–59, 61, 73, 101, 102, 178, 191

www.ingramcontent.com/pod-product-compliance
Lightning Source LLC
Chambersburg PA
CBHW021825300426
44114CB00009BA/323